Dedication

To my wife Wilma

whose patience and encouragement
have helped in the completion
of this book

also

to my children Sandra and Graeme

A Jas Graesan Publications Book

First published in Great Britain in 2006

ISBN 0-9536408-2-5

Typeset in Times New Roman 10

Printed in Great Britain by
Printagraph Ltd
Berryden Business Centre
12 Berryden Road
Aberdeen
AB25 3SA

Bound by
Glasgow Laminators Limited
20 Clydesmill Drive
Cambuslang Investment Park
Glasgow
G32 8RG

Jas Graesan Publications
'Càrn Dearg'
Burnieboozle Crescent
Aberdeen
AB15 8NR

Contents

L.L. = Loch Lomond

Maps

Illustrations (between pages 80 and 81)

Land's End

To

John O' Groats

A Winding Journey Of Over 2000 Miles

By A Bicycle And Its Friend

Vol. 2

Across Scotland

George Philip

JGP

The Author

George Philip was born in 1937 in Huntly, Aberdeenshire. At some stage after graduation he was a Principal Teacher of History and Geography, then a Principal Teacher of Religious and Moral Education and he also taught French and German for a number of years in Further Education.

As well as completing his Land's End – John O' Groats journey, he has cycled in other parts of Scotland and England and to a much lesser extent in the Netherlands and Norway.

He is also into backpacking, camping, bothying, hostelling and solo hill walking but has also tried skiing, canoeing and rock climbing. He has recently completed the ascent of all the Munros and is working his way through the Corbetts and Donalds.

This book 'Vol. 2 Across Scotland' covers only that part of his bicycle journey north of the Border, for the author has already published 'Vol. 1 Across England' of his non-stop End - End travels.

The author's other published work so far is a slim volume of poems in English entitled 'Lines For An Adder', but he has written three more volumes in Scots and these will be published eventually. His work has appeared in newspapers, magazines, journals, anthologies and on the radio.

Other interests include church, voluntary community work, many European and Asian languages, history, music and art and he is looking forward to further physical and mental challenges.

He is a Baillie of Bennachie, a FSA Scot., a member of the Scots Language Society, a member of the Aberdeen & North East Scotland Family History Society, a member of the Buchan Heritage Society, a member of the Cyclists' Touring Club and, not given to all life forms, a member of the human race.

And now, if you can stop yawning, the author invites you to read the rest of the book.

Won Ohw Serac

Acknowledgements

I wish to thank the following institutions, museums, exhibition, visitor and heritage centres, National Trust For Scotland properties and their staff (at the time of writing) for information and help: Matthew Constantine, Keeper of Social History, Tullie House Museum, Carlisle; the Blacksmith Shop Visitor Centre, Gretna Green; Dryfesdale Cemetery, near Lockerbie; Annan District Council Chambers, Annan; DFS Caskets, near Annan; the Savings Bank and Church at Ruthwell; the Caerlaverock National Nature Reserve; Lesley Armstrong, Supervisor Dumfries Tourist Information Centre, Dumfries; the attendant ladies at Greyfriars Church, Dumfries; the Old Bridge House Museum, Dumfries; the Robert Burns Centre, Dumfries; the Globe Inn, Dumfries; the N.T.S. Ellisland Farm, near Dumfries; Jane Insley, Senior Curator of Engineering Technologies, Science Museum, London; John Crocket, 'Fairview', Dunscore; Maxwelton House, near Moniaive; Gerard Godfrey, Manager of the Museum of Lead Mining, Wanlockhead; the Sanquhar Tolbooth Museum, Sanquhar; New Lanark Mills; the Tourist Office, Lanark; the library staff, Lanark; the Chatelherault Hunting Lodge Museum, near Hamilton; the Hunter House Heritage Centre, East Kilbride; Hairmyres Hospital, near East Kilbride; Paisley Abbey, Paisley; Paisley Museum and Art Gallery, Paisley; Coats Observatory, Paisley; Antartex Village, Lomond Industrial Estate; Lucille Furie, Cemeteries and Crematoria Officer, Glasgow City Council; Mark O'Neill, Head of Museums and Galleries, Glasgow City Council; Kelvingrove Art Gallery and Museum, Glasgow; the Clydebank District Museum; the Scottish Maritime Museum, Dumbarton; the Rob Roy and Trossachs Visitor Centre, Callander; the Scottish Wool Centre, Aberfoyle; the Queen Elizabeth Forest Park Visitor Centre, N. of Aberfoyle; C.J.S. Sangster, General Manager, the Gold Mine, Cononish, near Tyndrum; A. Smith, Vice-President, Glencoe and North Lorn Folk Museum; the N.T.S. Visitor Centre in Glencoe; Margaret Donaghy, Manager, 'The Aluminium Story' Visitor Centre, Kinlochleven; the Ballachulish Slate Exhibition, S. Ballachulish; West Highland Museum, Fort William; the Glen Nevis Visitor Centre, Glen Nevis; the Clan Cameron Museum, Achnacarry; the Commando Museum, Spean Bridge; Fort Augustus Abbey, Fort Augustus; Jean Thomson of Open Software Technology, Dhivach Lodge, Drumnadrochit; the Inverness Museum, Inverness; the N.T.S. Culloden Moor Visitor Centre, Culloden; Joe Lindsay, Targe Maker, N. Kessock, near Inverness; Kath MacLeman, Avoch Heritage Centre; Groam House Museum, Rosemarkie; the N.T.S. Hugh Miller's Cottage, Cromarty; Barbara Cheney, Research Assistant, the Lighthouse, Cromarty, Research Station for the University of Aberdeen;

Tain Heritage Centre, Tain; Clan Ross Centre, Tain; Dornoch Cathedral, Dornoch; Skibo Castle; Dunrobin Castle, near Golspie; Iain Sutherland, Wick Heritage Centre, Wick; Caithness Glass Visitor Centre, Wick; Elizabeth Munro, Northlands Viking Centre, Nybster.

I would thank also Dr. Rennie McOwan, journalist and author; Annette McNamara of Branklyn Garden of the National Trust for Scotland; Robin Satow, Senior Land Agent for the N.T.S.; Katie Carr, Public Relations Officer for the West Region of the N.T.S.; Douglas Mathieson, Assistant Reference Services, National Library of Scotland, Edinburgh; E.W. Powell, the Librarian of Innerpeffray Library, near Crieff; Dr. David H.Caldwell, Deputy Keeper, History and Applied Art, Royal Museum of Scotland, Edinburgh; Sean Newsom, Deputy Travel Editor, 'The Sunday Times'; Joan McAlpine, 'The Sunday Times Scotland'; J. Derrick McLure, Senior Lecturer in English, University of Aberdeen; Jim Fiddes, Librarian for Art and Architecture, the Robert Gordon University, Aberdeen.

I am also grateful to the 'Dumbarton and Vale of Leven "Reporter"' for permission to quote from a letter; South Lanarkshire Council, the successor of East Kilbride District Council in which lies the copyright for the text and research of the booklet 'The Hunter Story' from which I obtained some information; Kirsty Lingstadt, Senior Museums Officer; South Lanarkshire Council; Constable and Robinson Publishing Ltd for information from 'The Prophecies Of The Brahan Seer' by Alexander Mackenzie, Foreword, Commentary & Conclusion by Elizabeth Sutherland; Jack Saxon for information from 'The Kildonan Gold Rush', Northern Printers, Thurso; Iain Sutherland for information from his 'Wick Heritage Centre Guide' and for information about the Sinclairs in his publication 'Sinclair & Girnigoe Castles' published by Signal Enterprises, Wick; Historic Scotland for permission to use information from 'Dumbarton Castle' by Iain MacIvor; the National Trust for Scotland for information from an interpretative board at Gartmore; Mr. D. Ken Cunningham, Head Teacher of Hillhead High School, Glasgow for permission to quote from 'Hillhead High School 1885-1961'.

My thanks also go to 'Encyclopedia Britannica' for biographical dating. By kind permission of the Automobile Association Developments Ltd. LIC080/00 all the mapping is based on maps in the A.A. 2005 Road Atlas.

I also acknowledge information gleaned from Tourist Information Centres over many years and from public monuments, memorials and plaques. My thanks also go to the staff of the Reference Library of Aberdeen Public Library. I am indebted also to many local people who, proud of their heritage, gave generously of their knowledge and time. Furthermore I acknowledge the help given by those whom I have met over the past 40 years in the course of walking, cycling, hostelling, camping and bed and breakfasting in Scotland and England. Furthermore there is a debt to any book, magazine, newspaper and T.V. programme, from which I have absorbed and retained information over the years in the course of my professional work in education.

Hopefully all the information I have gathered is accurate but I take responsibility for any mistakes made.

In addition I wish to thank those staff who went out of their way to help at Wanlockhead, New Lanark, Glasgow, and Crianlarich youth hostels; Alex McAllister in Lockerbie for mending my tyre; Jim Keir in Bankend for walking in the rain to show me the headstone of 'Old Mortality'; Jacqueline Morton and Pat Sutherland in Killearn Coffee Shop for providing me with a free scone and pancake for the road; my uncle Douglas and late aunt Mary Eglington in East Kilbride for sandwiches and tea; Mr. Bobby Main, senior janitor on duty on the night of my visit to Hillhead High School, Glasgow for giving me a free copy of the school's history; the lady in the local shop in Thrumster for going out of her way to fix me up with accommodation in Wick.

I am grateful also to Knight's T.V. & Computers Aberdeen for expert repairs and supplies; Kelvin Park of EC-PC Computer Training, Aberdeen; Johnny Dalgety of Cushnie, near Alford for his patient support and lengthy contribution to the preparation of the maps and the following staff of Printagraph, namely, Allan Hogg for overseeing the production of this book.

Lastly, but not least, I wish to thank my good friend Won Ohw Serac for his contribution to the book, my son-in-law Tony Rafferty for his computer advice, my son Graeme and daughter Sandra for their help, my mother Agnes, my sister Nora and her husband Art and my neighbours Hugo and Thelma Fletcher for their interest and encouragement. Above all I have to thank my wife Wilma for her moral support, not only during the trip but throughout the writing process, and for putting up with my laboured struggles with the computer and faulty software.

My apologies are offered to any organisation or person omitted from the above list of acknowledgements.

George Philip

Map 1

John O'Groats

Inverness

Fort William

Glasgow

Carlisle

Chester

Shrewsbury

Hereford

Bristol

Plymouth

Land's End

Route

0   40   Miles
0   50   Kilometres

Introduction

The author's winding 2171 mile journey from Land's End to John O' Groats was the fulfilment of a dream born over 40 years ago and modified to the extent that it was done by bicycle rather than on foot. Note that the mileage includes cycling within towns and villages but the mileage itself is the least important part of the book.

It was the author's intention neither to complete the trip by the shortest possible route and in the shortest possible time nor to produce a book to guide or nanny others, depending on one's point of view, along his route. Therefore, although a traveller would be well rewarded by visiting the places he went to, there are no details about the distances to be travelled before turning left or right or recommendations about the equipment or eating places or accommodation to be used. Indeed such was his determination to pack as many experiences as possible into each day that he ate irregularly, and often thought of accommodation only well into the evening. It must be stressed, however, that there was no shortage of eating or sleeping places. Again, although the book is not into the mechanics or technology of cycling, there are some cycling tips to be gained from the narrative.

Instead this is a book about a self-selected journey, about exploration and self-education, a book which looks at legend and our historical, literary, scientific and industrial heritage. It contains many unusual facts which will interest the general reader and the author lightens the narrative with dialogue and humour. The story is in diary form so that the reader can take up and drop the book from day to day.

Although this book stands on its own, there are content links with 'Vol. 1 Across England'. The story continues where it left off on 30 May at the border between England and Scotland.

The author has enjoyed writing about his journey, but it has been held up mainly by his initial computer illiteracy, computer, printer and software inadequacies, family illnesses and obligations, home decorating, holidays, producing a booklet of poems, attending computer classes and countless other interruptions. C'est la vie.

At last, however, 'Vol. 2 Across Scotland' is published. Hopefully, you the reader will enjoy it, even if you use it only as a teapot stand.

Won Ohw Serac

People who spend most of their natural lives riding iron bicycles over the rocky roadsteads of this parish get their personalities mixed up with the personalities of their bicycles as a result of the interchanging of the atoms of each of them and you would be surprised at the number of people in these parts who nearly are half people and half bicycles:

Flann O'Brien. Real name Brian O'Nolan

One of the pleasantest things in the world is going a journey; but I like to go by myself:

Hazlitt

He travels fastest who travels alone:

Proverbs

Journeys are magic caskets, full of dreamlike promises:

Claude L vi-Strauss

Still a child in a world of wonder,
Heir of the sky and the earth thereunder,
Colours and songs and seas and thunder:

W. K. Holmes

Travel broadens the mind:

Proverbs

Liberavi animam meam – I have freed my spirit:

St. Bernard of Clairvaux

I've lived a life that's full, I've travelled each and every highway
And more, much more than this, I did it my way:

Paul Anka

Inspiration And Preparation

For those of you who have not read 'Vol. 1 Across England', I repeat here what I said there about why I embarked on the journey and some of the preparation made.

First, let me recall an incident from the Scottish part of my journey. On 7 June I was in Glasgow after 5.00 p.m. and in among the gravestones of the Necropolis, Glasgow's famous cemetery near St. Mungo's Cathedral, when stones came thudding and bouncing off the grass and path and rolled down past me on either side. A handy place to die, I thought, as I halted my search for a particular memorial. Higher uphill, amongst those perhaps privileged to be interred nearer heaven, a gang of yelling yobos, or disadvantaged citizens, were hurling their missiles from the relative obscurity of the trees and bushes.

What was I doing putting myself in that situation? On my journey from Land's End I was often asked whether I was doing it for charity. Although I received many kindnesses on the trip, I certainly wasn't getting any charity in the process of being sacrificed, nor was I doing it for a particular charity. To a certain extent I regretted that but my preparations had taken up too much time, I had no support team and the investigative nature of the journey and its inexact timetable would have created some difficulties. Furthermore, what if I failed to complete the run to John O' Groats? Twice from sprinting on foot I had torn the muscles or ligaments in my left leg, I was still getting some twinges and had done little training. No, the reason for my cycling trip was to write a book.

I suppose the roots of my motivation extend back to my early days as a country boy in Aberdeenshire. I have long loved the outdoors and a challenge and, even as a primary schoolboy, disciplined myself to achieve certain standards of fitness and skills, although some of that came naturally. I remember how, aged twelve, I cycled some three miles to climb the hill of Bennachie (associated with Orde Wingate) and had the route and summit to myself. My Latin teacher, Mr Begg, at the Gordon Schools, Huntly, also influenced me with his words 'mens sana in corpore sano' (a healthy mind in a healthy body). It could be argued, however, that these aims were not met, seeing that I cycled some 2171 miles, instead of the shortest route of 874 miles, and lost two stones in weight on the way. After university I discussed with a fellow student and friend, Malcolm Robertson, now a retired teacher in Nairn, the possibility of walking from End to End but it wasn't until more than forty years later that I fully caught the 'disease'.

Without doubt my greatest inspiration has come from writers such as Bettina Selby, whose book 'The Fragile Islands' tells of her journey through the Outer Hebrides and whose 'Riding The Desert Trail' describes her cycle to the source of the Nile. The second writer to affect me was Roger Leitch who wrote 'By Bicycle In Scotland' but the greatest influence has been Alastair Scott, whose book 'Native Stranger' about his cycle tour in Scotland, and the illustrated talk he gave in Aberdeen, fired me to saddle up and hit the trail.

To prepare for this odyssey, I gathered over the years snippets of information and sent off letters asking for tourist literature, free maps and street plans on the areas and towns through which I hoped to pass. It was then a case of buying all the Ordnance Survey Maps of the route chosen, if I didn't have them already. In that respect I was very lucky, for I already had many 1:50000 maps, bought for hillwalking purposes. I also wrote to The Cyclists' Touring Club of which I am a member and was offered routes using either youth hostels or B&Bs. However, I preferred to use my more detailed maps and choose my own way, because my route was determined more by what I intended to track down. Among places I wanted to visit were mines, caves, castles, cathedrals, churches, National Trust properties, battlefields, ancient ruins, museums, factories, the birthplaces, homes and graves of famous writers, inventors and historical figures and, with a bit of luck, reach John O' Groats.

I then bought a fair number of camera spools for transparencies and small camping gas cylinders. Obviously there was no sense in carrying all the maps, street plans, tourist literature and spools all the way. The answer was to post material ahead of its use and to post what I was finished with back to Aberdeen. Certain hostels and a camp site were chosen as pick up points and this worked well.

I had an old bicycle which I would have used but for the poor brakes. Whenever they were serviced they just went again within a week and I decided to buy a brand new hybrid bike, an Alpine Trek with a springy, padded seat. A cycle computer was added and I asked that particular care be taken to set it properly, so that it would record distance travelled as accurately as possible.

My old tent was rather heavy, so I bought a lighter one from a Tiso shop in Dundee after catching an early train to the city. A tent provides great independence, for normally I didn't intend to book accommodation in advance, for such a commitment could force me to travel in atrocious weather conditions and pressurise me into curtailing some investigations.

I had been given dire warnings that the traffic was heavy in the south of England, particularly in Cornwall and Devon. Thinking that I might be exposing myself to a greater danger than usual (not so) and determined to have a grand funeral, if I came to a sticky end, I took out some life insurance. I was into death rather than injury for, if I were killed, the sum of £100,000 was to be paid to my wife. The premium of £200 nearly gave me a heart attack but the fact that you are reading this explains why my wife is not taking repeated holidays in the Bahamas.

As for training I did two twenty-five mile runs, one of thirty miles and one of fifty miles and felt great apart from the odd twinge related to my old injuries. This was no surprise as my legs were in reasonable condition after years of cycling around parts of England and Scotland with heavy loads, and walking to the summits of hundreds of mountains and hills.

I made a list of relevant hostel and camp site telephone numbers, tourist literature provided B&B information, and I drew up a list of cycle shops and their phone numbers on or near my route.

Trains from Aberdeen went directly to Penzance at full fare. On the other hand, there was an east coast special offer of £19 return to London, which I had never visited, and from there I could catch a train for Penzance. I opted for the latter course, bought tickets for myself and the bike and reserved a bed in St. Pancras International Hostel, London for one night, a bed in Penzance hostel for the following night and a place on Trevedra Farm camp site near Land's End for the night before 1 May. As it turned out, instead of camping, I opted for the hostel at St. Just a few miles from Land's End.

It was a case then of loading the bike with four panniers, two large ones at the back and two smaller ones at the front. In addition, on the front carrier went my sleeping bag and on the rear one the tent and a large rucksack. The latter, of 70 litre capacity, is useful for carrying the contents of one's panniers, if walking becomes a necessity or for hiding one's enormously large head at journey's end.

Finally the day came when I set off with the simple aim, not of breaking records in terms of speed or distance, but of writing my long dreamed of book. This was to be a book about particular people, places and activities in the past and present. Hopefully I would educate and entertain myself and others, and perhaps inspire those with the time and energy to embark on a similar adventure.

Land's End – John O' Groats

Vol. 2

Across Scotland

30 May   The Border – Gretna Town – Langholm – Gretna Town   O.S. 85

I soon arrived at the Blacksmith Shop Visitor Centre in Gretna Green, a village famous for its anvil marriages, and spoke to a kilted stalwart.

'I first came here when I was 18 years old, when I was hitchhiking from Carlisle to Ayr,' I said.

I was disappointed that he didn't recognise me and was even more miffed that there was no plaque to say I had passed through then, but there had to be a reason. Could it have been that he wasn't born then? Remain philosophical and rational, I said to myself, just as I would if I were to step into a deep, dirty puddle in my best suit.

For better or worse, I changed my mind and decided to leave my Gretna Green explorations until the next day, and so made for Gretna Town close by. This was the first new town built by the British government, and it was founded in 1915 to accommodate munition workers in a nearby cordite factory. The town was completed by 1917 and was completely self-contained. It had its own police and fire services, school, hospital, laundry, shops, offices, halls and clubs. Every building, not just the houses, had running water, mains drainage, a bath, and was wired for electric lighting. The town had also churches, a railway (125 miles of track and 34 railway engines), its own power station, water treatment plant, electric street lighting, state controlled pubs and a cinema. The bakeries produced 14,000 meals and 13,000 loaves daily and 6000 items were laundered each day.

Gretna Town and the new township of Eastriggs to the west were built to house 30,000 workers required in H.M. Factory Gretna, one of the largest factories built. Buildings stretched over nine miles from west of Eastriggs, on the outskirts of Annan, across to Longtown. Previously this was a stretch of moorland and fields, and Gretna Green parish had about 180 families and Eastriggs, in Dornoch parish, one family. Officially, for a long time, these towns didn't exist and the government referred to them by the code word 'Moorside'.

The job of the workers was to help make ammunition which our troops desperately needed. When Sir Arthur Conan Doyle visited the factory in 1918, he described the explosive paste as the 'Devil's Porridge', for it was a highly dangerous mixture of nitro-glycerine and nitro-cotton. The girls and

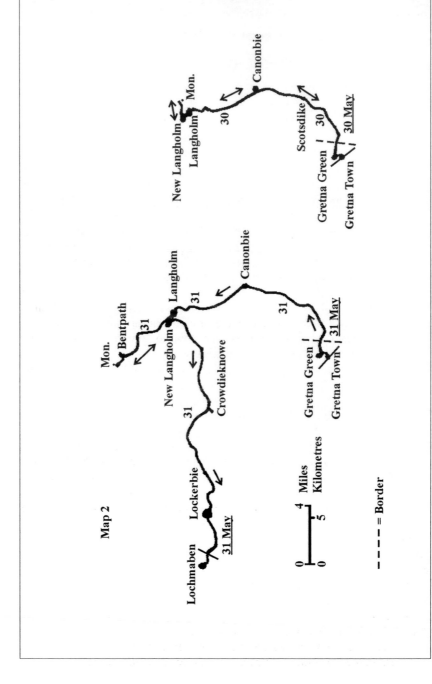

Map 2

New Langholm
Langholm
Mon.
Canonbie
30
Scotsdike
30
Gretna Green
Gretna Town
30 May

Mon.
Bentpath
31
Langholm
Canonbie
31
New Langholm
31
31
Crowdieknowe
31
Lockerbie
Gretna Green
31 May
Gretna Town
Lochmaben
31 May

Miles
Kilometres
0 4
0 5

– – – – = Border

some of the men who mixed the 'porridge' were forbidden to wear anything loose in case it fell into the mixture, or to wear metal buttons in case a spark caused an explosion. The dried paste was then hand kneaded into lengths of 'rope' called cordite, which was inserted into bullets and shells. A thousand tons of cordite were produced each week, an output greater than that of all the other factories in Britain engaged in similar work.

Feeling hungry, I went into a shop and bought some sandwiches which I started eating outside. I stopped several people and asked if there was any trace of the munitions factories, but only one man gave me information.

'Out in Central Avenue here there used to be a railway track, but the factory buildings have gone. There is or was, I believe, the remains of a glycerine factory and the chimney of an ether plant. Out at Eastriggs I've heard there are a few wooden bungalows that were once occupied by the workers. Your best plan is to go out to Eastriggs, where there's an exhibition about all this in St. John's church.'

I thanked him and cycled to the outskirts of Gretna Town to look for any such industrial relics, but found nothing I could be absolutely sure about. Back in town again I paid particular attention to two buildings. One today is a hotel, but during the World War I years it was the social club for military staff. The other I focused on is a registry office, which has been at one time described as the busiest centre for civil marriages in the UK.

'Excuse me,' I asked some older men, 'but do you know where Benny Lynch, the great boxer, used to live in this town?'

No use. They simply didn't know. Lynch (1913-46), born in a Gorbals slum in Glasgow, became the world flyweight boxing champion of the world when he was 21 years old. He defended his title four times, but lost it in 1938 when he didn't make the weight. He died as a penniless drunk in Glasgow's Southern General Hospital.

For some time Robert Carlyle, the Scots actor, has wanted to act as Lynch or direct someone else playing the part, but Lynch's son in Toronto was said to have been against his father being exploited. However, Carlyle will be involved later, I'm told, in a T.V. series about the boxer.

I was more successful with my next question. I decided to look for the Gretna Public School, where A.S. Neil had taught as a young man. He became the controversial headteacher of Summerhill in England, not to be confused with Aberdeen's Summerhill Academy, where there was also a controversial head by the name of R.F. McKenzie. In the English school, pupils were given the freedom to attend classes or not and to smoke and swear. When I found Neil's old Gretna school, it was a heap of rubble. As I stood looking at it hesitantly, a young girl looked out of the window of her house and came out asking if she could help.

'Is this the school where A. S. Neil was a teacher?' I asked.

'Yes,' came the emphatic reply. Somebody had educated her.

As I cycled back into the heart of Gretna Town, I had the 'bright' idea of setting up the tent and dumping all my luggage, except for tools and waterproofs. I found a camp site on the outskirts of the town and pitched the tent on a nice piece of grass among some caravans. It was lovely and sunny and so it was a pleasure erecting the tent. After that I was 'away with the fairies', so to speak. Without calculating the mileage I had the brainwave of cycling to Langholm, then west to Lockerbie and Lochmaben and back by Ecclefechan to Gretna Town. There was nothing wrong with that, except I hoped to do it starting in the middle of the afternoon. The next day then I could go west along by the Solway. Perhaps it was the sun and I should have lain down a while. It's one thing to cycle but it's another thing to cycle and heritage hunt.

'Fool' of hope, I set off back along the A6071 towards the fork whose right branch leads to Longtown. I veered left and cycled north up the A7. From studying the O.S. map earlier, I knew that just over three miles on was the Scots Dike, the trench/earth wall barrier between Scotland and England. I thought it started behind the Marchbank Hotel & Sportsman Restaurant, uphill off the road. I pushed the bike up to the hotel and spoke to a cook who came out of a side door. I should add that he wisely opened it first.

'Excuse me, but is there access from here to the Scots Dike?' I enquired.

'No, and we don't own the land behind. If you go back to the main road and continue on, you'll come to a sign marking the line of the Dike as it reaches the road.'

Thanking him, I pushed the bike down the path to the road and cycled on, until I found the marker just as he had said. A steady pedalling soon brought me to peaceful Canonbie, where I cycled past its old coaching inn, known today as 'The Cross Keys Hotel'. It was in such establishments that guards once exchanged the keys to the turnpike gates. Canonbie was originally a village of canons (ecclesiastic big guns?) and the village still has its priory. I wondered if the 'bie' part of the name was the same as 'by' of Viking origin meaning 'town'. Apart from that I could see no Scandinavian influence in the area. Not even a swede was to be seen growing in the neighbouring fields.

Canonbie was in the middle of the Debatable Lands and fought over until the frontier was settled in 1552, the year the trench/earth wall of Scots Dike was built for several miles between the rivers Sark and Esk to keep the Scots and English apart.

The road beyond Canonbie runs through lovely woods beside the Esk, which offers good salmon and sea trout fishing. Standing beside the river is Gilnockie Tower, where once lived the wild Border reiver Johnny Armstrong, whose betrayal led to his death in 1531. The boy king James V ordered him to be hanged without trial yet Armstrong 'lives' on, immortalised in a ballad.

Once I crossed Skipper's Bridge, I was soon into Langholm long known for its fine woollen textiles. The town is in horse riding country and the Langholm Common Riding, held annually in July, is one of the oldest in the Borders. Langholm claims it has the oldest Rugby team in the Borders, if not in Scotland. It became in 1871 an alternative sport after mild winters spoiled the curling. The town is also the place to be or was if you like pies, for started there was a pie club, whose members meet or met to eat pies. What a pioneering idea! Perhaps there should even be clubs for members to eat Kellogg's cornflakes, created originally as a health food for mentally ill people.

Born near Langholm was Sir William Beattie, a surgeon on the 'Victory' at Trafalgar in 1805. In the famous 'Death of Nelson' painting there is a picture of Beattie alongside Hardy, who was born too prematurely for kissogram activities.

Langholm's most famous son, however, is Christopher Murray Grieve, better known as Hugh MacDiarmid. He was born in 1892 and died on 9 September, 1978, and was hailed as one of the world's great poets, although not always popular because of his political views.

My main reason for going to Langholm was to track down places connected with him. I noticed a sign about the MacDiarmid Memorial and followed the road up to Whita Hill, where just off the moorland road I found a small cairn with an inscription and farther uphill a memorial sculpture provided by public subscription. It is constructed of Corton steel and bronze and takes the form of an open book full of images and symbols from MacDiarmid's poetry. It was unveiled in 1985 by Valda, his second wife. I read the following: 'I have known all the stones that rolled. I have been a singer after the first fashion of my people – a poet of passion. All that has passed. Quiet has come into my soul. Life's tempest is done. I lie at last a birdcliff under the sun. Hugh MacDiarmid.'

A man in his fifties, I reckon, came up from his car and joined me as I studied the memorial. I smiled but being security conscious never turned my back on him.

'It's an interesting sculpture,' I said, 'but it's a pity it looks like a chunk of rusty metal.'

'Yes, I've heard it being criticised. It's a bit controversial like the man himself. Maybe that's part of the reason it's outside Langholm. He wasn't too popular with some people.'

It was interesting to read the following: 'The MacDiarmid Memorial was organised by the Scottish Sculpture Trust with the support of the Scottish Arts Council, the Langholm Community Council, the Langholm MacDiarmid Committee, Buccleuch Estates and many hundreds of people with courage.'

MacDiarmid, as a teenager, taught in Sunday School in Langholm and in

World Wars I and II he served in the R.A.M.C. and in a Glasgow shipyard respectively. At one time he worked as a journalist and as a councillor in Montrose. Often controversial, MacDiarmid joined and was expelled from the National Party of Scotland and the Communist Party. His Communist beliefs led him to support the Russian invasion of Hungary in 1956. Perhaps that is why Langholm, while it claims him and acclaims his poetry, symbolically distances itself from him.

'Have you seen the house in Langholm where he was born?' I was asked before the man returned to his car.

'No, not yet but I'm just going back down to do that.'

The run downhill was great and when I pedalled through the quiet streets of Langholm, I asked a lady where MacDiarmid's house was. Once directed I pushed the bike up a steep brae (slope) to what I thought was the house (confirmed by a local man there) and photographed it. It is house No. 17 in Arkinholm Terrace.

On another occasion in the future, I was to walk again along the Terrace and speak briefly to a white haired woman, who lives near MacDiarmid's birthplace.

'I was of his time,' she said. 'He and my mother were first cousins. I don't think he would have liked his big memorial up on the hill. He was also not too popular, partly because of his politics and partly because of his relationships with women.'

However, to go back to my earlier bicycle journey. After leaving No. 17, still a private house, I went to see the church in Drove Road where MacDiarmid had taught at Sunday school from 1905-1906. From there I returned to the High Street to stop at the Old Library (already passed on entry to Langholm), where MacDiarmid's mother became the caretaker. There, in a street level, since gutted house below the books, the family lived from 1899-1913. The library today is known as the Thomas Telford Library and was partly endowed by him in 1834, the year of his death. MacDiarmid attributed his literary interest to his long familiarity with the books above his house. As he himself said: 'Before I left home I could go up into the library in the dark and find any book.' Believe that if you like.

I noticed outside the library a memorial inscription to William Julius Mickle (1734-1788) who died near Oxford. It said that he was the translator of the 'Lusiad', author of 'Cumnor Hall' and the writer of the well known Scottish song 'There's Nae Luck Aboot The Hoose'.

If I wasn't running out of luck, I was running out of time. I would have to shorten my journey and get back to Gretna Town. Accordingly I left the local female teenage talent to keep Mr. Mickle's memorial company, then cycled back the way I had come.

MacDiarmid's father had been a postman but I left behind an even greater man of letters, when I soon cycled back to the tent in Gretna Town.

There was plenty luck about my 'hoose', as I enjoyed a small snack before settling down for the night.

31 May   Gretna Town – Nr. Lochmaben   O.S. 85, 79, 78

It was raining in the early morning when I woke briefly, but when I finally rose the rain was off. I breakfasted and in the process of tidying and packing my panniers, I came across a leaflet I had picked up previously. It mentioned Langholm cemetery, which could be reached from Skipper's Bridge by turning off from the A7, about one mile south from the town. After MacDiarmid died of cancer in Edinburgh, he was taken to the cemetery, where he was buried in a simple grave beside his father and mother. He is in Lair E73 under a headstone to Christopher Murray Grieve, which was his real name.

The grave is part of the MacDiarmid Trail which consists of ten places to visit. Eight are in Langholm of which I visited five and two outside, namely, Whita Hill and the cemetery. I decided to pay a visit to the latter before going through Langholm again on the way to Lockerbie.

Outside the tent I started talking to one of the caravanners about going on to Gretna Green. He said he was into railway history and mentioned that Gretna Green was less than a mile from Quintinshill, where Britain's biggest rail disaster had occurred in 1915. I had heard of this years ago but he refreshed my memory and added some new information.

'I've been reading something about it in Friday's "Annandale Observer",' he said. 'A man called Andy Murray has been doing some research into the disaster.'

'It was the signalman's fault, wasn't it? And two trains crashed,' I added.

'Three actually.'

'So what happened exactly?' I asked.

'A train carrying soldiers ordered to Gallilopi smacked into a local train and the wreckage of these was then hit by an express train. More than 200 died from being torn apart, crushed, burned or carbonised. Nothing left of them. Practically all the carriages were made of wood, which caught fire quickly because of the gas lighting. The gas had been made in Germany and was a version of the poison gas the Germans used on the battlefield. Before this tragedy, some of the officers who perished at Quintinshill had captured a German trench at Ypres in Belgium, and six of them were allowed to draw lots for some days' leave in Scotland. Three of them happened to be on the troop train. A Gretna farmer went by motor bike into Carlisle to get the fire brigade.'

'That must have been some blaze and mess.'

I thanked him and said I might go to Quintinshill, even if it wasn't part

7

of my original route. After going to the toilet for the last time, I cycled up through Gretna Town and over to Gretna Green and its Visitor Centre. I entered the shop, which was selling the usual tartan, tweed, knitwear, Gaelic jewellery, crystal, china, shortbread, marmalade and confectionery, along with books on Scotland.

'What a load of tat,' I heard a dissenting voice say.

Maybe so and maybe we don't want tartan items made in Hong Kong, although imitation is a form of flattery, they say. Many foreigners as well as ourselves admire our tartans, so why not enjoy them without attaching too much historical importance to them? Why shouldn't we be proud of our knitwear, tweed, jewellery and shortbread? They give employment to people and help the economy. Nobody's forced to go into such shops and nobody's forced to buy anything. These things have their place within reason. There's plenty books, museums, art galleries, orchestras, universities and industrial works to illustrate Scotland's cultural, technical, economic and scientific contribution to the world. How many of those who sneer at the aforementioned shop goods are active themselves in promoting Scottish culture or providing employment? Or are they trying in some cases to impress others with their 'superior' attitude? Perhaps if we had full self government, Scottish T.V. might do more to promote the more worthy aspects of Scottish life.

From there I entered the museum, where I learned much about the anvil marriages which have taken place there at Gretna Green. In 1754 a law was passed in England to stop secret runaway marriages, such as were performed at the Fleet Prison in London. From then on all marriages had to be done through the church. In Scotland it was different, for all that Scots law required was that a couple expressed their wish to get married in front of two witnesses, and the marriage was recognised as legal everywhere.

Little wonder that elopers from across the border came to the first place, in which they could get married without a clergyman. From the beginning of the 18th century, it was mostly the Gretna Green blacksmiths who married couples over the anvil. One of the first so called anvil 'priests' was Joseph Paisley (1754-1814) who was a fisherman and smuggler. He was born just south of Gretna and was said to be so strong that he could straighten a cold horse shoe with his bare hands – as if he would try it with a red hot one. One story tells of how two couples required his services at the same time, and he ended up marrying the wrong brides and grooms. He wasn't upset and told them: 'Weel, jist sort yersels oot.' Later in life he was described as ignorant and coarse, 25 stone in weight and fond of a good drink. It was obviously a 'big' day for him as well as for the happy couple. He was reported to have married even from his deathbed around 1814.

Another 'priest', David Lacey (1792-1827), had been selling drapery and haberdashery (obviously a man of the cloth) in Lancashire when he was seized by the press gang. The ship he was on was captured by John Paul Jones, a great sailor. (See later.) Robert Elliot (1814-1840) was another 'priest' and he collected his memories and published them. He claimed to have presided over between 4000 and 8000 marriages but unfortunately the registers were lost, when his handicapped daughter set fire to her bed and burned herself and the registers.

One of the last anvil 'priests' Richard Rennison (1920-1940) married 5147 couples over the anvil. He told couples he must be a good man, because his surname spelt backwards was 'no sinner'. Apparently in Langholm cemetery there is a headstone to a Stanley Rennison who died aged 86 in 1998. In earlier times these 'priests' would charge 10 guineas for officiating, but a half hour in one of the blacksmith shops would cost about £130 today.

Many thought that these marriages were disgraceful and immoral and the church complained. Angry parents came on horseback or in carriages to try and stop these marriages, but were often too late. To slow down these marriages a new law was passed in 1857, whereby couples could get married only if they had been in residence for 21 days before the marriage.

Anvil marriages continued until 1940, when they were made illegal after pressure from the church. However, Gretna Green still attracts couples because, unlike England where couples have to be 18 before they can be married without parental consent, in Scotland they can be married at 16. Today marriage takes place in church or at the registry office, and then after that couples undergo the Old Blacksmith's Marriage Ceremony. Royalty, politicians and film stars have come to Gretna Green and at least one ageing cyclist, who married elsewhere and thus gave Gretna Green a bypass without working for the Ministry of Transport.

I learned so much from that museum but it was time to go. In my haste to get on the road, I forgot to go to Quintinshill which was less than a mile away. Once I was beyond the place, I remembered but decided not to return and pressed on towards the cemetery which, I repeat, is about a mile south of Langholm. I turned off to the left just before Skipper's Bridge and pushed the bike up a winding road among trees. Eventually I reached the lovely cemetery laid out on a flat piece of ground at the top of the hill. After an inspired guess and short search, I came across MacDiarmid's headstone and grave. Incidentally, I find it fascinating the connection between our word 'grave' and the Norwegian verb 'grave' which means 'to dig'.

It was then back downhill, over the bridge and into Langholm again. The Langholm band failed to greet me as I entered the town, which claims to have the oldest town band, presumably in Scotland. After Waterloo the band of the time marched through the streets with the Royal Greys. I imagined the stirring sound as I took the B709 to Bentpath.

My aim was to see the Thomas Telford (1757-1834) Memorial, established to commemorate arguably Eskdale's most famous son. Born in the parish of Westerkirk, this son of a shepherd was employed as a young craftsman to build Langholm Bridge, and his mason's marks can still be seen there. In 1788 he was appointed county surveyor for Shropshire, and he also educated himself as an architect and designed churches and docks. Telford, however, is more famous for building bridges, canals and roads. One of the bridges he built was a cast iron one at Buildwas, and it was stronger and bigger than the very first iron bridge downstream at Ironbridge in Shropshire. Telford also built the Menai and Conway Suspension Bridges, and the three arch bridge over Mouse Water at Cartland Crags near Lanark. In fact he built more bridges in Britain than anyone before or after him. Telford was also the engineer for the Ellesmere Canal, the Caledonian Canal and the Gotha Canal across Sweden. He built about 1200 bridges and 1000 miles of road in Scotland. Robert Southey the poet was one of his great friends. Telford was so busy that he was 64 before he had his own house.

Upon arriving at Bentpath I turned down to the right and went to the churchyard, where I hoped to find some reference to him. I found nothing and returned, knocking first at a house door before reaching the main road.

'Excuse me, but can you tell me where Telford is buried?' I asked a man who came to the door. 'I found nothing down there.'

'He's not buried there but his memorial is just along the road.'

Of course, I could see that on the map, but the churchyard had seemed a natural place to look for his grave. I thanked him and walked along to the memorial which had three plaques. The one on the left said that the seat was erected in 1928, the middle one gave his place of birth, mentioned his F.R.S., and that he was the First President of the Institution of Civil Engineers from 1820-34, and the third showed a poem about the seat.

After photographing the memorial, I went up to the library close by and read the plaque which said: 'Westerkirk Parish Library established 1793.' I knocked, a man appeared and we talked about Telford.

'There was a Thomas Telford in the old kirkyard and he was a brother who died earlier. From him Thomas Telford took his Christian name. Telford is buried in Westminster Abbey. Did you know that the libraries in Langholm and Westerkirk have benefitted from endowments he left? This is the fourth library, you know. The first was built near Megget and was provided by Telford, the second was at Kirktonhill, which is on the outskirts of Bentpath. Thomas, the brother, was buried there. The third at Westerkirk got transferred to the present one, where the memorial is. Telford left a legacy of £62.80, which is still being paid to the present library. It's just enough to pay the electricity bill.'

So Telford took his Christian name from his brother Thomas! Talk about cloning.

After leaving the library, I cycled back along the B709 to Langholm, where from a tourist signboard in a car park I quickly read about the Clan Armstrong Centre, but didn't grasp exactly where it was. My ignorance, however, made no difference to my day, for I took the B7068 to Lockerbie some 18 miles away. The road climbed slowly to a point after which there was a general descent to my destination. Once I was past the summit, I intended turning off to the left down a small road to a cemetery at Crowdieknowe, in order to have a look for some of the forebears of MacDiarmid the poet. Presumably, I'd have had to look out for the name 'Grieve' on the gravestones, MacDiarmid's real surname. Unfortunately I missed the turn-off point as I whizzed along, and this was confirmed when I spoke to a man, who said I had passed the place.

'You're definitely past it,' he said. Very worrying. Did I look that old?

Lockerbie was to be my next stop but before reaching it, I passed Tundergarth Mains without realising it as I pressed on. It was at Tundergarth that the nose cone of the Pan Am Flight 103 aircraft and more than 100 passengers came down, when a terrorist bomb exploded aboard 6 miles up in the air on the evening of 31 December, 1988. The ages and nationalities of all the victims are contained in the Book of Remembrance, which is kept in the Tundergarth Memorial Room. It seems that the church there was for a while in danger of closing, because of lack of sufficient financial support from parishioners, but thankfully it has been saved.

I had been to Lockerbie before about seven months after the air disaster. My wife and I had rented a cottage for a week on the outskirts of Moffat, just off the A708 that leads to Tibbie Shiel's Inn. The let was at Craigieburn, mentioned in a poem by Robert Burns. The nearest station was at Lockerbie and from there we cycled north to Moffat and the cottage. Incidentally buried in the churchyard at Moffat in 1986 is a Nan Pont, a minister's wife, who survived the 'Titanic' disaster as a child.

On the return journey we had a B&B in Lockerbie and the next morning I went along to Sherwood Crescent, which had been badly affected. On the night of the disaster a fuel laden wing and fuselage had hit the houses just after 7.00 p.m., and created a trench 30 feet deep and as long as a football pitch. There on the ground 11 Lockerbie citizens died in that conflagration. Passengers, some still in their seats, had rained down into people's gardens. That night Lockerbie's population more than trebled as people converged on the town. On that holiday visit I took no photos, questioned nobody and tried to avoid standing and staring, as it was still a sensitive matter. I noticed then that they were making good progress rebuilding houses, and I couldn't avoid seeing some fire blackened garden walls. Apparently the heat had been so intense that no trace could be found of some people killed on the ground. They were simply vaporised. One policeman remembered seeing a wrought iron gate melting like a candle. I had also visited the local library, where I saw a collection of very moving letters from Americans to the people of Lockerbie, letters expressing gratitude for the love and care shown to relatives and friends of the deceased.

This time I wanted to see the cemetery where the air victims are buried, but first I cycled north to the outskirts of the town to see the Lockerbie County Manor Hotel, for it was in that building that the Queensberry rules of boxing were written, and then published in 1867 under the sponsorship of John Sholto Douglas, Marquis of Queensberry. Another member of the Douglas family was a poet and friend of Oscar Wilde, about whom I shall say nothing that is below the belt, particularly after reading about and seeing the latter's memorial in the Cimetière du Père Lachaise in Paris. From the hotel it was back into town again where, although I didn't see any boxers, I caught sight of a spaniel. I finally left Lockerbie by the A709.

It didn't take long to cycle to the Annandale and Eskdale District Council cemetery of Dryfesdale and the garden of remembrance. It was already evening when I arrived and perhaps there were about six or seven people there. A notice read: 'This garden of remembrance is in memory of the 270 victims, whose ages range from 2 months to 82 years from 21 nations.' The dead from the 747 jet numbered 259.

There were some very beautiful messages on plaques on a wall in the garden such as: 'Never forget how to laugh for laughter is the inner energy which cleanses the soul and lifts the spirit.' Another read: 'Those whom we hold most dear never leave us. They live on in the kindness they showed, the comfort they shared and the love they brought into our lives.' These words I was to use later at my own father's funeral.

Moved by the love and care lavished there and by the callous waste of so many lives, I took some photos, when there was no danger of disturbing anyone else.

I returned then to the bike, knowing full well that I wouldn't be able to see Lochmaben and the surrounding area or reach Annan to the south, as I had hoped. The map showed Halleaths camp site about a mile from Lochmaben and I headed for it. I booked in and bought some food in the shop before setting up the tent. It was good to eat something warm and have a cup of tea.

As I lay in my bed I thought of that disaster. Whatever the involvement of foreign powers in the Middle East, whatever the role of the bombers, others had questions to answer. I had read that some intelligence people knew that a bomb was likely to be planted at some time in a radio on a plane from Frankfurt, that some people in the know made sure that they were not flying, but the general flying public had not been told of the risk. What a contrast between the destructive actions of the perpetrators of that air crime, and the supportive, healing work of the people of Lockerbie and beyond. Such thoughts were, however, brief for soon I drifted off to sleep.

1 June   Nr. Lochmaben – Eastriggs   O.S. 78, 85

In the morning, I set off towards Castle Loch and arrived there on the outskirts of Lochmaben. A notice told me that permits for fishing from the bank could be had from the water bailiffs but, as far as I remember, there was no information as to where the latter were to be found when needed. Perhaps I missed seeing a telephone number for contact. Some ducks didn't want to be interviewed, for they moved off quickly. Fish such as pike, perch, chubb, roach and bream could be caught but the big catch was this – all fish had to be returned. There was a warning about the disposal of lines and hooks so as not to endanger wild life. Surely, I thought perversely, the young 'bucks' of Lochmaben would not be so crazy as to chew hooks and lines? Who knows?

There was also a warning against disturbing birds' nests and about scum and the latter word made me feel unwanted, until I grasped that the reference was to algal scum, which could be dangerous to children and pets. This place can become crowded with up to 16,000 pink footed and up to 2500 greylag geese roosting on the water, so I decided to move on. I was just about to go when I was joined by a man with binoculars. He was obviously a keen bird watcher.

'Hello,' he said with a clear and friendly voice. 'Are you thinking of fishing?'

'No,' I said with a laugh, 'I never fish. The only fishing I do is for information for my diary.'

'You're keeping a record of your journey are you?'

'I'm trying to.' I hope he didn't think I said: 'I'm trying too.'

From there I cycled into Lochmaben which was frequently visited by Robert the Bruce, who became a Freeman of the town he called 'Margery o the Monylochs', because there are five lochs near Lochmaben. I rode up to Bruce's statue in front of the Town Hall and paid homage to a man who, in spite of some failings, did help Scotland gain freedom from English domination. It was unveiled in 1879 and occupies the position of the old market cross. It has been claimed and contested that Bruce was born in Lochmaben Castle, but the town grew up around the old parish church and the Bruce's family motte and bailey castle, on what is now Lochmaben golf course. The O.S. map shows this motte on the course.

Breakfast in the tent had been basic, so I popped into a café for coffee and cake, before going again along the High Street to Lochmaben Church to speak to two ladies.

'Excuse me, but is this the church, which has the oldest bells in use in Scotland?'

'Well, I go to this church,' one of them answered, 'but I haven't heard of that.'

'Nor me,' said the other one.

'I think it's this church,' I replied. 'The trouble is I can't remember where I heard it.'

Turning back along the High Street, I passed Annandale House in which are incorporated blocks of stone from Lochmaben Castle. I then went to look for the old church off the High Street, a church which allowed 16 inch bottom room for worshippers, as compared with the larger new one which provided an 18 inch space. Perhaps something to 'bum' or boast about. The mind boggles. Did the seats have dividing walls to retain a worshipper's rear flab from overspilling into a neighbour's space? Talk about neighbours from hell. Imagine the preacher asking: 'And what is the measure of man?' The old manse there is now called Magdalene House, and I believe that there is in the new church a writing desk taken from there. On it Burns is said to have written a poem. I think it was about the minister's daughter.

Searching the graveyard, I found the memorial stone of Dr. James Mounsey of Rammerscales, who was born at Skipmyre near Lochmaben and died in Edinburgh 1775. He had been the physician to the then Emperor and Empress of Russia, but had to flee the country in danger of his life, when suspected of being a spy. He is said to have introduced the root of the rhubarb plant into Scotland, a plant the Romans are said to have found growing wild along by the river Danube, the 'rhu' part of the word meaning 'plant' and 'barb' meaning 'wild'. The root was used for medicinal purposes in the then well known 'Gregory's mixture'.

Also in the graveyard, I saw the memorial to William Jardine, who was a merchant and M.P. and for many years senior partner in the firm of Jardine, Mathieson & Co. in Canton, China. It was largely through him that Britain acquired Hong Kong to make drug trading easier. He is said to have been in his time the greatest trader in or pusher of opium worth millions, and had the backing of the British government in forcing it on the Chinese. Unfortunately some of the worst dopes in the world are humans.

I had heard that William Paterson (1658-1719) had been born near Lochmaben at Skipmyre, and had gone to school in Lochmaben. Paterson had been the co-founder of the Bank of England and the originator of the ill-fated Darien Scheme in 1698. The plan was to set up a trading company near Panama as a centre for trade between West and East. The scheme went disastrously wrong with many people dying of disease and that, plus opposition from English trading interests, led to failure. Much of Scotland's wealth was invested in the venture and the ruin which followed, plus some bribery, led to the union of the Scottish and English Parliaments in 1707.

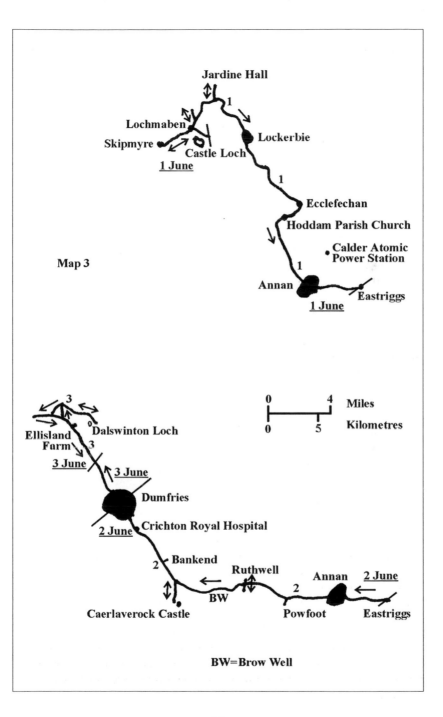

Map 3

Jardine Hall

Lochmaben

Skipmyre

Castle Loch

1 June

Lockerbie

Ecclefechan

Hoddam Parish Church

Calder Atomic Power Station

Annan

Eastriggs

1 June

Ellisland Farm

Dalswinton Loch

3 June

3 June

Dumfries

Crichton Royal Hospital

2 June

Bankend

Ruthwell

Annan

2 June

BW

Caerlaverock Castle

Powfoot

Eastriggs

0   4   Miles

0   5   Kilometres

BW=Brow Well

15

I next set off to find the house in which Paterson was born and met up with a farmer walking along the road.

'Excuse me, but is it far now to Paterson's birthplace?' I asked.

'No, it's just on a bit to the right.'

I was practically there and soon came to the farmhouse, where a plaque read: 'William Paterson, a founder of the Bank of England, was born here in 1658. This plaque was unveiled in June 1994 on the occasion of the 300th anniversary of the bank's establishment.'

From Lochmaben I cycled north along the B7020, before taking a secondary road to the right to Millhousebridge from which a road led to Jardine Hall. I resisted going there and cycled on towards and beyond Applegarthtown where, later in my wanderings on the narrow country roads, I met another cyclist, a robust, sun tanned man.

'I'm 84,' he said. 'My wife died some time ago and I come out cycling regularly.'

'Well, I think you are amazing both physically and mentally for your age. You're an inspiration. Keep it up. I'm doing the Land's End to John O' Groats run, but I'm heading now to the creamery to see how Lockerbie butter is made.'

We wished each other all the best but, not long after he had gone, I discovered that I had a slow puncture and the bike tyre wasn't in the best of health either. Better me than the bike. On top of that I became a bit disorientated, for the small roads didn't seem to match what was on the map and I didn't find the signposts very helpful. I had to ask a tractor driver for directions, and still to this day don't know where I went wrong. I had to make my way back to Lockerbie, where I hoped to get an expert to deal with the puncture. It took some time, but I reached Lockerbie and scoured the main street for a bike repair shop. Somebody recommended a particular cycle shop, but I discovered that it had been closed down for some time. I then tried a service station that was suggested.

'No, sorry, we don't mend tyres. There is a garage that might do it. Hang on and I'll phone up and see.'

Bless her soul but the young girl helping me managed to persuade someone in 'Express Tyres' to do the job. I wondered if he might be her boyfriend. She gave me instructions how to get there and off I went to the garage on the B7068.

'Hello,' I greeted a mechanic in the garage. 'Do you mend punctures?'

'No,' came the reply but a young mechanic by the name of Alex McAllister, as I learned, stepped forward and said he would do it. I waited until the job was done and gave him a £10 note, in spite of his unwillingness to charge anything. It was a relief to get the job done by someone accustomed to dealing with tyres, even if they were car tyres.

Satisfied with my explorations I pedalled off to Ecclefechan, initially along the B7068 and then the B7076. Upon reaching the place, my attention was caught by a statue of Thomas Carlyle, the great 19th century philosopher and historian. It stands on high ground looking down the main street. The memorial was gifted to the village by Carlyle's nephew Alex Carlyle and was erected in 1929. The words read: 'Thomas Carlyle born 4th Dec. 1795 at Ecclefechan Dumfriesshire died 5th Feb. 1881 at Great Cheyne Chelsea. Erected by Alex Carlyle 1929.' Thomas Carlyle was known as 'the Chelsea sage' and knew, among others, men such as Coleridge, Hazlitt, Thomas Campbell and Emerson.

Beside the statue was a warning: 'Haggs Putting. Anyone using this green does so at their own risk. Take due care of nearby householders and their property. For safety, this green is only to be used for putting, not driving or pitching.' I didn't see an arrow pointing to anywhere but may have missed it. There was a small piece of grass beside the memorial but surely that was not the putting area?

'Is this meant to be some local joke?' I asked a passer-by.

'I think so,' came the reply.

Had I been a very bad speller and believed in invisible, ugly old women, I would have accepted that there was some ongoing sporting activity, but I realised that 'Haggs' was a place name.

I cycled down into the village, whose name comes from the old Scots for 'the church of St. Fichan'. In the 18th and 19th centuries the village was an important coaching stop, and the production of strawberries was an important local industry. Today bus coaches arrive with their tourists to see Arch House built by Carlyle's father. There Carlyle was born and it is now a period museum situated on one side of the burn, which splits the main routeway through the village.

Carlyle, the son of a stonemason and later farmer, was educated at Ecclefechan and at Annan Academy up to the age of 13, and he was so keen to learn that he walked all the way to Edinburgh, where he attended the university from 1808-14. He studied literature and science, giving up his earlier religious vocation. He returned to Dumfriesshire to Craigenputtoch in 1828, where he wrote his masterpiece 'Sartor Resartus' which means 'The Tailor Retailored'. That was partly an autobiographical work, in which he describes a strong mystical experience and discusses creeds and human values, and partly a satirical work in which a professor discusses the value of clothes. In 1834 he and his wife left for London where he continued writing until his death.

As a writer, Carlyle attracted conflicting reactions from literary critics and he had an enormous effect on his age. While some people believed that impersonal forces rather than individuals had the greater influence on the course of history, Carlyle thought that the will of individuals had a major effect on the pattern of events and, in keeping with his right wing political attitudes, he believed that a strong, hero figure was necessary. It is interesting to think that in 1945 in Hitler's bunker in Berlin, Goebbels read Carlyle's 'Frederick the Great' to his Führer as the Russians closed in. Was this Hitler's *bad*time story?

I understood that when Carlyle died, his body was returned to Ecclefechan and he was laid to rest by Hoddom Parish Church. It was for that reason that I set out along the B725 to the south-west to find the church in question. Perhaps if his house in Ecclefechan had not been closed, I might have learned exactly where he was buried. I had heard that he was buried 'by' the church. I couldn't help thinking that perhaps he wasn't buried in the hallowed ground of the church and if not, why not. I read at the remains of the church that it had been destroyed by fire on the night of 2/3 February, 1975. Later when I phoned Arch House and enquired, I was told that Carlyle was buried in Ecclefechan.

Moving on, I pedalled down the B723 towards Annan and could see away to my left the towers of Chapelcross magnox atomic power station. I had hoped to go round past the station, even visit it, but my delay in Lockerbie had scuppered that plan as well as my intended butter factory visit. I had limited time left, but I wanted to track down a few things in Annan, before finding a place for the night. Consequently as soon as I entered the town, I started asking questions of the locals.

'Excuse me, but can you tell me where in Annan the Solway Viaduct started?'

In days gone by the viaduct carried a railway line across the Solway Firth to Cumbria, and during World War I trains carried coal and ammunition.

'Follow that road there,' I was told. 'I'm in the local historical society, by the way.'

I took the advice but didn't find any trace of the remains.

'No, you're going the wrong way,' another told me. 'It's away over there but all you'll see are a few bricks.'

Off I went in the new direction, only to be told by a couple in a car that I wasn't allowed down there. No doubt that, had I had better luck and more time, I would have succeeded. Perhaps I should have joined a hysterical society. I next tracked down the building, now a café or tea room, where Robert Burns the poet is said to have written the poem 'The Deil's Awa Wi' Th' Exciseman', when he was a customs officer there. Later outside the Old Church, I broke a commandment and stole a picture from the Annan born preacher and mystic, Edward Irving (1792-1834), who had turned up as a statue. I was aware that the 'crime' had been witnessed by the local gum chewing teenage 'neighbourhood watch', who eyed me suspiciously. Was that the same lot, the same rent-a-group I had seen in Langholm or as far back as Shrewsbury?

My old map showed a camp site in between the river Annan and the B722, but when I arrived there the place was devoid of campers, caravans and warden. It looked so run-down that I decided not to pitch my tent, and I even considered it possibly dangerous to camp there alone. Camping by myself in the wilds doesn't bother me but humans are the most dangerous animals around. Thus unsure of my water supply and security, I set off for a camp site at Lowthertown north of Eastriggs. Unfortunately, there wasn't one there either and the old map had let me down. I decided to try for a B&B and went to a local inn in Eastriggs, but it couldn't take me.

'Try along the road,' I was told by a barman. 'There's a farmhouse there that does B&B.'

Time was getting on and I crossed my fingers, as I didn't want to go back all the way to the Gretna Town camp site. Cycling was easy as I didn't have to cross my legs as well, and I was sufficiently lucky to find a room for the night and was very glad, because it was raining by then. Once I settled in, the lady of the house told me that she possessed a book written by a man, who had stayed with her in the course of walking round the coast. Hopefully one day she would be able to buy the story of my cycling trip.

Later as I relaxed in bed, I remembered asking somebody in Lochmaben the whereabouts of the Lochmaben Stone, a rocky lump 8 foot high and 20 foot wide. I learned that it was in Gretna. Very handy. Tomorrow I would head for Dumfries. Hopefully it would be there.

2 June   Eastriggs – Dumfries   O.S. 85, 84

Breakfast by, I departed for Annan to the west and made my first stop at the District Council Chambers, where I enquired about the famous African explorer, Hugh Clapperton (1788-1827), who explored the river Niger. In 1805 Mungo Park, a Scottish doctor born in Peebles, had explored more than 1000 miles of the Niger in the search for its mouth. Clapperton continued where Park left off and, when the former was killed by natives, his Cornish servant Richard Lander, already mentioned in my book 'Vol. 1 Across England', reached the sea by canoe via one of the river mouths.

'Good morning. I believe there's a plaque here about Clapperton the explorer,' I said at reception.

'O yes, it's upstairs,' said a friendly lady and I was taken up by a man to see the very plaque.

I thanked all who had been helpful and left the building. I remember thinking that it was possibly just across the road that Carlyle had gone to school in Annan, but wondered too if I was right.

On the way out of Annan, though not dead beat at that time of morning, I called in by a coffin manufacturer, which went by the name of DFS Caskets. I knocked at the door, entered and asked one of the men for information on coffin making.

'I'll get you something,' he said, entering his office. 'This is our product guide.'

The company, I learned, was a family owned business and, although now in Annan, it came originally from Coventry, where five generations of family members were funeral directors.

'We are environmentally aware,' he continued, 'and take our wood from carefully managed forests and use laquers which comply with guidelines about harmful emissions.'

This place was obviously politically correct. The man didn't even send me to Coventry when I asked my questions. Coffins could be made to the specifications of the customer, I discovered. Good. Maybe I could have one with an air tube and a bell I could ring, in case I got buried prematurely. It was possible to order one type of shell with one type of lid and with one kind of lager. Sorry, I mean laquer.

The average delivery time was about seven days. Old or damaged coffins could also be repaired. I was dead lucky to have arrived there. Perhaps if I ordered my box from there, I could arrange for it to be dug up, say after three years, and given a sandpaper, a lick of laquer, a screw tightened and have it treated for wood rot, a sort of M.O.T. . It was clearly a very busy place with guaranteed customers. I thanked the man for the time and care he gave to helping me.

It didn't take long to reach Powfoot, just off the B724, where long ago it was planned to create a holiday resort with a lake, a bathing pool and magnificent houses. From there I could look across at the wireless station masts in Cumbria and I wished I could have radioed for help, for the front tyre repaired the day before was giving me trouble again. The tyre was flat and there was no garage at hand.

It was down to me that time. I wheeled the bike into a tiny public park nearby, and took shelter behind a hedge from the wind and rain. Off came all the luggage and the tyre and I put in a spare tube. Luckily, it was the front wheel again, so that I didn't have the complication of gears to deal with. It was difficult doing the job in a cycling cape, and I was frozen in the shorts I'd worn all the way from Land's End.

'Not a very nice day,' greeted a man as I reloaded the bike.

What an understatement, for it was by far the worst weather I had encountered on the entire journey. Once ready for the road again I cycled on towards Ruthwell, a small community just off the B724, and not to be confused with Roswell of alien fame.

That Ruthwell is famous is due in no small measure to the Rev. Henry Duncan (1774-1846), who became a Church of Scotland minister there after turning down better opportunities in Ireland and in Lochmaben. He worked to help the poor and through his efforts the first Savings Bank was established in 1810. It should be noted, however, that it is also claimed that the first Savings Bank was established in Hamburg in 1778. As far back as 1697 Daniel Defoe had the same idea, but it was Duncan who founded it so well that, in the space of five years, there were Savings Banks modelled on his all over the UK. In order to establish and spread these banks, Duncan had to bear many of the expenses himself.

He was also an artist, writer, newspaper founder, essayist, church reformer and founder member of the Free Church of Scotland, when the Disruption took place in 1841. Duncan also delivered the first account of fossil footprints to the Royal Society of Edinburgh. His friends included Robert Owen (see later), Thomas Carlyle, James Hogg, known as the Ettrick Shepherd, Sir David Brewster (1781-1868), the scientist and inventor of the kaleidoscope, and he had even known Robert Burns.

Naturally I went to see the first Savings Bank that Duncan established, but when I arrived in the rain it was closed for lunch. Was it a money hungry bank? The obvious thing to do was to go and view the Ruthwell Cross, which I also had come to see.

This ancient cross, the most important Anglo-Saxon cross in Scotland, is about 18 feet high and over 1200 years have passed since some unknown artist created it in the early 8th century. On the edges of the Cross is the runic text of the Holy Rood, a Dream written by Caedmon, the shepherd poet, in the 7th century.

It was the Rev. Duncan who discovered and restored it after its bad treatment. The General Assembly had met in Aberdeen in 1640 and passed an Act requiring all crucifixes to be taken down, because they were considered to be idolatrous. Furthermore, late in 1642 in another Act, the idolatrous monuments in Ruthwell were specially mentioned. The cross was pulled down and broken in 1664, and the broken pieces lay for 130 years or more in the church earth or clay floor, and were consequently protected from the rough elements. It was daft breaking the cross, for it seems it was raised against Roman Catholic dominance, which the Reformers were also against. Duncan collected all the broken pieces, put them together and erected the Cross in 1802 in his manse garden, from which it was later taken to be put inside a specially built apse in Ruthwell Church in 1887.

While I was busy reading about and photographing the Cross, somebody was trying hard to get in at a locked door.

'Go round to the other side,' I cried and some minutes later a couple entered the church by the door I'd used.

'Thanks. We thought the door was locked.'

I spoke to them a while, before returning to the Savings Bank which was then open. As soon as I entered, the lady in charge gave me a guided tour of the museum. She was kind and well meaning, but I would have preferred to have gone round myself and asked questions, when I needed further information.

'This shows the Rev. Duncan himself along with another Church reformer, Hugh Miller of Cromarty,' she said, drawing my attention to a framed picture, 'and this is Duncan's chair and his desk and these are his books.' I was to learn more about Miller later.

From Ruthwell I cycled next to Brow Well, where Burns drank the water in the belief it would help his health. His doctor had sent him to bathe in the cold waters of the Solway Firth, a bad decision in view of the fact that it is now believed that Burns suffered from bacterial endocarditis and rheumatic heart disease. It was still raining, when I moved on from the rectangular shaped stone lined pool.

I decided to forego visiting a Wildfowl and Wetland's Trust Centre, where there were 20 hides, 3 towers and a heated observatory. My next destination was Caerlaverock, where there is a nature reserve and a castle. I photographed the castle from a distance but didn't enter. Instead I watched a video about it in the café next to the shop. Most of the area is part of the Caerlaverock estate and dates back to the time of the Norman conquest. The Caerlaverock National Nature Reserve is the largest wetland reserve in Britain and one of the few sites in Britain, where the natterjack toad, the rarest amphibian in Britain, is to be found. The hazel trees have provided wood for sheep pens, fences and building materials. Alder and oak have been used in the production of charcoal, gunpowder, medicines and clogs. Behaving myself, I spotted no woodpeckers nor did I see any of the roe deer, which are good at camouflaging themselves among the trees.

The castle, now in the care of Historic Scotland, lies 6 miles south of Dumfries and was built in the 13th century by Sir Herbert de Maxwell, who moved from an earlier castle south of the present one. In the 14th century, ownership of the castle see-sawed between the Scots and the English. Later in the 17th century, the castle was enlarged by Robert Maxwell, Earl of Nithsdale, and was besieged for over 3 months during the struggle between the Covenanters and Charles I.

The Covenanters had sworn to uphold the Presbyterian Church, which is Protestant and governed by presbyters, i.e. by ministers and elders. Many of them were also against the political philosophy of the Stuart kings, who believed that they had a divine right to rule. About 60,000 gathered in Greyfriars Churchyard in Edinburgh to oppose the rule of bishops and sign a covenant (agreement or contract).

Once refreshed in the tearoom, I set off for Bankend to find the grave of Robert Paterson, who took on the task of cleaning and repairing the Covenanter gravestones and restoring the names and epitaphs. In 1788, Sir Walter Scott, while staying with the parish minister of Dunnottar Church near Stonehaven, met by chance Paterson who was working on the

Covenanters' Stone there. This headstone in the churchyard is under 3 feet high and 28 inches wide and commemorates nine Covenanters who died as prisoners in Dunnottar Castle, including two who died from falling down the cliff face while trying to escape. Scott was so inspired by the man's devotion that he wrote his novel 'Old Mortality', in which the hero was based on Paterson.

Incidentally my daughter Sandra tried to become an extra in a crowd scene, when Zeffirelli was shooting at Dunnottar Castle for his film 'Hamlet'. She was rejected for being too smartly dressed. Later she married in the castle's old chapel and signed the marriage register in the drawing room in which her late grandfather Charles Garden, my wife's father, once scratched his initials up the chimney after he had restored the ceiling's heraldry.

It was still raining when I arrived at the old cemetery at Bankend, and walked in cagoule and yellow cycling cape round the gravestones. I searched in vain, perhaps too carelessly because of my discomfort, and was about to give up when a car drew up at the farm house beside the cemetery. Two men got out and I spoke to one of them.

'Excuse me, but do you know where the 'Old Mortality' gravestone is?'

'Yes,' he said. 'Follow me and I'll show you.'

'That's very decent of you, considering it's raining so heavily. Could I have your name? I'll mention it in a book I intend to write about my Land's End – John O' Groats journey.' I didn't always remember to ask names.

'It's Jim Kerr,' he replied.

I thanked him for his help, well aware that his companion was already enjoying the comfort of a warm house. I photographed the stone as he walked back to the cemetery gate. From Bankend I cycled towards Dumfries and searched for Crichton Royal Hospital. I missed it the first time, but took the right road eventually and steered the bike up the main drive to the door.

Originally the hospital, founded in 1839, was the Crichton Institution for Lunatics. That was where Sir Arthur Conan Doyle's father, an alcoholic, was admitted and, I've been told, somewhat neglected by his family. I too wanted to be admitted, not for that reason, but to see a chair Robert Burns had sat on to adjudicate a whistling competition which he recorded on paper. Some time later, the chair landed up in that hospital where the world's first hospital magazine, written monthly by patients, was produced. The issues from 1844-1937 are in the hospital museum collection.

'Excuse me, but is it possible to see the chair Robert Burns sat on?'

'I'm sorry, I can't help you. I just don't know,' said the first lady I asked.

Another lady appeared and I repeated the question.

'I'm sorry you can't be admitted just now and the lady to ask won't be in until tomorrow,' I was told. 'Why don't you come back then?'

'I can't. I'm moving on. I'll just have to leave it. Thanks anyway.'

I wasn't sure if I liked the implication of her word 'admitted'. It was definitely time to move.

Once into Dumfries, I enquired about and found a toilet and dived in quickly, in case my belongings left outside should disappear. There being no hostel or camping site that I knew of, I had to get a B&B in Dumfries. The tourist office was shut but, after I made some enquiries, a lady directed me to a street which offered such accommodation. I was lucky and was able to put my bike into a roomy garage at the back of a large house. It was such a relief to find a place at that time of evening and get out of the rain.

Once I had deposited my luggage in the bedroom, I went out to buy a snack. I found a small store in a street leading to Queen of the South's football pitch and bought some filled rolls and a can of juice. Back in the bedroom, I relaxed and enjoyed my food as I planned my next day. I had made it through the rain and had deprived no Solway Firth locals of a casket. At the same time I realised that I didn't know what the letters 'DFS' stood for, but thought it reasonable to eliminate 'Dead For Sure' as a meaning. Later, after reading the product guide booklet given to me, I learned that one of the partners was David Smith, which possibly explains two of the letters.

3 June   Dumfries – Nr. Dunscore – Just N. of Dumfries   O.S. 84, 78

I awoke early and decided that there was time to see some of the sights of the town before breakfast was served. Shortly after leaving the B&B, I walked parallel to the river Nith and arrived at the 'Coach and Horses', an old hostelry which existed in Burns' time. Just up Bank Street I saw the tenement, where Burns lived in 1791 in a first floor flat to which he moved with his family after leaving Ellisland farm. This house has been called the 'Sanghoose o' Scotland', for during his short stay there Burns collected, composed or improved many fine songs including 'Ae Fond Kiss', 'The Deil's Awa Wi' Th' Exciseman' and 'Lea Rig'. I read the words of the plaque: 'Here, in the Songhouse of Scotland, between November, 1791 and May, 1793, Robert Burns completed over 60 songs.'

On the same side of the river as Bank Street, I passed through the Whitesands area which was once the site of a farm animal market. There the herds were watered and drovers mixed with the tinkers who camped there. In 1659 at Whitesands, nine women deemed to be witches were strangled and burnt. I then trotted and walked fast to Dock Park, where I found a memorial stone or obelisk commemorating two citizens of Dumfries and Maxwelltown (the latter now part of Dumfries). One man was John Hume, a member of the 'Titanic's' band and the other was

Thomas Mullins, a steward. Both drowned when the liner went down. The ship left New York on 10 April, 1912 and four days later it ran into an iceberg and started sinking at 11.40 p.m. By 2.20 a.m. it was totally submerged.

If you have already read my 'Vol. 1 Across England', you will perhaps remember that I already touched upon the 'Titanic' when I visited Charleston, Cornwall, Leigh west of Manchester, and the Pendle Hill area, and this was why I was pleased to discover in Dumfries another link with the disaster. I might as well add here that engineers born in Greenock, Glasgow, Alloa, Aberdeen and Elgin and one educated in Stirling all went down with the ship.

But for lack of time caused by the two earlier punctures and the need to be back in Aberdeen by 18 June in readiness for a booked holiday in Wales, I had intended, prior to Dumfries, going to Dalbeattie, from which town one of the 'Titanic' officers by the name of Murdoch had come. His portrayal in the film 'Titanic' as a coward, who took bribes, caused quite a controversy and great anger was felt by some people, including a relative in Dalbeattie. According to survivors' statements, he shot himself on the bridge deck but there were no witnesses, it is said, to the claims that he took bribes to ensure lifeboat places for rich aristocrats. At the end of the 19th century, Lt. William Murdoch's father bought a cottage in Dalbeattie, and it was suggested recently that it could be used as an extension to the existing museum. This proposal, however, has not materialised.

Writing about Dalbeattie reminds me that, before that town, there were two other places I had planned to include in my 'grand tour'. Each has a connection with Dumfries as you will read. One was Sweetheart Abbey along the A710 south of Dumfries and the other was the Paul Jones cottage, south-east of Kirkbean and farther along the same road.

The 13th and early 14th century abbey, then occupied by Cistercian monks, was founded by Dervorgilla in memory of her husband John Balliol, the founder of Balliol College, Oxford and father of King John Balliol. When her husband died, she had his embalmed heart placed in an ivory and enamelled silver casket (not from DFS) and, when she died, it was buried with her, clasped to her breast. Dervorgilla had called the heart 'her sweet, silent companion' and the abbey became known as 'Sweetheart Abbey'. I visited it once years ago. It was Dervorgilla's husband's brother Sir Joscelyn who owned at Insch, Aberdeenshire, Dunnideer Castle, beside which I played as a youngster and learned my first German from German prisoners, waiting to be returned to their own country.

The cottage I had been keen to see is in the Arbigland estate near Kirkbean, and it was in that humble building that John Paul Jones (1747-92) was born. Jones, whose father was head gardener on the estate, became an eminent naval officer who fought boldly for America and Russia, but he has also been described as a pirate by those who did not favour him. In 1787 he was awarded a gold medal by the U.S. Congress, five years before he died in Paris shortly before his 45th birthday. In 1913 his body was taken to the U.S. and placed in a splendid tomb in the Naval Academy in Annapolis. He is after all regarded as the 'Father of the American Navy'.

The mansion on the Arbigland estate was built by a William Craik, a smuggler, linguist, architect, agricultural improver and merchant. Craik's son, Dr. James Craik, became George Washington's friend and personal doctor.

It was not to be and there I was in Dumfries earlier than expected. Across the river diagonally from the 'Titanic' memorial is Troqueer Church from which John Blackadder, a Covenanter, was forced to leave after an Act of 1662 was passed. Until it left in 1942 the Norwegian army, stationed in Dumfries during World War II, worshipped in that church. It was also in Dumfries that a Norwegian army store supplied some of the clothing for the four Norwegians, who were parachuted into Norway in 1942, as an advance party to prepare for a later attack in 1943 on the German heavy water plant at Vemork, near Rjukan in the Telemark region. I decided, however disappointing, that I would have to miss visiting the church that morning (probably shut anyway) for breakfast time was approaching. I hurried back for I like to be punctual.

'I've been out already,' I said when my delicious breakfast was brought to the table. 'I took some photographs.'

After breakfast, I paid a lady left in charge because the owner had to take her daughter to school. Once loaded, I visited the T.S.B. then went to take a good look at the Midsteeple building. That was built in 1707 and was the old Tolbooth used variously as town buildings, court and prison. On the front is carved an ell, the old Scots measure of 36 inches and also on the building is a table of distances from Dumfries, including the distance of 272 miles to Huntingdon in England. That was where the Scottish cattle drovers headed on their way to the London markets. There is also a royal coat of arms and a coat of arms of St. Michael, the patron saint of Dumfries.

The key of the Tolbooth had a second use as an instrument of punishment for those who stole peats in the burgh. The stolen peats were lit, the key was heated until red hot and then pressed against the thief's cheek. Even in days of yore they clearly had cheeky thieves.

Farther down the High Street, I came to the fountain built to commemorate the introduction of water to Dumfries in 1851. In 1850 a Bill was passed in the Commons, allowing water to be taken from Lochrutton Loch south-west of Dumfries. I saw too, next to Marks and Spencer, the original façade of the former Commercial, later County Hotel, in which Bonnie Prince Charlie set up his headquarters during his three days' stay in Dumfries in 1745. Charlie imposed a fine of £2000 on the burgh and demanded 1000 pairs of brogues. He and Imelda Marcos of the Philippines might have got on well, except that Charlie wanted the shoes for his men and not for himself.   It was rumoured that his enemy the Duke of Cumberland was approaching and Charlie left with only £1000 and 255 pairs of shoes. Riding rough shod, as it were, over the burgh, he left the town with two hostages, an ex-provost and a councillor. They were to be released when his demands were met.

Also in the High Street I came to the Globe Inn Close, along which I pushed the bike to a parking place outside the 1610 established inn. The rear courtyard there is attractive with paintings, wrought iron, arches, seats and wall written poems. In one painting, Burns is seen with four women mentioned in his letters and poems, and in the iron work I noticed a scene from 'Tam O' Shanter'. On an upstairs window there is some of Burns' poetry written on the glass with a diamond. With what else when Burns was fond of some of the hard stuff? There in the Globe Inn in 1819 was held the first, for Ayr, of what was to become the annual Burns Supper.

However, I had come to see another Burns' chair, the one he sat in when he came to drink in the inn. I approached one of the busy bar staff.

'Would it be possible for me to see Burns' chair and take a photo of it?' I asked.

'It's through here,' I was told. 'This inn was Burns' favourite drinking place.'

Burns became very friendly with one of the barmaids there and she bore him a son. I kept my distance from the barmaids and even more so from his chair, because I had heard that whoever sits in it and cannot recite a Burns' poem has to buy a round of drinks to all present. So far I had had no accidents on my travels and I didn't want to injure myself financially, just by failing the test and having my pocket hit hard.

Still sober I took the bike (not acting up at that moment) via Shakespeare Street to the Theatre Royal, claimed to be the oldest functioning theatre in Scotland. This theatre was co-founded and patronised by Burns who wrote prologues for it. Once, while with a group of friends, Burns was accused of singing revolutionary songs there and he landed in trouble. He was required, he was cautioned later, to be more careful when in government service as an exciseman.

My next stop was at the red sandstone building of St. Michael's church, believed to be the last church in Scotland in which Mass was celebrated during the Reformation. I was glad to see the roof looked in good order, for at one time sheet lead ordered for the roof ended up as musket balls for soldiers defending the town. This church too once had a minister who suffered for his Covenanting beliefs.

I specially wanted to see the Burns' family pew and inside the church on a pillar was a plaque, indicating where Burns and his family worshipped. I was told that, although the position would be correct, the actual seat having been replaced is no longer there. Jean Armour, Burns' wife, attended church there for 30 years after Rabbie's death.

There is also a wall memorial tablet to a James McLauchlan, who was involved in the cholera outbreak, which led to the burial in the churchyard of the victims. He took part in the first operation using ether anaesthetic in Britain and this happened three days before the Glasgow arrival of Lister, famous for his antiseptic surgery, but less well known for performing a mastectomy on his own sister.

Outside in the churchyard, which I had visited many years before, I walked to the Grecian mausoleum in which Burns, his wife Jean Armour and five of his children are buried.

'Burns was originally buried in a simple unmarked grave to the left of the mausoleum,' said a Dumfries man who joined me. 'In fact when William Wordsworth and his sister Dorothy came up to see it, they had difficulty in finding it. Eventually money was raised for the mausoleum and he was dug up. His features were well preserved but the head very quickly collapsed into a heap of dust.'

'Do you like coming here?' I asked. 'Presumably being a Dumfries man you've been here before.'

'Yes, there's an atmosphere here. Remembering his poems and songs leaves its mark on you and it's moving to walk here and think that these people were once alive and vital.'

'Yes, I know what you mean. It's an emotional thing to think of all the beauty Burns produced, that all his family and friends have gone. We don't want them, Burns in particular, to be gone.'

'The sad thing too is that some people feel nothing or very little for such matters. Have you seen inside the church and the graves of his friends here?'

'Oh yes,' I replied.

I thanked him and went off to find the Covenanter graves I remembered were there, and the memorial to those who succumbed to cholera. There was one stone with the names of two men who were killed in January, 1667 'for their adherence to the principles of the Reformation' and also inscribed was the name James Kirk who was 'shot on the sands of Dumfries'. I was relieved that the word 'Captain' was missing in front of 'James' and that 'Star Trek' would be unaffected, but also moved by the courage shown by such men as they stuck to their beliefs. There was also the Martyr's Monument raised by voluntary contributions.

On 15 September, 1832 Asian cholera hit the town and remained until 27 November. At least 900 people were affected of which 44 died on the first day, followed by another 376 deaths. The money for the cholera monument was taken from collections made in churches in the town.

I left the churchyard and went next to the house, where Burns and his family lived from May 1793 and where Burns died on 21 July, 1796. There scratched with his diamond ring is his name on an upstairs window. Then it was back to the High Street again, for I wanted to see where the King's Arms, the main coaching inn in Dumfries, stood. I branched off into English Street and on the right almost at the entrance was where it had been.

There again on a window, Burns scratched some lines of poetry and there too Robert Ferguson (1750-74) met with a local poet by the name of John Mayne. Like Burns, whose forebears came from the Mearns, south-west of Stonehaven, Ferguson's parents also came from N.E. Scotland. They moved to Edinburgh where Robert was born near the High Street, the father from Tarland and the mother from Kildrummy. After leaving St. Andrews University, Robert returned to work as a clerk in Edinburgh where he continued to write, producing work for the theatre, songs and poems in English and Scots. The latter were in a mixture of Scots dialects and literary Scots. When Ferguson died he was buried in an unmarked grave in the Canongate Kirkgate and it was Robert Burns, who erected a stone in memory of the man who was his chief forerunner.

Leaving the King's Arms in February 1829 William Hare, one of the two infamous body snatchers Burke and Hare, just missed a lynch mob of thousands. Hare should have been hanged like Burke, but was let off for turning King's evidence. That Dumfries crowd thought otherwise and would have strung him up as well, had not the local police used a decoy to get him out and away. Burke was later used for dissection and, had he realised, when alive, that that was to be his destiny, he might have been cut up about it earlier.

Farther along the High Street, I photographed the Burns statue erected in 1882 and made from Carrara marble, quarried and carved in Italy to a design by Amelia Hill, the wife of the pioneer photographer David Octavius Hill. I then turned down Buccleuch Street where, just after the entrance to Irish Street, stood the County prison erected in 1851. The last man and the last woman to be executed publicly, it is claimed, were hanged in that jail in Dumfries.

I knew it was time to get out of Dumfries because I intended to reach Wanlockhead that day, but there were many diversions and stops on the way. I decided to see one more place and have a quick look at Greyfriars Church. Two grey haired ladies were sitting at the door. Were they wardens I wondered? They were certainly volunteers and were keen to tell me about their church.

'Good morning,' one of them greeted me amiably. 'Are you wanting to see round?'

'Well, I can't stop long, for I've a long way to go, but maybe you can tell me something about the place.'

'Right, I don't know if this will interest you, but there was a castle just here over 300 years ago, and there was a monastery where these shops are. The church of that monastery is famous in Scottish history, for that was where Robert the Bruce in 1306 stabbed the Red Comyn, who supported Edward I's claim to the Scottish throne rather than that of Bruce.'

'I remember that story from my primary school days, but I didn't realise it happened here,' I said.

'And remember when Bruce was asked if the man was dead and was unsure,' continued the other lady, 'another man went in saying "I'll mak siccar."' (I'll make sure.)

'Yes, I remember that. These words have always been vivid in my memory.'

I thanked and left the ladies and looked for Glasgow Street. My route outwards from Dumfries now lay on the A76, with good cycling ahead in dry conditions very unlike the previous day. It wasn't long before I encountered some roadworks but there was no problem in getting by, for I was directed past any difficult bits.

'Go over that bridge there,' advised a yellow coated man, 'and you'll find it easier to get past all this.'

Moving on I passed Holywood with an 'l' less than its 'near twin' in America. The only stars to be seen beside Dumfries, however, are the ones you see in the heavens at night or if you bang your head on a suddenly braking bus. Speaking about the heavens, somewhere in the Holywood area a retired professor designed a special garden depicting the heavens. I wanted to see that garden and wrote to the Dumfries and Galloway Tourist Board to find out its exact location, and if it would be possible to visit it. A letter came back telling me that a Lady Keswick had passed away, and the Board was not sure what was to happen with the garden, which up to then had been open to the public. The Board had been asked not to make contact until it heard from the Trustees.

Some miles north of Dumfries I arrived at Ellisland Farm, a place I had long wanted to see. I arrived just before it opened, as I found out when I wheeled the bike round to what for me was a side entrance in relation to the road. Still suffering from the loss of my National Trust receipt, I paid my entrance fee when the man in charge eventually opened the door.

'I'm from Aberdeen,' he said in response to my informing him where I hailed from.

The house was full of information on Ellisland and the times and artefacts belonging to Burns. He had been offered the lease of the farm by his friend Patrick Miller, who introduced the Swedish turnip into Scotland, and Burns took over the place in 1788. The land was not the best but Burns tried to earn a living there for three years, until he moved to the already mentioned house in Bank Street, Dumfries in 1791. Burns, however, didn't make enough money from the farm, but managed to obtain a position with the Customs and Excise. The latter job sometimes saw him riding 200 miles a week and keeping records and, with his farm work as well, it's a wonder he found time to write.

It was while walking by the river that he is said to have written 'Tam O' Shanter' at a fast speed. Burns also wrote 'Auld Lang Syne' at Ellisland. For those who don't know, the 'S' is pronounced as an 'S' and not as a 'Z'. When Cliff Richard's song 'Millenium Prayer' to the tune of 'Auld Lang Syne' became a hit, it was reported that he wanted to visit Robert Burns' mausoleum. That was his choice but neither the Lord's Prayer nor the tune 'Auld Lang Syne' was written by Burns.

Patrick Miller lived at Dalswinton some miles farther north and I set off to see Dalswinton Loch, the scene of a very historic event. Before leaving the A76 and turning off to the right, I stopped at a small shop for something to eat.

'A Mars bar please and two ice creams,' I said to the lady. 'It's so warm today and my mouth's dry.'

The ice creams were delicious and I was sufficiently into astrology to be grateful for the benign influence the red planet's chocolate product had on my well being. I stood outside the shop and ate the lot before pedalling on, then turning off to the right. An easy run took me to the loch after a man gave me some advice about finding it. There on the water William Symington applied steam to inland navigation. Patrick Miller and Robert Burns, it is said, along with Alexander Nasmyth, the artist father of the inventor of the steam hammer, were present, when the first steam boat in the world set sail on 14 October, 1768. The design and construction were carried out by Symington and Taylor, engineers from Wanlockhead. A replica of the steamboat is presently at Dalswinton Loch.

It was very quiet as I stood at the water's edge and imagined the excitement of these men, experimenting with this new invention which would change the way people travelled.

It was an easy run back along the secondary road to the A76. I next cut westwards across country with the intention of reaching Dunscore to see something in connection with the Covenanters. As I cycled through the countryside, trouble started in the shape or lack of correct shape of a tyre gone flat. This was the third successive day I had a problem with the front tyre. Having pulled the bike into the side and removed all the luggage, I started on the front wheel. After inserting another inner tube I began pumping, but to no avail. The tube just wouldn't inflate and there was nothing for it but to return to Dumfries on foot. A decent man on a motor bike stopped to ask sympathetically about the health of my bike, and he was obviously very observant.

'Had a puncture, then?'

'Yes, it's the front tyre. The same one three days in a row.'

'There must be something wrong with it.'

He must surely be related to Sherlock Holmes, I thought or else he didn't know what to say in the situation.

'The tube or the valve must be faulty. The pump's okay as far as I know. I'll just have to walk back to Dumfries.'

'But how will you manage? You can't push the bike with all that stuff on it.'

Mentally I heard myself telling him that he could take me, the bike, four panniers, a tent, a sleeping bag and a large rucksack on the back of his motor bike to Dumfries.

'I'll pack as much as I can into this 70 litre rucksack and so take the weight off the wheels, particularly the front one. I don't want the front wheel buckled.'

'Best of luck then,' he said and roared off on his bike, perhaps having read my silent wishful thinking.

I loaded the rucksack, glad that I wasn't too far from Dumfries and walked several miles to the A76 and several more towards Dumfries. It was already evening and I knew that any cycle repair shops would be closed by the time I reached the town. I also knew that I would have to find some accommodation for the night, and didn't fancy having to do a last minute search late in the evening. Still some miles from Dumfries, I reached Newbridge camp site where I decided to stay overnight. I could walk in early next morning in time for any repair shop to open. There was one caravan and no tents on the small site, I noticed, as I advanced towards the reception where I heard a barking dog.

'That'll be £5 for the night,' said the man in charge, 'and here's your key for the toilet block.'

'I want to leave early,' I said. 'Will you be up when I return the key?'

'Post it through the letter box before you go,' he replied.

'You can rely on me.'

Soon the tent was up and with the luggage deposited inside, I phoned home as usual before having a quick snack in the tent. Thank goodness, I reflected, that none of my tyre problems had affected the back wheel. It rained before midnight but at least I had got back dry and I was soon asleep, knowing that Dumfries should welcome back my non-polluting vehicle. One problem, though. Should I see a doctor? I was having too much trouble with my inner tubes.

4 June   Just N. of Dumfries – Dumfries – Wanlockhead   O.S. 84, 78

I rose early and after breakfasting and packing up, I popped the toilet key through the reception letter box as requested, before taking the road to

Dumfries. No wonder I was overloaded - I should have left it where it was. Actually, the walk wasn't too bad and I arrived at the cycle shop, which I had found in Academy Street the day before. It was closed but I didn't have long to wait until it opened, and I was able to leave the bike and the luggage.

By then I was ready for a bite after the walk to Dumfries, but no dog appeared to accommodate me. However, just down the street was a takeaway where I bought a bacon roll and a cup of tea.

'That's really good value to get a bacon roll for 80p,' I said to the server, the boss himself, I believe. 'There was a place in the Lake District that wanted to charge me well over £2.00 for such a roll.'

'There's always some place trying to rip off people,' he replied.

The roll and tea were so good that I had a second helping of both, before setting off on foot to explore more of Dumfries. Across the road from the takeaway is the Academy which was established in 1897, but a school has been on that site since 1330. Former pupils include the already mentioned John Paul Jones, Henry Duncan, J.M. Barrie (1860-1937) and the actor John Laurie. Barrie, a Scottish author, is well known, of course, for writing 'Peter Pan', and the idea for the book is supposed to have come from Barrie's childhood memories of playing in a garden behind what was the Moat Brae Nursing Home, where Irving Street and George Street meet. I couldn't help wondering if this Irving was the same as the Annan Irving who was, shall we say, on very good terms with Carlyle's wife. Somewhere and sometime in my travels, I had heard there was a statue of Peter Pan in the garden, but I was unsuccessful in finding the latter, even after asking around. Barrie gave the profits from performances of 'Peter Pan' and of the book derived from it to the Great Ormond Street Hospital for Sick Children.

Across the road from the takeaway and nearer to Greyfriars Church, I spotted a wall statue high up. It was a statue of the Rev. Henry Duncan, erected above what a T.V. programme described as a 'Savings Bank building'. However, the building below the statue later became a Housing Association called 'Home In Scotland Ltd.'. The statue has long been known as the 'Stone Man', and is supposed to nod if you have more than £100 in the bank. He didn't nod to me and I was seized with panic, for I couldn't understand how so much of my T.S.B. money had disappeared, even allowing for the occasional bacon roll.

On leaving Academy Street I crossed the town to Dervorgilla Bridge built by Dervorgilla, believe it or not. Dumfries town council was later concerned about the safety of this bridge and James Birkmire, a barrel maker, built a house against the end of the bridge in 1660 and this strengthened it. Birkmire had to pay an annual feu duty and was allowed to possess the house, provided he informed the council before anyone brought across heavy loads of timber. Over the years the house has been an inn and

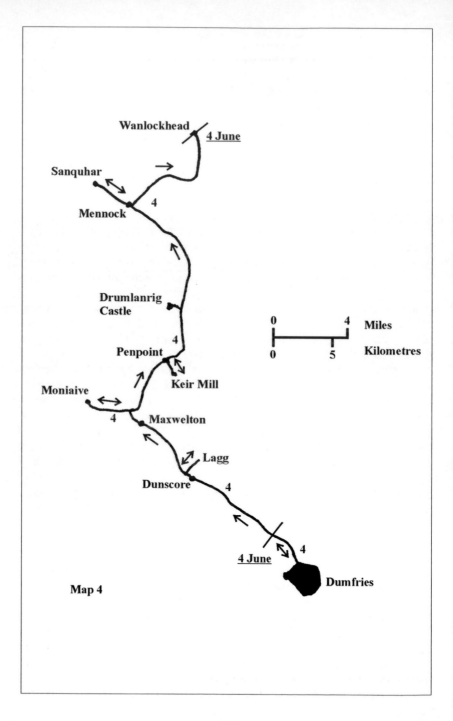

Map 4

a home, the last occupant dying in 1959. Today it is a museum and, after paying the entry fee, I had a good look around inside.

Since 1660 the bridge road has been heightened several times, and there are boulders at the corner of the building to protect it against being bumped.

'An interesting museum,' I said to the custodian. 'I've been to Dumfries before, but this is the first time I've been able to see the museum.'

From there, I walked down the bank of the river Nith to the Robert Burns Centre which opened in 1986. I discovered that the building was previously the old town mill, designed by the famous engineer Thomas Smeaton and destroyed by fire in 1985. Not only had it been a corn mill, but it became a hydro-electric power station in 1911. At one time there was a proposal to build a dock, between the river and the Centre, for a permanent exhibition of the replica of Patrick Miller's steamboat, but the idea fell through.

Who cares for history? I left the Centre and headed back for a third bacon sandwich and tea. I clearly had my priorities right, before I picked up the repaired bike plus a spare inner tube. That done I set off from the town, voted at one time as the best place to live in the UK. I cycled out along the A76 again, until I turned off for Dunscore via the B729. I understood that there was a Covenanter grave in the local churchyard but, when I reached it, I failed in my search.

'Excuse me, but is there a special Covenanter grave in there?' I asked one villager.

'Sorry, I don't know,' came the reply. 'Try that house at the end of the road. There's a man there who is a bit of an expert on local history.'

I took the advice and went up to the door of a house named 'Fairview', making sure that I had the bike between myself and any possible uncontrolled dog. I knocked and out came a man who identified himself as Mr. John Crocket.

'Good morning,' I greeted him. 'I was up at the churchyard there looking for a Covenanter grave, but I didn't see any and somebody recommended you to help me.'

'There's nothing like that up there,' he said, 'but I'll tell you an interesting place. Continue on the road through Dunscore, then take the first road to the right and go on until you see the remains of a tower on the right. That's Lag's tower, the ancestral home of the Griersones.'

Lag's real name was Robert Griersone (c. 1656-1733) but, as in N.E. Scotland, he was known by the farm name. He was so feared that children were told that Lag would get them if they didn't behave. I thanked Mr. Crocket and cycled out to see the ruined 15th century tower, which I found beside Lagg farm (O.S. spelling). At least I had found something near Dunscore connected with the Covenanters.

On communicating later with Mr. Crocket, he told me that Presbyterians were rolled in spiked barrels down a steep slope flanking the tower. Also within its eight foot thick walls, they were tortured with devices such as the thumbkins. It was from the tower, he said, that Griersone rode out with his dragoons and Highland mercenaries to persecute in south-west Scotland those people, who were opposed to the king's decrees.

Mr. Crocket also informed me that Griersone or Lag, knighted for his cruel repression of the Covenanters during the so called 'killing times', died later an old man, afflicted with dropsy and gout, in Dumfries. He added also that a memorial was erected to Griersone in 1897, 164 years after the latter's death, and is to be found in Dunscore Old Churchyard. I now realise that was what I had at the back of my mind, when I came initially into Dunscore.

Once back on the B729, I pedalled on in sunshine along the valley of Cairn Water to Maxwelton House. Having arrived there, I pushed the bike up the drive to the right and locked the bike outside. The House was originally called Glencairn Castle, but its name changed to Maxwelton when Stephen Laurie bought it in 1611. There his great granddaughter Anna was born in 1682. Anna or Annie Laurie (1682-1764) was made famous by the well known ballad written about 1700 by William Douglas, a rejected suitor.

The Laurie family kept possession of the house until 1966, but later a Mr. and Mrs. Hugh Stenhouse bought it in 1968 and spent three years restoring it. Locharbriggs Quarry near Dumfries was involved for over two years in the provision of stone and 65 men were employed.

As I left the house I had a word with the well spoken lady attendant at the door. I had already told her about the nature of my journey and she was really interested.

'I would have liked to have stayed longer,' I said, 'but I've a lot to see yet and a fair bit to cycle. I've taken a picture of the building, though. Are those the famous Maxwelton Braes mentioned in the song?' I pointed to the grassy hill slopes visible from the door and some distance away.

'Yes,' she replied and added: 'Good luck on your journey.'

I photographed those green braes then, fearful for my tyres under the heavy load, pushed the bike down the rough path to the secondary road. Just over a mile later I stopped to photograph the church where Annie got married. I didn't see if it was open but, after entering the A702, pressed on towards Moniaive where writers' courses have been held. I'm sure you the reader will find it easy to believe that I must have missed them.

I had to bike to the outskirts of the village before I found the monument to James Renwick, a Covenanter who was martyred for his beliefs. I locked the bike and climbed a short grassy slope from the road to read about him. James Renwick, newly ordained, returned from Holland and witnessed the hanging of Donald Cargill, a Covenanter, in the Grassmarket, Edinburgh.

Renwick joined the Covenanters after this and served as minister to 100 societies which Richard Cameron, another minister, had established. By 1688 Renwick was seized in Edinburgh and executed, also in the Grassmarket. It has been estimated that about 18,000 suffered, but Renwick was the last to be put to death. Some time after my trip was over, the Cutting Edge Theatre performed the play 'Blude Red', written by the theatre's founder Suzanne Lofthus. Over a six week period the play, whose main character is Renwick, was shown throughout Scotland.

On returning to the main street of Moniaive, I entered a small shop to buy a KitKat chocolate biscuit and something for my tea. On leaving Moniaive, I stuck to the A702 which took me up north to Penpont, from which I cycled in a south-east direction to the smithy at Courthill. There in 1838 or 1840, Kirkpatrick Macmillan made the first real bicycle by attaching a drive to the rear wheel of an earlier 'hobby horse', a two wheeled machine propelled by the rider's feet. Once in 1842, he rode his bike the 70 miles from Courthill smithy to Glasgow and he was fined for knocking down a child. The magistrate of the Gorbals Public Bar is said to have asked Macmillan to give a demonstration of his prowess on the bike, and to have paid his fine. A replica of his machine is in the Glasgow Transport Museum. Macmillan became famous long after his death for, following the accident, his invention was partly forgotten about for half a century.

Macmillan, who also pulled teeth and was a popular fiddle player, died in 1878, aged 65. He was obviously a man with a few strings to his bow.

I dismounted from the bike and took a photo of the building which was closed. What a pity Macmillan wasn't around, for I could have shown him my 21 gear bike. Back at Penpont I went into a small shop and café for a snack.

'Do you know if Drumlanrig Castle will be open?' I asked the lady behind the counter.

'Hm, you might make it,' came the reply.

The question was relevant, for the time was such I could expect places like that to be closing. I continued on the road to Thornhill but turned left along a secondary road and cycled north from Burnhead. Eventually I reached Drumlanrig Castle after passing Poets Corner near the river Nith. 'The boy stood on his bucking bike...'. O forget it, quickly!

I cycled up towards the castle but it was obviously shut. So disappointing, for I had hoped to see the bicycle museum. The castle was built for the first Duke of Queensberry round about 1680, but he was so annoyed by the cost that he spent only one night there and then went to stay in Sanquhar. Bonnie Prince Charlie slept in the castle at one stage and it is said to be haunted by a Lady Anne Douglas, who carries her head in her hands. The castle is now the home of the Duke of Buccleuch, one of the richest landowners in Scotland. Recently a valuable painting in the castle was stolen in broad daylight and it has still not been recovered.

Cycling on I returned to the A76, and left behind the quiet of the road I had been on for the more busy road. A good many miles later as I passed through Mennock, I recalled that there at Eliock House in 1560 was born James Crichton, who was famous for his achievements. It is said that he was a great singer, musician and dancer and could speak a dozen languages fluently while still a teenager. Still he proved that nobody's perfect by getting himself killed at the age of 22 in a street fight in Italy. Had I lived in his time, I might have used him to erect a fence for my garden, for reportedly, apart from being a great horseman, he was also an excellent fencer. J.M. Barrie used his life story as the basis for his play 'The Admirable Crichton' and Kenneth More starred in a modern film version of the story.

I cranked hard along the road towards Sanquhar and, once in the main street, came to the oldest post office in Scotland and, at the other side of the road, the Queensberry Arms visited by one of the Bonapartes. Some youngsters were playing beside the Tolbooth which is now a museum. I entered for a brief look, before going back down the main street to see a granite monument on the site of the former town cross. There the Covenanters produced the two Declarations of Sanquhar in 1680 and 1685 in their defence of Presbyterianism. Richard Cameron, a minister, became famous for his Declaration. As a result a price was put on his head and he was killed about four weeks later.

It was in Sanquhar too that Provost Andrew Crosbie and councillor Walter Riddle, taken hostage from Dumfries, were released by Bonnie Prince Charlie after he received the rest of the £2000 fine he imposed on Dumfries.

I still had nowhere to stay for the night, so I phoned Wanlockhead hostel and the conversation sounded like a repeat of that, when I phoned from Clitheroe to Slaidburn hostel in England.

'There's a bed available but you'll have to be in before I close the door,' I was told.

'I think I'll make it,' I said, 'but it's a long steep road and I'll have to walk a good bit for I've a heavy load.'

'Oh, it shouldn't take you that long. Don't worry. I'll stay up until you get here,' he replied most helpfully.

I set off expecting the worst when I reached the B797 but was pleasantly surprised to find that the gradient wasn't too bad for several miles. William Wordsworth, Dorothy his sister and Coleridge also came up this pass once, without bikes, and met some boys without shoes and stockings. Burns too went up there, not for exercise but for excise reasons, as a government officer. The road was quiet along by the Mennock water and it only became more difficult to cycle nearer the summit. From there, however, it was a great run to Wanlockhead, the highest village in Scotland. For the record, and to clear up any confusion, Tomintoul is the highest village in the Highlands of Scotland.

I arrived at the hostel earlier than expected and found that the warden was an older man doing the job on a temporary basis. I had just time to get a shower before going to bed in this basic but admirable hostel, which formerly was the home of the local mines' surgeon.

5 June   Wanlockhead – New Lanark   O.S. 78, 71

I rose to find another fine morning. After a scrappy, self-made breakfast, I left the hostel and pushed the bike uphill to see what was described by my Wanlockhead street plan, as the highest house in Scotland. I found it but, as far as I remember, it wasn't exploiting its fame by offering B&B or, even perhaps more appropriately, high teas. Walking down Goldscaur Row, I passed what the village map showed as the Gold Museum, but it was closed.

This is an area noted for its mineral wealth including gold. Scottish gold is amongst the purest in the world and the gold from the Mennock area is about 22.8 carats. Gold extracted locally was used in the making of the Scottish regalia and the Queen Mother had a brooch made from that gold. In 1424 the Scottish Parliament passed a law stating that any gold mine was to belong to the King. A Dutchman was one of the first prospectors, as was a Nicholas Hilliard, an Elizabethan goldsmith and painter, whose work is to be found in Drumlanrig Castle.

Farther downhill I came to a hut occupied by two men. This was where I could have arranged for a gold panning session, but I knew I couldn't spare the time. If only I had taken the right photographic equipment, I could have done some video camera panning instead. Gold has been extracted from most of the area's burns and, although the occasional nugget is found, most of the gold is in alluvial sands and gravels which have to be panned. When the rubbish or paydirt is washed away, the lucky prospector is left with a few gold grains or flecks which, being heavier, sink to the base of the pan.

There were a few men beside the hut and I engaged one of them in conversation.

'It's a pity you weren't here earlier in May,' he said. 'We had the annual British and Scottish Open Gold Panning Championship. There was an Italian team and an Italian won the British Open Championship Trophy. That's the first time a foreigner has won it.'

'Where did the competitors go to pan?' I asked. 'Was it in the Mennock?'

'No, each competitor was given a bucket full of sand and gravel and hidden in it were a few grains of gold. They put on waders and had to go into a bath of dirty water and start separating the dirt from the gold. The person who got the most gold in the shortest time became the winner.'

'So who organised all this?'

'The Wanlockhead Museum Trust. You must look into the museum and go and see the lead mine.'

'I intend to,' I answered.

The Museum of Lead Mining he had been referring to was described, at the time, as the largest industrial museum in the south-west of Scotland. After a quick visit to the tea room attached to the museum, I toured the museum and learned that lead had been probably mined locally since Roman times. Near the beginning of the 18th century, lead mining increased because of its use in glass and pottery making, and as a building material. When cheap foreign lead was imported into Britain in the first half of the 19th century, this resulted in a decline in lead mining which, apart from brief increases in production, ended completely in the 1950s. Famous engineers such as Smeaton, Murdoch, the Taylors and the Symingtons were employed in the Wanlockhead mines. It was Symington who helped build the second Watt engine to be built in Scotland and it was used at Wanlockhead.

From the museum, I walked to the other side of the valley and climbed a small slope to a shop to buy a Mars bar, before going to see the Straitsteps Cottages, where Wanlockhead mining families used to live. Life had been very hard for the miners what with scurvy, poor food and lack of hygiene. Next I made for the lead mine entrance with my ticket ready, and waited for the guide to appear at the appointed time. I was really keen to enter the mine for, as you'll be aware if you have read my 'Vol. 1 Across England', I had already been inside tin, copper, iron and coal mines. The guide was very late and I was short of time. A sign said that nobody should enter without a guide but, as there was still no sign of the guide or anyone else, I had to make a decision. I'm not saying whether I entered or not and the reader may draw his or her own conclusion.

As I prepared to leave, some people arrived having walked presumably from the museum, and then along the path to the mine.

'I thought the guide was supposed to be here some time ago,' I moaned. 'Anyway I can't wait to hear what will be said.'

I returned to the bike and pushed it back up towards the hostel. My first stop on the road uphill was beside the school built by the Duke of Buccleuch. I hope he had others to help him. The school closed in 1976 and is now a community centre. When the Wordsworths met barefooted local boys in the Mennock Pass, the lads told them that they studied Latin and Greek in the village.

Unfortunately the Lead Miners' Library was closed as I found when I went up the path. I noticed on the wall a brass plaque to a Robert Reid, who wrote under the pen name 'Robert Wanlock'. He went to Montreal, Canada where he wrote verse and died in 1922. Hopefully his demise was not the consequence of his writing. The library, founded in 1756, is said to be Scotland's second oldest and highest subscription library and has over 3000 rare books. I later learned that the library has a drum taken from Waterloo, presumably from Belgium and not from its namesakes in Britain, U.S.A. and Canada, and correspondence from famous people including R.L. Stevenson. Sir Walter Scott was an honorary member. The curling society also keeps there the curling trophies, which it has won playing against Sanquhar. I suppose it's not surprising that I didn't see any women with curlers, for it was only June after all.

I had seen much of what was worth seeing in Wanlockhead and, as I prepared to leave, I took a last look across to the Lowther Hills with their radar masts and dishes, which were set up in 1948. The summit of Lowther Hill was once used for burying suicides. Some day I shall climb these hills, having already climbed two-thirds of the lowland hills of that type, namely the Donalds. Lowther Hill also forms part of the Southern Upland Way of which I have walked a small part. Apparently on a fine day there are great views from the top of the hill. To the north are the Pentland Hills near Edinburgh, to the east the Cheviots, to the south the Isle of Man, Skiddaw and Helvellyn and away westward Ailsa Craig (a source of granite for curling stones), Ben Lomond and the Paps of Jura.

Someday too I'd like to walk the path from the village to the Enterkin Pass where Covenanters, bound for execution in Edinburgh, were rescued. Prince Charlie's army is said to have used the pass in 1745 and Daniel Defoe, who once stayed at Drumlanrig Castle, came to see that famous throughway.

It was time, however, to cycle to Leadhills, which claims to have the highest golf course in Britain, and whose Leadhills and Wanlockhead Railway is said to be Britain's highest adhesion railway at 1498 feet above sea level. It was built originally to carry lead to Scotland's Central Belt.

First I went looking for the Allan Ramsay (1685?-1758) library founded in 1741 and described as the oldest and second highest subscription library in Britain. It originally began as a reading club with 21 miners, the schoolmaster and the minister, according to one source. I found it on the main road on the right as I cycled into Leadhills.

'It's been called the "Allan Ramsay Library" for some time,' I was told by a resident, 'but maybe it was only his idea. We know that 23 lead miners established the library and that a mine manager called James Stirling was very much involved. Stirling was into social reform before Dale and Owen (see later) at New Lanark and he cared for the welfare of the miners.'

It is now called the 'Leadhills Reading Society' because there is no direct link with Ramsay. However, the idea of having a library in Leadhills may have come from Ramsay, who was born in the village and later founded a circulating library in Edinburgh.

Apart from a spell as a wigmaker (a good job, for wigs were always required by professionals such as lawyers or by those who wanted to be in the fashion), bookshop owner and publisher, Ramsay pioneered the use of Scots in his own poetry, at a time when most Scottish writers had abandoned Scots for English in their writing, and he also preserved the work of earlier Scots poets. He even built a theatre in Edinburgh at his own expense and co-founded the Easy Club, a society with Jacobite leanings.

Leaving behind the library I went to search for Ramsay's birthplace. I had a street plan, but I wasn't absolutely sure if I was at the right house. I asked a man out walking and was told how to locate it, but I can't remember what he said except to find a particular building first. Whatever, I found Ramsay's house and it was occupied by someone. A man outside in the street was keen to help when I told him what I was doing in Leadhills.

'You're into that old stuff, are you?' he asked. 'Go and see the curfew bell as well. That was rung to get the miners off to bed at a decent hour, and it was also rung when a John Taylor, aged 100, went missing for a long time in the snow. His grave is in the cemetery.'

I thanked him and went off to see the bell, which hangs in a kind of frame and then, by using the village plan, I arrived at the cemetery where I found the grave in question. Taylor's gravestone said that he died at the age of 137 years in 1770. As I stood there I thought of the gravestone in the cemetery at the entrance to Glen Muick near Ballater, Royal Deeside. It tells of a man who died ten years younger at the age of 127 years. Is the grave in Leadhills that of the engineer Taylor (or some relation), who was involved in the construction of the canal at Tavistock?

I climbed apologetically over the cemetery wall and dropped down into a grassy field, where there was a large monument to William Symington at the top of the slope. Symington, the son of a mine manager, was born in 1764 at Leadhills but he was brought up in Wanlockhead, where his brother George was a mine engineer. William worked on steam pumps for the mines, before developing a steam engine for a canal tug boat. This was the 'Charlotte Dundas', which was successfully tested on the Forth and Clyde canal, but nothing came of it, because the canal owners were frightened that such boats would eat away the canal banks. Consequently orders for steam powered boats for canals near Manchester were cancelled. Later Bell in Scotland with his 'Comet' and Fulton in America with his 'Claremont' were successful with their use of steam power. Both, however, are said to have studied Symington's 'Charlotte Dundas'.

Symington's engine, designed and made in Wanlockhead and tried out as said previously on Dalswinton Loch, is now in the Science Museum in

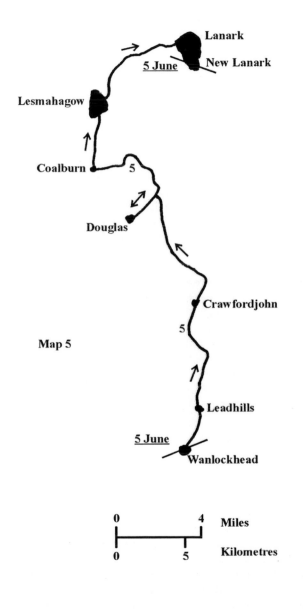

Lanark

New Lanark

<u>5 June</u>

Lesmahagow

Coalburn

5

Douglas

Crawfordjohn

5

Map 5

Leadhills

<u>5 June</u>

Wanlockhead

| 0 | | 4 | Miles |
| 0 | | 5 | Kilometres |

London.

After photographing the gravestone and Symington's monument, I climbed back over the cemetery wall, for I saw no obvious way in or out. Cycling on and stopping, I asked several people what proof there was about John Taylor's age and at last found a man, who put me more in the picture.

'Right,' said my informant, 'according to his own story he was mining underground when he was called to the surface to see an eclipse of the sun in 1652. If he saw an eclipse then and died in 1770, he must have been 118 years old plus his miner's age of at least 15, for you couldn't be a miner before then. That would make him 133 years old when he died.'

'Sounds a bit far fetched to me,' I said.

'They say he came in 1732 from Strontian in the west of Scotland to work here as a mining engineer and was supposed to be very old even then.'

I thanked him for his time and interest and pedalled off carefully, in case the approaching car reduced my lifespan.

Leadhills was into gold production as well, and in 1542 its gold was also used in making the Scottish Regalia now viewable in Edinburgh Castle. The lead miners used to use their spare time occasionally to pan for enough gold to make a ring for their lady friends.

I certainly had no time for panning, as I left with the memory of Wanlockhead and Leadhills, set in an area nicknamed 'God's Treasure House In Scotland'. After climbing a bit, I had a tremendous run downhill, which took me far from Leadhills to reach Crawfordjohn. Once I left the B797, I cycled in a north-westerly direction for about three miles. The only thing I knew about this small place was that Sam Bor, a former leader of the Scottish National Orchestra had settled there for a while in a cottage with his wife Dorothy. Both were friendly with my wife's sister Caroline Garden, for all three were once members of the Orchestra.

On entering a local bar, I checked that I had the right road for Douglas, my next destination, for I had an old map for this part of the route. I had to take the B7078 (formerly the A74) running roughly alongside the M74. Travelling along the B road was wonderful, for it was so quiet and I can remember only one or two cars on it. I came abreast of two men in yellow jackets and helmets and spoke to one of them.

'This road is going to be closed to vehicles,' one said.

'That's a pity for it's a great route for cyclists,' I replied.

'Oh, they're going to develop a route for cyclists and walkers, I believe.'

It was such a pleasure in the sun and soon I arrived at the A70, where I turned left and sped on towards Douglas. There I stopped at a little shop to buy a pint of milk and a Mars bar. I altered the tone of the place by eating and drinking outside the shop, but maybe redeemed myself by depositing the empty carton in a waste bin across the road.

There used to be a castle there by the name of Douglas Castle, not to be confused with the town of Castle Douglas in Dumfries and Galloway, but it was demolished in 1938 because of subsidence. This was the castle referred to in Sir Walter Scott's 'Castle Dangerous', a name given to it by the English.

I then took up the Covenanting connection again, for there was a particular stone I wanted to see.

'Excuse me, but can you tell me where I can find the stone with the shears carved on it?'

'It's in the main street,' came the quick reply from a smiling lady.

Sure enough I found it just back from the pavement. Built into a cairn was a lintel taken from a cottage which had belonged to a James Gavin, a tailor and Covenanter, whose ears were cut off as a punishment for adhering to his beliefs. Carved into the lintel are shears and a tailor's goose.

I next went looking for old St. Bride's clock tower, whose clock is said to have been gifted by Mary Queen of Scots, when she stayed in Bell's Wynd in 1565 with her cousin Darnley. The clock is set to strike three minutes before the hour, because of the Douglas motto: 'Never Be Late.' It is said to be the oldest working public clock in Scotland.

I tried to go into the church which unfortunately was locked but, when I enquired, I was told that I would have to get the key from a house nearby.

'Good afternoon,' I said to a lady who appeared at the door I knocked at. 'Would it be possible to have the key to go into the church?'

'Certainly,' she replied. 'Just lock up and bring the key back here when you're finished.'

I set off and walked round the building, until I found the door which the big key fitted. The place was well worth visiting. I came to Inglis Aisle, named after a man called Inglis who once lived on a nearby farm. He learned that the English were about to storm the nearby castle, and warned the local Earl who, as a reward, allowed him to be buried in the churchyard.

My attention was drawn to a piece of Sir James Douglas, who was killed on the way to the Holy Land with Robert the Bruce's heart. Douglas's own heart was brought back to St. Bride's and enclosed in a lead casket, which I could see through a glass case on the floor. There too, enclosed and visible through a similar glass case, is the heart of Archibald Bell-the-Cat. How did Archie get his nickname? A faint memory suggests it was something to do with a brave mouse and a cat. Did a mouse attach a bell to a sleeping cat so that when the cat moved the mice were warned? Whatever, James III of Scotland had a great passion for music, dancing, good clothes and fencing, and he preferred the company of people keen on that rather than the company of his nobles. The latter became jealous and annoyed and Archibald, Earl of Angus, seized the king's favourites and hanged their leader over Lauder Bridge. Afterwards Archibald acquired his new name. I've yet to learn why his heart is there in St. Bride's. Come to think of it, if his ghost had appeared it might not have had the heart to tell me.

As I exited from the church and locked the door, I met up with an elderly man who greeted me cheerily.

'Hello. Been in St. Bride's have you? Did you see the tomb of Lady Lucy Elizabeth Douglas Home?'

'Yes, I did,' I replied, 'but I was more interested in the hearts.'

'That was the mother, you know, of the Earl who restored the church when it was falling to pieces after the Reformation. Cromwell is even supposed to have used the ruined building as a stable.'

'I see. Do you know anything else of interest?' I enquired.

'Hm. Anything of interest?' He thought for a minute. 'Have you heard of Bell's Wynd?'

'Yes.'

'Right, Mary Queen of Scots stayed in a house there. It's now called Dower House and it's used as a Heritage Centre today. Sir Alec Douglas Home and Sir Harold MacMillan, who used to be British Prime Ministers, have both worshipped in there. Sir Alec used to come up here to Castle Mains for the shooting and the flower show.'

'And where is Castle Mains?'

'If you go out along the A70, until it meets the road to Lanark, it's close to there.'

I thanked the man for his help and returned the key, before going back to the shop for another drink and some chocolate. That done I went to look at Dower House and the memorial to the Cameronians, originally a regiment of Covenanters raised at Douglas in 1689. Each man was kilted and issued with a Bible. Cameron took part in the battle of Airds Moss and, when he was captured, his head and hands were cut off afterwards and were said to have been kept overnight in the Douglas Tolbooth, which later became the Sun Inn and then a private house.

The memorial is a statue of the Earl of Angus, first Colonel of the Cameron Regiment. The Cameronians, I read at the memorial, were disbanded in 1968 and had to amalgamate because of army cutbacks.

It was time, however, to move on so I cycled out of Douglas and back to the B7078. I turned left, for my next goal was Lesmahagow but I had gone less than three miles, when I decided to turn left again into a secondary road, which took me through Coalburn, a former mining village. According to the poet Blind Harry, and add a pinch of salt, William Wallace took shelter there in a cave in 1296 after attacking the English. I drew level with a man working in his garden and, because he looked up at me and seemed willing to talk, I engaged him in conversation.

'Hello,' I greeted him less formally than usual. 'Is there anything interesting about this place?'

'There used to be rows of miners' houses here,' he said after considering. 'Things have changed now. Land is being bought up by people with money. See these woods. That's where there were many Polish soldiers during World War II. After Dunkirk, 7000 Poles arrived here and the people in Douglas had to provide them with food and soap. They had to wash in the lochs near the village.'

My ears pricked up when I heard about the Poles, for I knew that General Sikorski (1881-1943) of the Free Polish army had had his headquarters at Carmichael, about 7 miles from Douglas. The general was killed later when his plane crashed after taking off from Gibraltar.

During our conversation we learned that we had both been to Ruthven Barracks at Kingussie. He was a reader of the 'Scots Magazine', he said, and I told him I once had a poem printed in it. He said he would look through his back numbers to find it, and then we talked about Auchlochan House and its reported ghost, the Black Lady. Mere speculation, but could she have had a secret lover who was a coal miner?

'I was thinking of going to the House en route to Lesmahagow,' I added.

'Well, that's now a private nursing home or home for the elderly,' he informed me.

Perhaps that would have suited me. I left the man busy with his garden and made my way out of Coalburn, which I found a rather depressing and run-down place, and the sight of a coal bing didn't help. Whatever my aspirations had been about seeing the haunted house, I lost the opportunity for I took the wrong road and settled for Lesmahagow alone.

As soon as I arrived, I went looking for the church graveyard where I understand Burns' sister Isabella was buried. She had married a man by the name of Hope and had been in a horse driven carriage, which had overturned and this led to her death. Unfortunately the church cemetery gate was locked and there was no way of seeing Mrs Hope's grave, if there.

'There's no other entry,' said a passing man I questioned, 'and the gate's locked to keep out vandals. Personally I haven't heard of anyone called Isabella Hope.'

'Is there anything else of interest in this area?' I asked, still full of hope.

'The Craighead Mill on the outskirts of the town,' he continued. 'Some people say it's the oldest working mill in Scotland but I don't know.'

There was another 'attraction' as I learned later. A Sikh millionaire apparently took up residence in Lesmahagow in a 19th century mansion called 'Little Castle'. He made his money, I'm told, as a property developer, has his own tartan, is madly keen on Burns and wants the name 'Prestwick Airport' to be changed to 'Burns Airport'. And why not? Burns certainly had some great flights of fancy.

I thanked my informant and studied the map. The mill was marked but, with the map being old, I wondered how much time I might waste searching for it with some of the roads being differently designated. Instead I called into a service station for some filled rolls and asked the best way to leave the town for New Lanark.

On leaving Lesmahagow I must have been quite near the mill, but I didn't realise it at the time. I eventually took the B7018 and came out on the A72. Had I turned left, I would have arrived at Linnmill farm which was close by. I probably had looked across at it from the higher ground I had covered on the way to the junction. I decided time was against going to it, but it was quite exciting to be so near to it for the following reason. In 1993, I was fortunate to win the Hugh MacDiarmid Silver Tassie and £40 prize money by means of a poem in Scots, entered in the Scots Language Society's literature competition. On top of that Dr. George Philp (no relation or misspelling) of 'Scotsoun', which produces tapes of Scots writers and their work, sent me a free copy of 'Linmill Stories' in Scots. Note that the O.S. map has 'Linnmill' whereas the book has 'Linmill', which the author, Robert McLellan (1907-85), always insisted was the correct spelling. He was born at the farm and the stories, written between 1960 and 1965 for the radio, were based on his experiences as a young boy on the farm run by his grandparents. For a while he lived on the east side of Arran to which he moved with his wife in 1938 and, once on a cycling holiday there with my wife, I saw the house in which he had stayed.

I was aware by then that I was in an area of glasshouses, for bedding plants, flowers and vegetables have been grown there for some time. However, I turned right at the junction and pedalled along the A72 and then the A73 to Lanark and from there down to the hostel, which is situated in the 200 year old conservation village of New Lanark, right down in the woodland gorge beside the Falls of Clyde, once visited by Burns, Wordsworth and Turner. The village is one of Scotland's top attractions and has won a European conservation award, as well as being a world heritage site.

The youth hostel was originally a row of mill workers' homes, which had lain in ruins for many years before being restored. The workers were required for the mills set up by Richard Arkwright and David Dale and improved by Robert Owen, the social pioneer and son-in-law of Dale. In 1784 Arkwright visited Glasgow, and Dale, a linen merchant and banker, brought him to see the Falls of Clyde. Arkwright realised the industrial potential and Dale financed the building of the mills to be powered by the Dundaff Falls. A tunnel at the top of the falls carried water to the waterwheel and a road was made to Lanark. It took ten years to build four mills and houses for over 1000 workers.

Owen (1771-1858) was born in Newtown, Montgomeryshire and at the age of 29 this Welshman helped set up the cotton mills, which became by 1799 the biggest in Scotland and the country's greatest industry after farming. In the same year Owen married Dale's daughter and Owen became the managing partner in 1800. His own house, in which he lived with his wife and seven children, is still there in the centre of the village, as is the store set up in 1813 to improve the living standards of his workers.

Owen believed that if the welfare of his workers improved they would become better people. To this end he shortened the working hours to provide time for dancing and music. He gave them decent wages and there was a nursery and schooling for workers' children, as well as evening classes. It was so advanced that a future Czar of Russia, Nicholas I, came to see what Owen had done. Later Owen went to America and promoted schemes for village cooperatives.

I walked the bike down the steep slope to the hostel but was a bit puzzled as to where the entrance was. As it was I knocked at the wrong door.

'This isn't the hostel entrance. It's farther along,' said a woman who indicated that I was at the warden's own house, while at the same time a big collie came flying out at me.

Inwardly I was a bit annoyed at this but perhaps I was dog-tired. I have never appreciated rowdy, strange dogs, as I have had some nasty experiences with them. Anyway I didn't think that the warden was very friendly, but any interruption of the warden's time off could have been avoided by better signposting. I was also to become annoyed at having to wait so long at reception, when there wasn't anyone else waiting to be served. I also arrived without food and found that there was no evening meal service provided, and not even a hostel shop where I could buy something for self catering. Surely a hostel in such an important showcase of a village could provide some of these facilities. Also I didn't like the idea of the bednight fee including breakfast, particularly after being in various English hostels, where I had the option of paying or not paying for breakfast.

'What if someone is sick in the morning,' I asked 'and can't manage breakfast?'

Of course, breakfast included in the price saves time for those running the place. Breakfast was also being started far later than in any other hostel I had been in.

'Would it be possible to have my breakfast earlier?' I asked. After all it wasn't a cooked breakfast. 'I have a lot to see on my travels before reaching Glasgow.'

It was finally agreed that I would get my breakfast early and I paid my fees and put the bike round to the shed at the back of the building. I then had to cart my luggage up in stages to a room which I had to myself. A machine downstairs provided a chocolate snack which prevented me from gnawing my arm.

Up in my room I thought over my next day's plan. I wasn't going to go round the village or along by the river Clyde, for I had paid a visit there before. In fact I wasn't among the first visitors, for once wolves hunted in the woods, and bears fished and beavers built dams in the river. Of course, there had been changes since I was last there such as the 'Annie McLeod Experience', a history tour through Robert Owen's New Lanark with the ghost of a ten year old mill girl as a guide. Perhaps there was a thimble museum at last. Certainly in 1985 there was a plan to build the world's first (so claimed) thimble museum in an old workshop.

As I lay there in my bed thinking of the story I would be writing up later, I hoped that Annie's ghost would not appear and tell me she could spin a better yarn. Who would I be to argue with a smart mill girl? Anyway I didn't need a ghost writer.

6 June   New Lanark – Glasgow   O.S. 71, 64

Full marks in the morning to the young lady who provided me with an early breakfast of fruit juice, cereal and milk. That is not a full continental breakfast, of course, but I wasn't expecting that and I wanted to minimise to staff any disruption caused by my early start.

Breakfast over I loaded the bike again, going through the usual ritual of taking all my luggage downstairs in stages. Once ready, I pushed the bike up the steep brae from the gorge and cycled into the heart of Lanark, one of Scotland's oldest burghs and a royal one since around 1140. From the time of King William the Lion (1165-1214) this was a favourite royal hunting area.

Although not a king with a horse, I decided to do some hunting by bike and track some of Lanark's history. I started by cycling along the Castlegate to see the site of Lanark Castle, which had been a motte and bailey type. This was where William used to live when he was in that part of the country and, if he wasn't there, he might have been in his palace somewhere behind the closed Tivoli Theatre in Aberdeen. Robert the Bruce also used Lanark Castle in 1321 to hold court and there too it is claimed (disputed) that Scotland's first Parliament was held. Later the motte was used for soldiers training and grazing or, more precisely, for training soldiers and for animals grazing, until it was levelled out and a bowling green established on the site. This was confirmed when I arrived there surprised to see the green. I went into the clubhouse and spoke to a man.

'Is this where the castle was?'

'Yes, but as you can see it's just a bowling green now.'

Surprise, surprise. Cycling back along the Castlegate I missed seeing the 'girnin dog' at eaves' height, an ornamental dog turned towards a neighbour's house to annoy a neighbour long ago. However, it didn't take me long to find the site claimed to be that of William Wallace's house, where a plaque read: 'Here stood the house of William Wallace who in Lanark in 1297 first drew sword to free his native land.'

Next I went searching for the Clydesdale Hotel built in 1791 as a coaching inn. Beneath the later Assembly Rooms at the back once stood a Franciscan Friary established by Robert the Bruce, and possibly the skeletons discovered were of monks buried there. The vaults are said to be haunted by the ghost of a grey abbot. Important hotel guests in the past included William and Dorothy Wordsworth and Charles Dickens. Along in Hope Street I entered the library to make some enquiries.

'Good morning. Do you know where I can find the burial place of William Lithgow? He's supposed to be the first Scotsman to write a travel book. That was in 1632.'

Nobody knew, so I came back along the High Street to the Tolbooth which isn't so tall today. It was designed as a three storey building but only the top two floors are visible now, because the High Street has risen by 12 feet in 200 years. Next to the Tolbooth, setts in a circle have marked the position of the Tron or weigh scales at least until recently. For hundreds of years Lanark was responsible for all the official weights used in Scotland.

I decided next to go and see the old St. Kentigern's Church, often called the Out Kirk or High Kirk, but became aware that my tyres were a bit soft. Enquiries led me to a garage that sold and repaired bikes and I approached a senior man, possibly the manager or owner.

'Good morning. My tyres are becoming a bit soft. Would you please pump them up for me, for I'm not entirely sure yet of my new pump. Anyway your car pumps are better.'

In hindsight I should have pumped up the tyres myself, as I do now without giving it a thought. Had I failed I could have called for assistance, but at the time I was too anxious to risk making my tyres softer.

'Let's have a look at them,' he said and he soon had them inflated.

'How much is that?'

'No charge,' I was told but I insisted that he take something.

I was ready then for the ruined church, which is thought to have been built before 1124. William Wallace, Scotland's greatest patriot, is said to have married Marion Braidfute there in the 13th century, and I wandered past the gravestones to stand and imagine Wallace with his bride. However, there is no hard evidence, if any, that he had a wife by that name or that he was even married. The death of Wallace's wife at the hands of the governor of Lanark and his men is said to have set Wallace on the path of resistance to English rule, but that traditional story too is probably fictional. Wallace truly received a cruel death when ought, for he was hanged, drawn and quartered at Smithfield, Of course, previous to that, Edward 1's treasurer, Cressingham, was said to have been skinned and Wallace is supposed to have used a part of the skin to make for himself a dagger sheath. Wallace

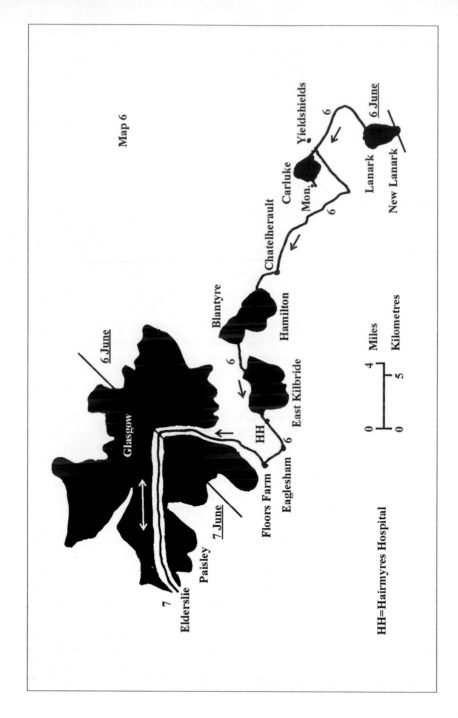

Map 6

Glasgow

6 June

7 June

7

Elderslie

Paisley

Floors Farm

Eaglesham

HH

East Kilbride

6

Blantyre

Hamilton

6

Chatelherault

Carluke

Mon.

Yieldshields

6

6

Lanark

New Lanark

6 June

Miles

Kilometres

0   4

0   5

HH=Hairmyres Hospital

52

was later betrayed to the English by Sir John Menteith, who at one stage in his life became the governor of Dumbarton Castle. The strange thing is that Menteith signed the Declaration of Arbroath, which was a pledge not to surrender freedom to the English, the very thing that Wallace had fought for.

By writing about Wallace's sheath, perhaps I am continuing some of the fiction written by William of Wintoun, the Abbot of Lindores in Fife and by Blind Harry, the 15th century poet. If so, it may add a touch of colour to and even create an interest in local history, but it is not real history.

Coming back from the church I passed the Lanark auction market. I learned later that the toll gates from the Cartland Bridge are built into the market, and are said to be the oldest surviving toll gates in Scotland. The bridge itself was described in the early 19th century as the highest road bridge of its kind in Scotland.

While on the subject of records, the Lanark town bell is said to be the oldest in Europe and on the steeple face is a statue of Wallace. I didn't see, as far as I can remember, the Covenanters' Memorial. Apparently 3000 Covenanters met before the old Mercat Cross to oppose bishops being imposed on them.

'Excuse me, but what are these pennants for?' I asked a passer-by.

'Oh, that's for Lanimer's Day,' I was told.

I had heard of that special day but I didn't know exactly what it involved. That was quickly put right.

'It'll soon be here. It's the largest celebration of its kind in Scotland. It goes right back to the 12th century to the time when Lanark became a royal burgh. Following the king's orders, the burgesses had to inspect the march or boundary stones and report on their condition, and this still is done today at the beginning of Lanimer Week. The kids take part in a procession on Lanimer Day and there's a queen and her court.'

Remembering that the 18th century lawyer Lord Braxfield, perhaps too harshly labelled 'The Hanging Judge', was associated with Lanark, I decided not to hang around any more but to leave Lanark. I set off on the A706 and turned left when I reached the A721. At that stage I was less than two miles from Carstairs, the mental hospital, and I was relieved to find no men in white coats waiting for me at the junction. Just over four miles farther on, I reached the B7056 and I was then less than a mile from Yieldshields. It seems a horse from there went down with the 'Titanic'. Had it shown more horse sense, had mair or 'mare' money' and travelled first class it might have survived. (See 'Vol. 1 Across England'.)

It was time to leave Lanark and I cycled to a brickworks in Carluke. There I was 'dead jammy', or 'very lucky' for the linguistically impoverished, not surprisingly in a place famous for jam. After locking the bike, I ran up some stairs and entered the works' yard and, as I was taking some photos, I tripped backwards over a low wall or kerbing. This gave me quite a scare momentarily, for I was so absorbed in taking some photos that I didn't know where I was falling, and I imagined for a second or two that I could be falling down some shaft or well in the ground. I fell heavily and dropped the camera, but I was relieved to have landed safely and found that the camera was undamaged as far as I knew.

'Are you okay?' asked one of the men who worked there.

'Yes, I'm fine, thanks. I've just been taking some photos and I'm collecting some information for my diary. Have you any facts about this place that you can give me?'

'Come round to our office,' he invited me and there he introduced me to another man.

They had no leaflets on brick making but they were real 'bricks' themselves, and I thanked them before cycling farther into Carluke to buy something to eat. That done I made enquiries as to how to reach the site of the birthplace of General Roy.

'Go back the way you came in and turn right along a secondary road. It's less than three miles to the memorial.'

I was told to watch for a landmark on the main road and this would warn me when to turn right. What it was I can't remember but it might have been a tall chimney I reached. No matter, for after cycling along a wooded road, I came to the memorial, which was grossly vandalised with red and black paint.

There at Miltonhead near Milton Lockart Farm was born General William Roy, an ex-pupil of Lanark Grammar School and founder of the Ordnance Survey. After the 1745 Jacobite rising, the Duke of Cumberland was keen to have Scotland mapped for military purposes and Roy, still in his twenties, had the job completed by 1755 on a scale of 1 inch to 1000 yards. I was so pleased to see this memorial to a man who had done something so important. It was one more piece in the jigsaw for me, for I had been also three times up Shiehallion, the Perthshire hill on which map contours originated from scientific work done there to establish the mass of the earth.

As for the vandalism, was it a political protest against Roy for carrying out 'Butcher' Cumberland's work? I doubt it. Probably it was just one more example of the mindless, moronic behaviour of some of our ill disciplined youth.

From there I retraced my route then took the B7056 through to the A72, which was to lead me along a busier road to Hamilton. However, before entering that town I turned off into Chatelherault, which was built in 1732 as a summer palace and hunting lodge for the 5th Duke of Hamilton. William Adam, a Scottish architect, designed it and it was built on high ground as an attraction at the end of the Grand Avenue of trees, stretching north from Hamilton Palace. Coal mining subsidence led to the palace being demolished and Chatelherault became a sorry ruin. The latter in time was restored, and what were previously the kennels for the Duke's hunting dogs have been turned into a museum display gallery. There are more than 10 miles of woodland walks in the High Parks, which were once part of Cadzow Forest, the medieval hunting ground of Scottish kings.

I knew that I wouldn't be able to see everything because of the time of day. I took a photo and secured my bike, but didn't spot the cycle rack mentioned in the tourist literature. On entering the visitor centre, I made an enquiry before going round the place.

'Excuse me,' I asked one of the staff, 'but why has this place got a French looking and sounding name?'

'Well now, the Duchy of Chatelherault was gifted by the French king to the 2nd Earl of Arran, a Hamilton, for his help in securing the betrothal of Mary Queen of Scots to the French heir. That was in 1548, I think.'

Back outside, a group of tourists were chatting and some were studying an O.S. map. Roy would have been proud of them.

'Where does that name "Cadzow" come from?' asked a stout lady 'It looks like a Polish name.'

'Originally Hamilton town was called "Cadzow" for the Cadzows were an important local landowning family,' explained another lady.

'Speaking about "Cadzow",' interrupted a short man with a moustache, 'there's oaks here called the "Cadzow Oaks". They're supposed to have been planted by King David I. He used the castle here as a base for hunting. Some of these oaks are over 600, maybe nearly 1000 years old.'

As I cycled out of the grounds (only allowed on the tarmac paths), I wondered if there were still white cattle in the park, the last descendants in Scotland of the wild, white cattle in Britain. I didn't know, but was sure that Chatelherault would be no white elephant.

I returned to the A72 and cycled on towards Hamilton, which wasn't as busy as I expected. A few enquiries brought me to the right road for East Kilbride. It grew much busier on the road leading to the Whirlies Roundabout, but I was lucky again to have a narrow strip between the white line and the grass verge. It made for safer cycling.

Not far past Whirlies, I cut into Maxwelltown Road in East Kilbride and whizzed down it to Hunter House Heritage Centre, where John and William Hunter had lived in the 18th century. The house was formerly a thatched farmhouse on the farm of Long Calderwood and roughly a mile from the village, around which the new town of East Kilbride was developed.

The House is an interesting place with a bodywork area explaining 18th century surgical practices, touchable limbs, medical instruments and an inter-active C.D. Rom. There is also a large screen theatre where one can learn about the Hunters.

John Hunter (1728-93), aged thirteen when his father died, disliked book learning. He was more interested in birds, plants and insects and he used to dissect reptiles and other animals. As for a job, he had at first no idea of what he wanted.

Meanwhile his older brother William (1718-83) studied under some of the great Scots medical men in London and later in Paris, where he learned the importance of human dissection. He then opened his own school of anatomy in London and gained a great reputation as an anatomist. William sent for John to help and soon was so impressed by John's skill at dissection that he took him on as a pupil. One of John's tasks was to acquire dead bodies and he worked closely with body snatchers to achieve this.

John continued to study anatomy and also surgery under two important surgeons. After spending some time as a surgeon in the Seven Years' War (1756-63), John returned to London and opened his own surgical practice and anatomy classes. He went on to produce part of a treatise on human teeth, the first proper work on teeth written in English. After he married, his wife gave receptions and these attracted famous guests, including Lady Byron and Oliver Goldsmith. In time John Hunter became one of the surgeons at St. George's Hospital and one of his pupils was Edward Jenner, who later was given the credit (arguable) for discovering the vaccination against smallpox.

Many honours came John's way and he became an F.R.S. and Surgeon-Extraordinary to King George III in 1776, a job William had held for years. John Hunter also was one of the founders of the Veterinary College of London, now called the Royal College of Veterinary Surgeons, and had his portrait painted by Joshua Reynolds. Lister respected Hunter so much that he kept an engraving of him in his study. John Hunter was buried in Westminster Abbey.

Both the Hunters knew Joshua Reynolds, Benjamin Franklin, William Hogarth, Adam Smith, Oliver Goldsmith, Edmund Burke and David Hume, all prominent men. John's wife Anne also wrote the libretto for some of Haydn's work, and in recent years a play has been written about Anne by north-east of Scotland playwright Charles Barron.

The Hunters were great collectors with their own private museums. When William, that great anatomist, teacher and obstretician, died, he left his varied collection of coins, art, books, anatomical specimens, fossils and shells to Glasgow University. He also left money to house the collection and this is now the Hunterian Museum there. John, the father of scientific surgery, died and left a collection of thousands of anatomical specimens, stuffed animals and fossils, which are now part of the Royal College of Surgeons.

When I came out of the house, I looked around and imagined young John Hunter roaming around the countryside, before it became covered with houses of the new town of East Kilbride. Some of that very countryside became famous in Europe through the work of David Ure in carboniferous palaeontology.

From Hunter House I sped downhill and arrived at my aunt Mary and uncle Douglas Eglington's house. They had met when my aunt was a nurse in Aberdeen and my uncle was in the R.A.F. and stationed at Dyce near Aberdeen. (Dyce is now part of Aberdeen.)

'I can't stay long,' I said, 'for I've to go to Hairmyres Hospital then across to Paisley before going to Glasgow.'

'Help yourself to these sandwiches, anyway,' I was told. 'What are you going there for?'

'George Orwell, the writer, was a patient at Hairmyres for a while and I want to find out a few other things for my diary.'

I certainly enjoyed the salmon filling and the cup of tea, for that was the best food I had enjoyed all day. I thanked them and said goodbye. Little did I know that I would see my aunt only one more time before she died.

After cycling through some of East Kilbride's quieter streets, I joined the A726 then branched off to cycle along the B764 to Hairmyres Hospital. I went there because that is where George Orwell (1903-50) spent some time in ward 4, when he was suffering from T.B.

In 1946 Orwell, whose real name was Eric Blair, went to the isle of Jura off the west coast of Scotland and settled in Barnhill, a farmhouse about 23 miles north of Craighouse. It was pretty basic inside and he tried to live off rabbits, garden vegetables, fish and lobsters. He slept on a camp bed, had a paraffin heater and no telephone. Apparently it would have cost £40,000 to connect him. While there Orwell worked on his book '1984' which he completed in 1948 and, by reversing the last two numbers, Orwell obtained the '84' part of the book title. The book gives a gloomy picture of a totalitarian state and it is from the book that we get the expressions 'Big Brother' (yes, long before the T.V. programme of that name) and 'Thought Police'.

In 1947 he became ill and had to be moved to Hairmyres where he continued typing his book. Some people believe the grimness of the book is a reflection of the side effects caused by the streptomycin drug used to treat his T.B. The drug was licensed in America but it was used experimentally and possibly illegally on him at Hairmyres. Too great a dosage resulted in him having hair fallout, peeling skin and mouth ulcers, and his treatment had to be changed.

After months there he went back to Barnhill in Jura to finish the book, until he became too ill to stay there any longer and went to a London hospital. He died in January 1950.

When I reached the Hairmyres Hospital it was very difficult trying to decide where I would enter. Eventually I locked the bike and went through a door. No pain, no gain.

'Excuse me,' I said to a nurse, 'but can you tell me where George Orwell, the writer, was a patient? He wrote "1984", remember.'

'I'm sorry, I don't know. Wait here and I'll see if I can find someone who does.'

A nurse came back and said that I would have to go to another part of the building. I passed along some corridors until I was stopped quite rightly by a senior nurse.

'Where are you going?' she asked authoritatively.

'I was told I could go along here. I'm searching for where George Orwell was a patient and the veranda where he and other T.B. patients were put out in the fresh air.'

'You shouldn't be in here,' she said disapprovingly. 'If you go out of here and then outside, I think you'll see the veranda you're looking for.'

I thanked her, followed her instructions and found the veranda which I photographed.

Back on the bike I continued along the B764 to Eaglesham, a pretty village four miles from East Kilbride, and one of the first to be designated as a place of special interest architecturally. The village was built in the 1790s and modelled on an Italian village seen by the 10th Earl of Eglington.

Near the village a paw print was once found and identified by someone from Calder Park Zoo, Glasgow as that of a puma. It seemed that the Renta Puma business was doing well. If there was a puma about it was quite safe from me, for I could only have eaten a horse.

I headed next north-west to Floors Farm now shrouded in mist. I had had to cycle into East Kilbride with my waterproofs on and had worn them to Hairmyres. It was still wet but the sky was by then heavy with low cloud. It was at Floors Farm on 10 May, 1941 that Rudolph Hess, Hitler's Deputy, had literally dropped in by parachute and was taken prisoner by a farm worker called David McLean. When the latter heard the low flying plane, he looked out from the window and thought that his wife had not taken in her washing. What in fact he was looking at was the German's white parachute. Hess asked to be taken to the Duke of Hamilton, but he was taken to Busby three or so miles away along the B767, and then to Maryhill Barracks, Glasgow before being transferred elsewhere.

Apparently Hess had come to contact the Duke, whom he had met before World War II, but had mistaken his landing place. Hess had hoped to negotiate Britain's exit from the war. It seems British Intelligence wanted to make the Germans think that Britain wanted peace in the hope that the Germans would ease up on Britain, thus giving us more time to build up our defensive and attacking forces. Also if Hitler felt safer on his western front, he would be more ready to attack Russia, which would be to our advantage.

With respect to any English and particularly any foreign readers, please note that I said 'Britain's' exit, for Scotland and Wales were also in the war.

Some people, however, do not believe that the man taken prisoner at Floors Farm was Hess, for it is said that, when he was medically examined, he showed no trace of a bullet wound he received in his lung during World War I. Hess later died in Spandau prison, Berlin, and there is even controversy about that, because the suspicion arose that he was murdered.

As I stood in the mist, I remembered searching for the English airfield west of Hereford from which he was flown to be tried at Nuremberg in Germany. Another circle was complete.

I knew that Paisley was out of the question timewise, and so left Floors Farm and cut across country to the B767 to cycle via Busby out of the hill mist and into Glasgow, the city which provided an air squadron, which fought longer in the Battle of Britain than any other.

My bed was already booked in the hostel, having arranged that en route. To make sure I kept fit when I arrived, reception allocated to me a room far upstairs. With the bike locked away and my bed made up, I went out to search for a fish supper. This became an all consuming passion, which filled the rest of the evening until I got back to the hostel. No bones about it I slept well that night.

7 June   Glasgow – Paisley – Elderslie – Glasgow   O.S. 64

After a cooked breakfast I took my bike on a mini tour of Paisley, reportedly at one time to be Scotland's largest town, whose Gleniffer Press in 1985 printed 85 copies of the world's smallest book ever printed and gained entry in the Guinness Book of Records. The pages are so small (1mm. x 1mm.) that they can only be turned with a needle. For a short time a minister by the name of Ernest Gordon served in the town. During World War II, he was a captain in the 93rd battalion of the Argyle and Sutherland Highlanders. Captured by the Japs, he was forced to work on the railway of death and the bridge on the river Kwai. Fortunately he survived and a film was made of his life.

Perhaps I would be discriminatory if I omitted a story about a Paisley snail, especially after writing about snails in England in my book 'Vol. 1 Across England'. A Glasgow woman by the name of Donoghue found a snail in the bottle of ginger beer she was drinking in a café. She decided to sue Stevenson the manufacturer and, after taking the case as far as the House of Lords, she was awarded compensation. Her win made legal history for it is now the basis of the Law of Negligence. Today the café is gone but a bench and wall plaque mark the spot.

Interesting as these facts may be, that was not why I pedalled across the river Clyde (I used a bridge) and headed out Paisley Road West that fine morning in unbelievably light traffic. No, among other things, I wanted to learn about wordsmiths, weavers and witches. Cycling along, about a mile from Crookston, I was aware that away to my right was Craigton Cemetery where there is a memorial to John Harper, a minister famous for his preaching. He perished on the 'Titanic' but made sure his tiny daughter (later Nan Pont of Moffat) was safe on a lifeboat. The Harper Memorial Church in Govan is a reminder of the man.

After entering Paisley by the A761, I began my quest by stopping to look at a statue commemorating Alexander Wilson, who was born in the town in 1766. He was a weaver poet who took to the road at the age of 20 to sell his poems. He emigrated to America in 1794 and continued in his previous work, before becoming a school teacher. He developed a great interest in birds, took part in expeditions to study them and became known as the father of American ornithology. He used to correspond with Thomas Jefferson (1743-1826), the third President of the United States.

Another Wilson, a John Wilson, was a scholar who published two volumes of poems when he was 27 years old, and he was a friend of Wordsworth and the other Lake poets.

Also opposite the Town Hall, I found a monument to Robert Tannahill who became the most famous of the weaver poets. At the beginning of the 19th century, the Paisley weavers were among the best paid working men in Britain, and were probably the first truly organised trade unionists in the town. I photographed his monument, and a man smiled and nodded as I packed away the camera.

'Do you know much about Tannahill?' he asked.

'Just that he was a weaver poet and drowned in a burn (stream) after a bad love affair.'

'Well, you go to Castle Street. That's where he was born and then go to Queen Street, where you'll see the thatched cottage which his father built, and where he worked at his loom and wrote some of his poems.'

'Are these places far from here?'

'No, Paisley isn't that big. Oh, and he's buried in the Canal Street cemetery. One of his poems 'Jessie, The Flower O Dunblane' used to be sung all over Victorian Britain. After he felt that his girl friend Jessie had jilted him, he went south to work in Lancashire. He was also one of the founders in 1805 of the Paisley Burns Club, which some claim on documentary evidence to be the oldest in the world.'

'You're a fan of Robert Tannahill, are you?' I asked.

'You could say that. I just find the whole story of his life so romantic.'

'Well, nice meeting you anyway. Thanks for stopping to tell me about him.'

'You're touring, are you?'

'Yes, Land's End to John O' Groats.'

'Best of luck to you then,' he added and with a wave he was off. People were so helpful and this was typical.

I went then to have a look at Paisley Abbey, once featured in the T.V. detective series 'Taggart'. In one of the programmes there appeared an actress I have known for a number of years, which goes to prove you don't have to be a bishop to speak to a thespian. A monastery and church were established there in 1164 and monks were brought in from Much Wenlock in Shropshire. It became the farthest north of the Cluniac houses in Europe and was granted the status of an abbey in 1219. The local saint St. Mirin (St. Mirren is the local football team) attracted pilgrimages, and it became one of the main pilgrimage shrines in Scotland. The abbey was nearly totally destroyed by Edward of England in 1307, but was rebuilt after the battle of Bannockburn in 1314. In fact the site has been built over twice after previous demolitions. Inside the abbey is the tomb of Margery Bruce, Robert the Bruce's sister. By 1560 Paisley Abbey was the fourth wealthiest monastery in Scotland.

Another thing which drew me to Paisley was the desire to learn about the famous Paisley shawls. To that end I cycled to the Paisley Museum and Art Gallery, where the world's largest collection of such shawls is to be found. Ever since 1905, the museum has been building up a collection of these colourful textiles. There are now over 900 examples, but only a small amount of the shawls can be seen at one time.

The Paisley pattern is the name of the teardrop or tadpole pattern, but Paisley did not invent it. It can be traced back over 2000 years and can be found in Celtic art (the Celts, I once read, originally came from the heart of Europe, but I have also read that they came from near the Black Sea) and in India but the pattern was first used in Kashmir. Presumably that is from where we get the word 'cashmere'.

Incidentally, I would not be trying to pull the wool over your eyes by saying that Shahtoosh is the finest woven wool, even finer than cashmere. It can take the fleece of five Tibetan antelopes to make one such shawl, which could cost at least anything from £1000 to over £5000.

In the middle of the 19th century, examples of the Paisley shawl pattern were brought to Britain by the East India Company, and the pattern was modified to suit European tastes. The Edinburgh, Paisley and Norwich weaving centres received masses of orders but Paisley, through the good organisation of its workforce and mass production, became dominant and the name 'Paisley' was applied to the textile. For about 100 years, Britain became the leading place for shawl fashion, but Napoleon's Empress Josephine also influenced the fashion. Production in Paisley began in 1805.

Strict standards came to be applied to the production of shawls. If the weave was slack, for example, this could distort the pattern and also affect the length of a shawl. In a 3.35 metre (11feet) long rectangular shawl, the weaver was only allowed to be out by 6 millimetres (1/4 inch). Only if the shawl was passed was the weaver paid. The shawls were finished in the warehouse, where they were clipped to remove unwanted threads at the back and the fringes made. The shawls were then washed, dried, stretched on frames and steam pressed.

I had no sooner entered the museum than I was offered help by one of the attendants, who was very helpful and keen to show and tell me about the shawls and Paisley pattern, when he learned what I was about. He was also forthcoming otherwise.

'I used to sing when I was younger. I was a bit of an entertainer.'

He certainly sang the praises of the place and seemed to be very keen on his job. Like another guide, he wouldn't give me his name for my diary.

'No, no,' he said. 'I'm just glad to help. I'll give you these leaflets.'

When I left the museum I had a closer look at the Thomas Coats Memorial Church, which was a gift from the Coats family to Paisley. It has been described as one of the finest Baptist churches in Europe and has even been called 'the Baptist Cathedral of Europe'.

Two incidental pieces of information. The first Baron Glentanar of the Coats family of Paisley bought Glentanar estate on Royal Deeside in 1905, and I have had many a pleasant forest and hill walk in the area. Also in 1907, the firm J. & P. Coats established a mill in São Paulo in Brazil and one of its Paisley engineers, Archie McLean, became known as the 'father of Brazilean football'.

I noticed a sign informing that there was an exhibition about Thomas Tait (1882-1954), the Paisley born and educated architect famous for the 1938 Empire Exhibition in Bellahouston Park, Glasgow, St. Andrew's House, Edinburgh and the Sydney Harbour Bridge in Australia.

Moving on, I went up a steepish brae to visit the Coats observatory and was allowed to take the bike inside the ground floor. I think that was the first observatory I had ever visited. Since 1882 this place has recorded astronomical and weather information, but it is also a seismic station and has a satellite picture receiver. I walked round the displays on weather, earthquakes and astronomy.

At one point I was speaking to a member of staff and I mentioned that I was going to return to the museum to pick up something I had forgotten.

'I'll let you through the back way,' he said. 'It'll save you a lot of time and effort.'

It certainly did. This was far easier than going back down the steep slope at the front and then round to the front of the museum.

Later when I returned to the observatory and came out of its front door, and was attending to one of my bike panniers, I heard the friendly voice of an old man with one of those spotted dogs. I was in luck for it wasn't a spotted man with an old dog.

'Touring are you?'

'In a sense,' I replied. 'I'm looking up things of historical interest.'

'Have you seen the Sma Shot Cottages?' he asked when I listed some of the things I had seen.

'No, what are they?'

'There's an 18th century weaver's cottage and a worker's house.'

'Right thanks. I'll go there.'

I was glad his dog had behaved itself or I might have had to knock spots off it. Some dogs are a treat but others are quite objectionable.

'I can't remember what street it's in. It's some time since I've been there. I'm from Glasgow and I'm here to visit my sister.'

I thanked him again, freewheeled downhill from the observatory and cycled to the cottages, when I learned where they were. They were shut, as was Tannahill's cottage, and I failed again when I attempted to find his birthplace. However, that triple 'disaster' was followed by success when I went in search of his burial place.

'He's buried at Castlehead Church,' said a lady whose help I had sought. 'That's also the church that Ronald Reagan came to in search of his ancestors.'

Obviously it could have taken time to check every gravestone in the churchyard but I was dead lucky, you could say, for I managed to 'bag' a young man passing by.

'Excuse me, but can you tell me exactly where Robert Tannahill's grave is?'

'Yes, follow me and I'll show you.'

He brought me to the grave where I thanked him, and I read and photographed the stone. As somebody who writes poems, which will be left behind when I'm gone, it's difficult to explain to people who have not written what my feelings are, when I stand before the graves of men or women who once breathed and expressed their feelings in print. It's an awareness of the fragility and transience of life, an awareness of the beauty that is lost, an awareness of kinship of spirit, of being a link in the chain.

However, all that can be lost on some people, as it was on one former woman headteacher I know. I had expressed interest in a namesake of the past and wondered if there could be any family link. She impudently and strongly tried to put me down in front of colleagues, because she was too dumb or insensitive to grasp what I was saying. Professional criticism I can take, ignorant rudeness certainly not!

For some time I knew from holiday makers that Paisley had had its share of witches and that, as a reminder, there is a special marker on the road where George Street and Maxwellton Street meet. Hopefully safeguarded by the garlic bread I had eaten before leaving home, I set off from the church and scanned the road ahead. Then I saw it. I locked the bike and watched for and dodged the traffic, as I stepped out on the road to photograph a stone sett circle, at the centre of which is a horseshoe fixed in a block of granite. This I knew was where the remains of burned witches were put on display after those poor women were executed on nearby Gallow Green, at least up to the end of the 17th century.

As I sped back to the safety of the pavement after taking a photo, an old couple came by and the man spoke.

'You're taking your life in your hands, I see.'

'You're right. I was out taking a picture of the stones there.'

I quickly recounted what I knew and asked them if they could tell me anything more. The lady then spoke.

'Not very much. The horse shoe is there to keep off evil, of course, and there's a story, I don't know if it is true, that a weaver once stole it. Some of the local weavers started to commit suicide and it didn't stop until the shoe was replaced. I wouldn't walk over these stones myself. Oh, and there's something else. One of the girls suspected or accused of witchcraft or who accused others, I can't remember exactly, went on to develop a thread which helped Paisley take a lead in weaving.'

'Not very much!' I exclaimed. 'That's great information. I'll be putting that in my diary.'

After I thanked them, they went off and a thought passed through my mind. How did that old lady know so much and why was she scared to go on the stones? It was obvious, of course.

My speculation ended and, not requiring a broomstick, I cycled to Elderslie, the claimed birthplace of William Wallace. It was staring me in the face that I had arrived when I saw a large statue of Wallace, in fact more of a large memorial than a single statue. Its impressiveness was marred by the unsightly paint grafitti provided by some Turner prize aspirants. I recalled Roy's vandalised memorial near Carluke, and wondered if there might be some viral disease affecting brains in the neighbourhood.

Just down the road a short distance from the memorial, I stopped at a service station where I bought something to eat and drink, for Wallace had offered me nothing. A filled roll and a can of juice were sufficient to perk me up for a straight run (apart from a public park toilet stop) back to Glasgow.

I entered the city, still with time to see some interesting things and there is plenty of that in Glasgow. For example, the city at one time had the longest Post Office counter in Britain until the place in George Square (the latter built to look like Trafalgar Square in London) was closed down, the Broomielaw Bridge built over the Clyde by Telford was the widest in Britain when completed, the city has the longest bar in the British Isles at the 'Horse Shoe', Drury Street, the first purpose built teacher training college at Cowcaddens, Park Crescent has been described as the best example of 19th century planning in Europe, and it has been said that Glasgow has more park space per head of population than any other city in Europe. And that's nothing. Glasgow has been reported as having the highest rate of lung cancer in the world!

I went through by George Square, past the former post office and past the City Chambers, which I once visited before with a party to be received by the then Provost (Mayor in England). The marble interiors are well worth seeing and the Chambers have been used by film and T.V. crews to represent the Kremlin and the Vatican. Moving on from the Square I revisited Provand's Lordship, the oldest house in Glasgow, but it was shut, not that I was too disappointed because I had been inside it before. Glasgow Cathedral, the only Scottish mainland medieval cathedral to have survived the Reformation complete (except for its west towers), was also closed, but again I had been before to see the baptismal font and St. Mungo's Well. The building is reputedly built over the tomb of St. Mungo or St. Kentigern, as he is also known.

I did, however, go just beyond the Cathedral to the Necropolis, Britain's first garden cemetery, whose design was based on the Paris cemetery of Père Lachaise which I have explored. I wanted to track down the grave of William Miller, the poet who wrote 'Wee Willie Winkie', the nursery rhyme. I hadn't a clue where it was, but I had been told that it was near the entrance. For all I knew there could have been several entrances. When I arrived at the cemetery, there was a brass band taking some refreshment from a mobile van manned, if you'll pardon the expression, by two women. I bought a filled roll and tea and made some enquiries.

'Do you know where the writer of "Wee Willie Winkie" is buried?'

'No, I haven't a clue,' one woman answered and then asked her companion the same question.

She didn't know either, so I decided that I would have to go in and search systematically. While doing so I almost got stoned, not with what I drank at the van but, as I said in my introduction, with stones flung from the higher ground in the cemetery. A gang of the native underclass so called, perhaps mindful of their nursery days, were maybe trying to protect the hallowed ground of Wee Willie Winkie's creator. I resolved to discuss the matter with them in a civilised and restrained manner.

'Cut that out before I get injured!' I shouted 'The police are on the way!'

I couldn't help regretting that there was no citizens' advice bureau just outside the cemetery, and that I had not carried with me a 'Parliamo Glasgow' book. No matter they must have thought I said 'polis' instead of 'police' for the pelting, if not the vocal war cries, stopped. I continued my search and found a small cenotaph, which informed me that Miller had died in 1872.

Before leaving Aberdeen, I had written to Glasgow Tourist Board to enquire about Miller's grave, but the reply didn't arrive until I had left for London. On reading the letter after I returned home, it said that a memorial to William Miller, the 'Laureate of the Nursery', was in the Necropolis and enclosed was a cemetery plan showing the location of the memorial. The letter also said that Miller's body was buried in Tollcross Cemetery, Corbett Street, and close to the entrance gate.

From the Necropolis, I went to the Royal Infirmary along from the Cathedral to see again the plaque commemorating Lister, the surgeon who had been a pupil of John Hunter. It reads: 'On this site stood the surgical wards in which from 1861 to 1869 Joseph Lister Surgeon to the Royal Infirmary and Regius Professor of Surgery in the University of Glasgow initiated the method of antiseptic treatment.'

That done I went to St. Vincent Street to track down John Smith's bookshop, which is probably the oldest trading bookshop in Scotland. From there I cycled to the Empire Theatre and after that to the Mitchell Library, certainly at one time Europe's largest public reference library, in which is preserved the original manuscript of Robert Burns' 'Auld Lang Syne'.

There were still three places I wanted to see before returning to the hostel. Firstly I wanted to see a mission hall just off the city centre end of Great Western Road. Leaving the latter, I branched off along the quiet narrow North Woodside Road and stopped when I saw a wall plaque, which said that there in 1883 the first Boys' Brigade meeting was held. The movement was started by a Thurso man called William Smith, who was later knighted. Originally a company of 30 Glasgow boys met but today the organisation is world wide. The Boys' Brigade was also the first uniformed organisation for boys to be established for the whole of Britain.

Something else of interest took place in North Woodside Road, although I didn't discover the exact site. Roughly about 1911, two brothers Robert and Tom McColl set up a factory there to supply the 30 sweet shops they owned throughout Glasgow. When Robert returned from World War I, they began to sell cigarettes and newspapers and developed shops beyond Glasgow, so that at the time of writing there were about 250 R.S. McColl outlets throughout Scotland. No update was available in August, 2005.

At Celtic Park in 1900, the year both brothers went into business, Robert, who became known as 'Toffee Bob', became the only Scot to get a football hat trick in Scotland against England. Truly a sweet moment.

There was one more place to see that evening. Back on Great Western Road, I cycled a little farther out then turned left into the Hillhead area, which is between Glasgow University with its Hunterian Gallery and Great Western Road. I was on the trail of Hillhead High School, which was attended for a while by Robert Service (1874-1958), the poet whom my father brought to my attention when I was a boy. I could see that some sort of activity was taking place inside the school and I approached a mixed group of adults outside.

'Excuse me, but do you know anything about Robert Service, the poet who, I understand, went to this school?'

'I don't know anything about that,' said one while another said, 'I think I heard something about that. Ask inside.'

I took the bike in through the door and asked a young black woman the same question. She said she didn't know but would ask someone.

'Nobody knows,' she said on returning, 'but come and join us for a cup of tea and a chat.'

She was very persistent but I didn't have the time and I wondered if she was trying to inveigle me into some religious group. Perhaps she was simply being friendly as Glaswegians in general are.

'Try the janitor,' was her final comment, 'for he's an expert on the school.'

This to a certain extent proved to be true, for Mr Bobby Main, the janitor, gave me a slim book about the school. I thanked him and headed back to the hostel, where I settled down to look at the book after putting away the bike.

The book is entitled 'Hillhead High School 1885-1961' by A.D.C., which the Head Teacher thought, as he told me later, stood for 'A.D. Campbell', and was published by Hillhead High School Pavilion Improvements Fund Committee in 1962. On page 19 the comment is made that there had never been a Former Pupils' swimming section: 'This is more surprising when we remember that John Thomson and John Service have swum for Britain in the Olympic Games, Thomson also in the European Games, and Irene Service, on emigrating, for Canada in the Empire Games.' I wondered if John and Irene Service were the parents of Robert Service.

Robert's father was called John and a John Service worked in a Glasgow bank, as did Robert before emigrating to Canada, where he became famous for his 'Songs of A Sourdough' and for the Yukon and Rockies characters in his poems, such as 'The Shooting of Dan McGrew' set in the Yukon at the time of the gold rush. Service became very wealthy from the royalties he received for his poems.

Skimming over more pages, I came to a bit about several former pupils, who had distinguished themselves in some kind of literary work. Alistair MacLean (1922-87) is mentioned and also Robert W. Service, but it is a Walter Owen, poet and translator, whose work is greatly praised. Some of the latter's work should be in the Mitchell Library according to the book.

In 1959 W. Menzies Campbell, M.P. was one of two debaters who won two debating trophies. It was bedtime, however, and there was no debate about that.

Breakfast over, I made for a cycle shop I had passed the night before at the city centre end of Great Western Road. I had noticed that the shop sold Alpine Trek bikes and felt that I would get good service there for my own one.

'Can you do my bike now?' I asked on entering. 'I'm on a bike tour and I need new brake pads and a new front inner tube. I've had punctures three times, and I want to make sure I don't have problems once I go into less populated areas beyond Glasgow. Oh, and could I have new batteries for my front light, please?'

I was lucky to have the jobs done quickly and I thanked and paid the mechanic, who told me that the front tyre problem had been caused by not having the right size of tube. Along the road, I purchased a spool for slides and headed for Glasgow Art Gallery and Museum at Kelvingrove. From newspaper publicity, I knew that there were in the museum two items that I wanted to see in particular, namely, the Dead Sea Scrolls Exhibition and a famous North American Indian ghost dance shirt. Glasgow was the only British venue that year for the Exhibition, which was created by the Israel Antiquities Authority supported by some manuscripts from the Mitchell Library. I soon arrived there and, after locking the bike to a railing, I entered.

'Is photography allowed?' I asked hopefully, with regard to the Scrolls, but received the expected but understandable negative reply: 'No, flash can damage.'

The Scrolls, unique in being the oldest known manuscripts of Judaism and Christianity, were written over 2000 years ago and were discovered accidentally in caves in 1947. Between then and 1956 more than 800 scrolls and tens of thousands of scroll fragments were found in 11 caves. The Scrolls are thought to be the library of the Essenes, a sect of pious Jews, who took to the Judaean desert as a protest against the corruption of society and of worship in the Jerusalem Temple. They were an all male community (John the Baptist may have been a member) which used a solar calendar of 364 days, while other Jews used a lunar calendar of 354 days. Threatened with destruction by the Roman army, they hid the Scrolls in caves high above the north-west shore of the Dead Sea. Some scholars believe that the Scrolls, preserved in the dry desert heat, were part of the library of the Jerusalem Temple, which the Romans later destroyed in c.70 C.E.

Almost all the books of the Old Testament (the only part of the Bible used by Jews) have been found, whereas none of the New Testament books have been definitely found among the Scrolls.

As well as the Scrolls, the Exhibition showed diverse objects from the

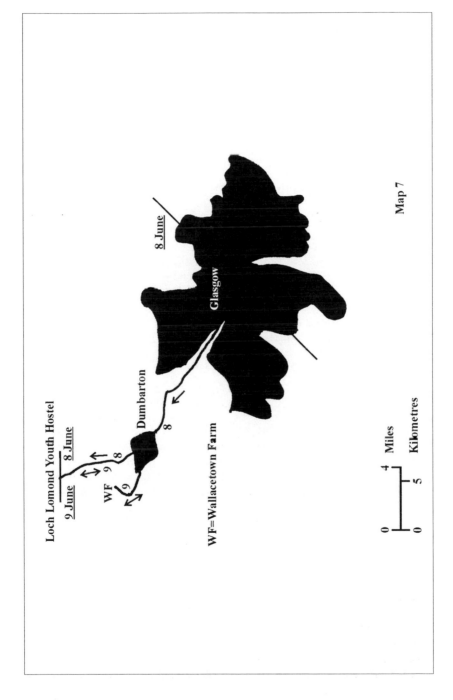

Loch Lomond Youth Hostel

9 June   8 June

WF 9

9

8

8

Dumbarton

8

Glasgow

8 June

WF=Wallacetown Farm

0   4   Miles

0   5   Kilometres

Map 7

69

archaeological excavations at Khirbet Qumran, the Essene settlement near the Dead Sea. Combs, pottery, baskets and sandals, for example, were found.

When I had seen enough of the Exhibition, I went to see the North American Indian ghost dance shirt which was attached to a dummy. Thank goodness I was too late for the role.

'Am I allowed to photograph this?' I asked an attendant.

'Yes,' was the brief reply.

I could hardly believe my ears but quickly cocked the camera and pressed the button. The attendant must have been psychic for there was no flash. I left the museum and cycled back to the shop, where I had bought the spool and purchased a new battery. I was back in business again and hurried back to photograph the shirt.

With its raven and eagle feathers, it was of religious significance and was thought to protect its wearer from enemy bullets. The stained and bullet holed ghost dance shirt of the Lakota Sioux on display was apparently acquired after the Battle (or Massacre, depending on your viewpoint) of Wounded Knee in 1890, when 300 men, women and children were slaughtered by the U.S. cavalry, who were certainly not all clones of the late John Wayne, the former film star who acted sometimes in Westerns.

It arrived in Glasgow in 1891, when Buffalo Bill's Wild West Show came to the city at the end of its European tour. William Frederick Cody, better known as Buffalo Bill, was in residence at Parkhead and attended a football match at Ibrox between Rangers and another team. The shirt was donated in 1892 by an interpreter employed by Buffalo Bill, and taken to Kelvingrove.

In recent years the shirt became the subject of controversy, ever since an American of Cherokee descent learned of its presence in Glasgow, when on holiday in Scotland. Some time afterwards a delegation of Sioux descendants proposed displaying the shirt in a heritage centre at Wounded Knee. It was argued that it should be returned to America, in order that the dead warrior's soul might rest in peace. The Kelvingrove Museum was unwilling to return the shirt, however ordinary it looked compared to some in America, for it was the only one it had and was, as far as was known, the only one outside America. The shirt, however, is today over in America as requested, and only a replica is to be found on display in the Kelvingrove museum.

It seems the eagle and raven feathers give the shirt a dating back to the end of the 19th century. To establish the authenticity of the shirt, a test of the stain was tried but proved inconclusive. Apparently after the massacre, fake ghost shirts were dipped in chicken blood and then sold as mementoes of the battle.

After seeing the ghost shirt, I repeatedly turned over the same question in my mind. If it was the genuine article, why was I allowed to subject it to the flash of my camera? Upon further inquiry after the trip, I was informed that it was the authentic ghost shirt that I saw and that there are a lot of myths about exposure to flashlight. Certainly there didn't seem to be any restriction on the use of flash in the Louvre in Paris, when I paid a visit there later and photographed paintings in the presence of attendants.

I didn't see the ceremonial waistcoat which, according to the interpreter who was at Wounded Knee within two weeks, had belonged to Chief Rain-in-the-Face. The latter is said to have killed General George Armstrong Custer, who fell (Custer's last stand or rout) with 266 of his men at the Battle of Little Bighorn in Montana in 1876. At that battle five Scotsmen in the cavalry buried their bagpipes before being killed. No more pipe dreams for them. An unusual find on the battle site was a pair of jeans believed to be the oldest in the world.

When I left the museum, I cycled to the Scottish Exhibition and Conference Centre down by the Clyde. From there a cycleway leads all the way to Loch Lomond Hostel, the route being part of the National Cycle Network promoted by Sustrans to popularise cycling. I cycled past the S.E.C.C. until I came to a footbridge over the A814, where I dismounted and crossed to follow the signed cycle route alongside the A814. As this is not a guidebook, I do not intend to describe here all the twists and turns of the route, for these are dealt with adequately elsewhere in a Sustrans publication. A shower came on and I stopped to put on my waterproofs. So far the route was good, but care had to be taken under bridges or flyovers, where glass sometimes lay strewn.

By the time I reached Clydebank, the home of the Singer sewing machine, and the worst place in Britain for asbestos caused cancer, I had already left behind places I had been relatively close to, such as the Clyde Tunnel and Victoria Park with its fossil tree stumps. Soon I was beside John Brown Engineering, the name a reminder that the John Brown shipyards had built in their heyday the famous 'Queen Mary' and 'Queen Elizabeth', as well as 'Britannia', the Royal yacht I visited sometime later at Ocean Terminal, Leith. During World War II Clydebank suffered heavily from German bombing and, if I remember rightly, only five houses were left undamaged. I would have liked to have visited Dalnottar Cemetery, where victims of the bombing were put into a mass grave, and to have seen around Clydebank District Museum. The problem was that I thought it would take too much time to come off the cycleway, find and see these places, and get back to the cycleway to Loch Lomond

Soon I passed Dalmuir, where aeroplanes were made during World War II, then came along the Forth and Clyde Canal path. As I cycled under the Erskine Bridge which spans the Clyde at that point, I recalled that in the days of the ferry a fiddler used to entertain the waiting motorists. Over at the other side of the water from where I was is the Erskine Hospital, the Princess Louise home for limbless soldiers and sailors.

By this time, I had met up with a mixed group of cycling schoolchildren, with two teachers to whom I talked and commented on their mountain bike tyres.

'At least with these fat tyres you won't get punctures.'

'Oh, we do, believe me. Glass can still get through.' He broke off the conversation and shouted: 'Right, are you all ready?'

The youngsters rallied and set off, and I followed at a discrete distance or overtook at times. I was glad to follow, for the group was also making for Loch Lomond Hostel and it saved me time, when the route became unclear. At a later halt I mentioned the signposting of the route.

'The path's not always obvious,' said the male leader. 'Sometimes the signs are removed or turned. I know the way because I've been along here a few times.'

I remembered that road signs had been interfered with during World War II, in order to create confusion in the event of an invasion by German soldiers. However, the problems the leader had referred to were caused by silly pranks or sheer vandalism.

At times the run was through rather grim, grafittied areas, but it was more attractive along by the canal, where there were trees and bushes as well as locks. In places I noticed a green slime on the canal water, and it was only later that I learned that this is a pond weed unique in the world. Shopping trolleys have been deliberately put into the water to hold the plants in place during dredging. Or was this an April Fool story?

We passed Old Kilpatrick, which was the western terminal of the turf Roman Antonine Wall, and at Bowling the canal towpath came to an end. There beside the canal was a cycle repair shed, where some of the teenagers' bikes were attended to, for slow or full punctures. I moved on and, after crossing the canal, stopped at a shed shop for refreshments. It had some very tasty rolls and icing cakes, which some of the youngsters enjoyed as well. However, those who had had tyre problems were given no time to linger, and had to get on the way as soon as they were ready. I followed the group across the road, through a park and back to a tarred road and into Dumbarton. I was particularly glad to follow them, through the traffic and maze of roads, to beyond the town and into the country.

All was going well, or so I thought, as I tailed the group on the cycleway through that wooded and grassy country. Suddenly my chain snapped and some parts went flying, not that I could have done anything with them even if I had found them. Hardly gutted but downhearted, I watched as the last of the party disappeared round a bend. I could scarcely take it in that the chain of a new bike had broken. I removed the chain, packed the big rucksack for a second time on the trip, and walked the bike several miles back into Dumbarton.

By the time I reached the town, the rain was falling heavily and it was pretty miserable. I made a few enquiries about a cycle repair shop but initially drew a blank until I spoke to some schoolboys.

'Halfords store does bike repairs,' they said and pointed me in the right direction.

'Can you repair my bike now?' I asked when I entered the shop. 'The chain broke.'

'Bring it in,' I was directed.

I wheeled in the bike and pushed it to the distant back of the store (a chain store?), where I unloaded the panniers, and the bike was fitted with a new chain at a cost of £14. Back on the bike went the panniers and, once outside, I unloaded the big rucksack and put the contents back into the panniers. Luckily there was a canopy outside, which sheltered me from the rain during this aggravating and lengthy exercise. Once bitten, twice shy they say. I decided not to go to the hostel by the cycleway in case I had any more problems, either with the bike or the route, and so opted for the busy A82. At least the route was clear and, if I did have more problems, there were vehicles passing by. That was the good part, but the rain and constant traffic made the journey hazardous and unpleasant, and I was relieved to reach the hostel.

I booked in and as I struggled upstairs with my luggage, I was greeted by the friendly youngsters I had been with earlier.

'What happened to you?' asked one of the teachers when I came downstairs.

'My chain broke and I had to go back to Dumfries.'

'We wondered. I feel a bit guilty. I should have come back.'

'Not at all. You're not responsible for me.'

The two leaders offered me some food they had left over but I accepted only a cup of coffee. After a girl had finished a lengthy call, I phoned home then washed some clothes and had something to eat.

Later as I lay in bed I reflected on the day. Repairs to the bike in the morning and repairs at tea time. Yet I counted my blessings, for the broken chain might have happened between Loch Lomond and Fort William, where there are many places not within easy range of a shop with spare parts. I thought too of the ghost shirt. If that was worn by the warrior chief who killed Custer, an Aberdeen man might have noticed it on the killer, for I believe there was at least one Aberdeen man amongst those who died at Little Bighorn. I hope the latter didn't 'lose his shirt' when attacked.

I recalled too that inside a church at the west end of Princess Street, Edinburgh, there is a plaque to a man who died at Little Bighorn. I believe it was placed there by some family members.

'I hope the weather's better tomorrow,' I said to a hosteller just before the dormitory lights went out.

I closed my eyes for I, Rain-in-the-Face-Neck-Hands-Feet-All over the Waterproofs, had spoken for the last time that night. In the darkness of the quiet room, I listened to the steady sound of the rain on the window panes.

9 June   L.L. – Wallacetown Farm – Dumbarton – L.L.   O.S. 56, 63

In the morning people waited patiently outside the dining area in the hostel, possibly hungry or eager to get on the road. I shared a table with an American group, but it wasn't very appetizing and continued with a normal breakfast. It was obvious that there was a fairly large American party in, for other tables were filled with Europe's relations from across the 'pond'.

I wasn't too sure about biking to Crianlarich, my intended destination, because the rain was pouring down that morning, and eventually I decided to stay another night in the hostel and booked in accordingly.

'There's no way I'm going out in that,' said a girl to her boyfriend and it wasn't her clothing that displeased her.

About forty years had passed since I was last in that hostel, when I had taken the opportunity to fill an empty seat on an Aberdeen bus taking S.Y.H.A. delegates to a meeting there. I was still impressed by the place as I was then, and rightly so. It is a fine looking building with magnificent woodwork inside, and was built on the site of one of King Robert the Bruce's hunting lodges. At one time it was the world's largest youth hostel and, in the T.V. soap 'Take The High Road', it served as the 'Big House'.

Later in the morning it began to brighten up apart from the occasional shower. There was no time then, however, to cycle to Crianlarich so I resolved to return to Dumbarton and then follow the A814 towards Cardross. Accordingly, I cycled first through the leafy grounds of Cameron House Hotel and Country Estate. Many years ago when I had a car, I went there with the family to see the bear (or was it beer?) park which was Britain's first. There in Cameron House at that time was the world's largest collection of whisky bottles. The bears had all gone years earlier and Cameron House, set in 108 acres of ground, was instead a 68 roomed hotel and time share complex, voted 'Scottish Hotel of the Year' in 1995 by A.A. inspectors. Happily in this case 'A.A.' refers to the Automobile Association rather than Alcoholics Anonymous.

At the end of the 17th century Cameron House belonged to James Smollett, a judge whose grandson, Tobias Smollett (1721-71) was born nearby in Bonhill parish. Tobias was educated in Dumbarton and Glasgow University and became a novelist after giving up a medical career. When he didn't make enough money from his books, he used to sell off some of his black West Indian slaves at £80 each.

It was peaceful cycling through the wooded grounds, but I came back to the A82 and cycled towards Cardross on the A814, after passing through Dumbarton. Of course, the Cardross I was cycling towards is more recent than the vanished old village of Cardross, just across the mouth of the river Leven from Dumbarton Castle. There in the village castle in 1329, Robert the Bruce died of leprosy or at least some bad skin condition. Before he expired he commanded Sir James Douglas to take his heart to the Holy Land. (I hope he didn't say 'hat'.) Douglas died on the way and his own heart was brought back to the village of Douglas to which I have already referred. Bruce's heart was eventually buried at Melrose Abbey.

Before reaching Cardross I turned right and cycled on until I arrived at Wallacetown Farm. There was no sign of Gromit anywhere. I pushed the bike uphill towards the farm house and looked out on the fields which sloped downward. What an excitement there must have been there on 12 September, 1895, when Percy Sinclair Pilcher, a lecturer at Glasgow University, made the first properly controlled glider flight in Britain. His machine rose 12 feet into the air and remained aloft for about 20 seconds.

By the way, some aviation buffs believe that a Dundee Scotsman called Preston Watson flew a powered aeroplane, before Orville Wright in America was given the credit for being the first to do so in 1903. Watson is said to have made his powered flight on the bank of the Tay at Errol, and several people claimed to have witnessed the event. When Watson was killed in 1896, his brother went to the Royal Aero Club to argue the case. Lord Brabazon, whom he saw and who is credited with making the first British powered flight in 1909, refused to accept his claim. I believe Wright gave his plane to the Smithsonian Institute, on condition that no research was done into who was first to fly a powered aeroplane, and thus protected his own position. My own bike flies when I am in a hurry.

As I came down the road from the farmhouse, a car came uphill towards me and a man poked his head out of the window. Not too painful, I hope.

'Is this Wallacetown?' he asked.

'Yes,' I replied. I wondered if he thought I was a country yokel, but quickly dismissed that notion as I wasn't chewing a straw.

Looking back from below, the slopes were very noticeable. It didn't take very long to cycle back to Dumbarton where, in the process of looking for a place to buy a spool and a sandwich, I spotted the Cat's Head Inn. Being a reasonable chap I tried not to harbour any nasty thoughts about what was on the menu there. I was glad I hadn't seen a Man's Head Inn, when I remembered that at least one black African leader had allegedly kept human heads in his fridge. Mind you, some people think that potted head is quite tasty.

I then cycled along by St. Augustine's Church, whose foundation stone was laid in 1872, and which benefitted from the generosity of the Denny shipbuilding family. The famous Scottish architect Charles Rennie

MacIntosh was married within. Farther along the High Street I cycled past the Old Parish Church built in 1811. Watching of the dead began in 1830 because of body snatchers, and watches in the graveyard were maintained from dusk till dawn for up to eight years.

Beyond that I came to the bottling and blending complex owned by Allied Distillers Ltd. Originally the building was erected by a Canadian company before World War II. As I sat astride the bike and looked at the building, a man spoke to me.

'You see that building. They reckon it took 2,000,000 bricks and 600 men to make,' he said. 'There used to be a shipyard there.'

He sounded proud as he reeled off these facts. I discovered that the complex was built on the site of a former Archibald McMillan & Son yard that operated from 1846-1930. At one time the distillery complex was the largest in Europe. Like Rome it wasn't built in a day.

'There's a gate in the new office block. It used to be part of the main entrance to Denny's shipyard,' was his parting shot as he walked on. Had he escaped from the tourist office?

Denny's was famous for new ideas in the field of marine turbines, stabilizers and welding, and that was the yard which finished and rigged the famous tea clipper the 'Cutty Sark' after Scott and Linton of Inverbervie became bankrupt. It was launched in 1869 and was one of the fastest sailing ships ever. It was built to carry tea from China, but later became the fastest ship in the Australian wool trade.

The Scottish Maritime Museum in Castle Street, or at least Dumbarton's part of it, was something that really attracted me to Dumbarton. Outside I viewed the engine which came from the 'P.S.Leven', a wooden paddle boat which operated between Dumbarton and Glasgow. The engine, his first, was built by Robert Napier (1791-1876) in 1821 and was given to Dumbarton in 1877 by his son.

I locked the bike and entered the building which houses the Denny Ship Model Experiment Tank. This tank, which can hold 1,659,290 litres of water, was built in Victorian times in 1882 and was the first commercial ship model testing tank built in the world. It still has many of the first features such as a water tank as long as a football pitch, clay moulding beds for casting wax model ship hulls, and the original Victorian machinery for shaping models.

'Is it still in working order today?' I asked one of the staff.

'Oh, yes. It was restored by the Scottish Maritime Museum and is still used for testing ship designs.'

The Tank is the only surviving bit of the William Denny and Brothers shipyard, which operated from 1846-1963. There used to be several other shipyards in Dumbarton at one time.

After a snack I cycled to Dumbarton Rock and the Castle, which I had seen from a distance the day before. It was quiet and almost deserted in the neighbourhood of the castle, as I locked the bike and went upstairs to pay my money at the desk.

'It won't be long before closing time but you have time to go round,' said the lady custodian, who possibly considered me to be a shape shifter.

The rock itself is a basalt volcanic plug with two peaks, and is thought to have been a stronghold longer than any other place in the country. Dumbarton has had various names but the present one comes from 'Dun Breatan', which means 'Fort of the Britons'. In ancient times the castle was attacked by Picts, Northumbrians and Vikings, and by the Middle Ages it was a royal castle.

One of the past governors was Sir John Menteith who, as mentioned already, was behind the capture of William Wallace. The claim has been made that Wallace was held prisoner there before being transported to London for execution, but Historic Scotland's 'Dumbarton Castle' publication considers this is improbable. Note, however, there is no categorical denial, and maybe Wallace was in the area when one recalls the name Wallaceton Farm, but another explanation has been suggested.

In 1548 as a six year old child, Mary Queen of Scots was taken to the castle for her safety. She stayed there for five months, before sailing from Dumbarton to marry the French Dauphin. He became François II of France but when he died, Mary, then Queen of France as well as of Scotland, returned to Scotland in 1561 and revisited the castle in 1563. One of the governors of Dumbarton was the father of Darnley, her cousin, whom she later married, and another governor accompanied her to England in 1568, where she remained until her death.

Oliver Cromwell came to Dumbarton and yet another governor drank to his health. A visit from General Wade led to the castle's defences being improved and later, after the 1745 Jacobite rebellion, some rebels were held there including one of the seven men of Moidart, who had come with Bonnie Prince Charlie to Scotland. The Napoleonic wars saw the arrival of some French prisoners, and I visited the French prison indicated by one of the signboards. There was, however, no sign marking where they did a 'Oui Oui'. I also saw the magazine built in 1748 by William Skinner, the engineer also responsible for Fort George near Inverness.

Exiting from reception, the top of the castle is reached by some steep, stone stairs, and I was thankful for having the health and fitness to climb them. The view from the top is magnificent and is aided by having a notice board and a map of the surrounding area. From the Rock, which was taken over in wartime by the army and hit by enemy bombs, I could see where aeroplanes were manufactured during World War II.

'Would you like a look through my binoculars?' I asked a young man and woman who shared the view with me.

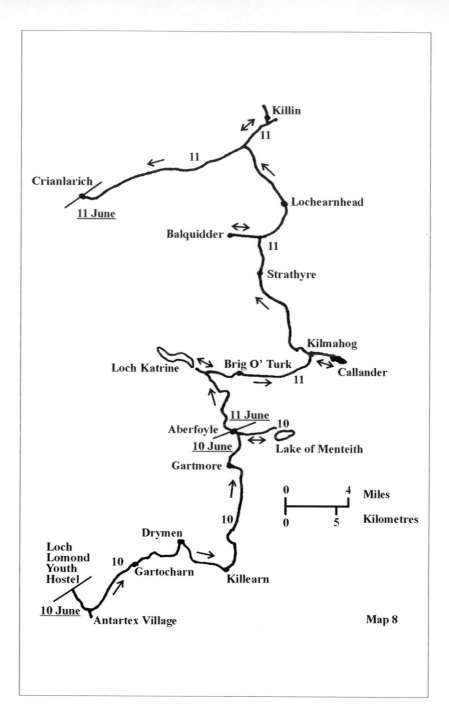

Killin

11

11

Crianlarich

11 June

Lochearnhead

Balquidder

11

Strathyre

Kilmahog

Loch Katrine   Brig O' Turk

Callander

11

11 June   10

Aberfoyle

10 June

Lake of Menteith

Gartmore

0   4 **Miles**

0   5 **Kilometres**

Drymen

10

Loch
Lomond
Youth
Hostel

Gartocharn

Killearn

10 June   Antartex Village

Map 8

'Yes, thanks. Great view from here.'

Shortly afterwards they handed them back and moved on, and I explored more buildings and battlements on the very striking peaks of the Rock.

I wasn't wearing a watch and was a little concerned about the time, although I felt I was still within the limits I had set myself. Back in the museum and reception, the lady had assured me that she wouldn't lock me in. To my relief she clearly said 'in' and not 'up'.

'I know you're here,' she had said, 'so don't worry.'

As I finally picked my way down the stairs, I was pleased that at last I had visited this landmark and castle, which I had seen on past train journeys on the Glasgow – Fort William line.

'Is there anyone else up there?' asked the custodian when I met her again.

'No, I don't think so. The couple I saw went down. I certainly passed nobody on my way here.'

I continued down to the bike and, close on my heels, she emerged from the castle and made for her car. I cycled to a shop for a bag of crisps, a chocolate KitKat, a can of juice and a local paper, before taking the A82 back to the hostel. The school party was gone but there were still plenty foreigners inside the hostel. A cup of tea and some biscuits refreshed me, while I read the paper and then made some plans for the next day. I was looking forward to it, because I thought at last I would be really flying north.

10 June   Loch Lomond – Aberfoyle   O.S. 56, 57

Breakfast was such a pleasure and afterwards I carted, not strutted, my stuff outside to the bike, which I had brought round from the bike shed at the back. The morning air and sky were good and I intended to go to Crianlarich. A lady was loading her bike too and she told me that she was doing the End to End run. The difference was that she was doing it in a fortnight.

'I intend going to Glen Coe today,' she said.

'Which route are you taking?' I asked, wondering in self-amusement if 'Glenn' could perhaps be a brother of Sebastian, the former great athlete.

'Right up the western side of Loch Lomond to Crianlarich and onward to Glen Coe.'

'I'm going by Aberfoyle, the Trossachs, Callander and Killin and from there to Crianlarich.'

I noticed that she was travelling very light, and I was aware that she wouldn't have time to look into things in depth on the way. She set off some time before me and I never saw her again.

Once ready I cycled down the driveway to the A82 and pedalled in the direction of Alexandria. Alexandria was one thing but I ruled out Cairo and turned into the A811. After a short time, I turned right into the Lomond Industrial Estate to the Antartex Village, which is a shopping complex and visitor centre with one of those ubiquitous Edinburgh Woollen Mill shops for visitors. In the complex you can buy country and leisure wear, souvenirs and gifts, sheepskin and leather and there is a golf shop, a craft village, and a very attractive restaurant and coffee shop. I succumbed to the latter. Somebody had to do it.

'Excuse me, but can you explain why the Village has the name "Antartex"?' I asked a well dressed male member of staff.

Had I engaged my brain first instead of my mouth, I would have realised that the word was a combination of 'Antarctic' and 'textile' just as the material name 'Goretex' comes from a Mr. 'Gore', a man encountered by a hillwalker I once met, and 'textile'.

'Oh, we have supplied the equipment, the clothing for the British Antarctic expeditions, and there's a mock Antarctic base set up in the Village. There you'll see the actual equipment used in Antarctic expeditions, and in particular clothes made at Antartex for over 40 years. Explorers need the right kind of clothes to handle temperatures well below zero. Since the late 80s Antartex has been part of the Edinburgh Woollen Mill Company.'

Unfortunately, as I discovered later, I lost some information describing some of the production processes. On leaving the complex, I moved on and passed Balloch in the neighbourhood of which G. Leslie Hunter (1877-1931), one of Scotland's leading painters, did some fine paintings. Balloch is also where Sweeney's cruises operate on Loch Lomond. I had observed in the 'Dumbarton and Vale of Leven "Reporter"' that Mr Sweeney, the proprietor, had written to say that his 'Skylark IX' was not renamed after one of the ships that evacuated hundreds from Dunkirk during World War II.

'This is wrong. The "Skylark IX" is the actual boat that was used in the evacuation of the Dunkirk Beaches, and two Dunkirk Veteran Association publications both recognise the "Skylark IX" as an original "Little Dunkirk Ship".'

Mr Sweeney was very concerned that everyone knew that his was the genuine article and the editor apologised for being 'under the misapprehension that the "Skylark" used at Dunkirk was no longer sailing'. Perhaps my uncle Bill had been on it or had seen it at Dunkirk I mused, as I cranked along the A811 to Gartocharn.

Just before reaching the village, I stopped at a sign indicating the farm of Tullochan, and I could clearly see the buildings at the end of the farm road. That was, I gathered, the home of Brigadier Alastair Pearson, the paratroops' most decorated soldier in the British army. By sheer

Hugh MacDiarmid's Grave (Centre Front), Nr. Langholm

Dryfesdale Cemetery, Nr. Lockerbie

William Paterson's Birthplace, Nr. Lochmaben

Brow Well, Nr. Ruthwell

First Savings Bank, Ruthwell

Grave of Robert Paterson, 'Old Mortality', Bankend

Robert Burns' Mausoleum, Dumfries

Birthplace Of First Real Bicycle, Courthill Smithy, Penpont

Scotland's Oldest Post Office, Sanquhar

William Symington's Memorial, Leadhills

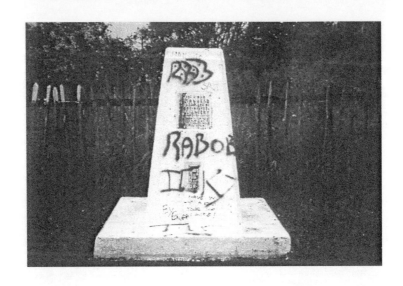

General Roy's Memorial, Nr. Carluke

Veranda Used By George Orwell, Hairmyres Hospital

Robert Tannahill's Grave, Paisley

Forth And Clyde Canal Cycle Path

Robert Bontine Cunningham Graham's Memorial, Nr. Gartmore

Supposed Grave Of Rob Roy, Balquhidder

Memorial to MacIain, MacDonald Chief, Glencoe

Neptune's Staircase, Corpach

Joe Lindsay, Targe Maker, N. Kessock, Nr. Inverness

Alexander Mackenzie's Grave, Avoch

Brahan Seer Stone, Chanonry Point, Nr. Fortrose

Hugh Miller's Cottage, Cromarty

Memorial (Nr. Lothbeg) To Last Wolf Killed In Sutherland

House Lived In By R.L. Stevenson, Wick

coincidence I had bought the 'Dumbarton and Vale of Leven "Reporter"' for that day and there was an article about him. According to the paper he was the only man awarded four Distinguished Service Orders for bravery. I learned later that he had been a Glasgow baker before World War II, but his bravery and leadership saw him rise through the ranks and earn also a Military Cross. According to his daughter, quoted in the paper, he 'was involved with 15 young organisations just before he died aged 80'. Today the Tullochan Trust tries to help people aged 12-25 develop their potential and they are expected to help their peers in turn.

I felt some excitement when I entered Gartocharn, for two old friends live there. I have known them since we were students doing summer work in a holiday camp. What a surprise or shock they would get if I turned up unexpectedly at their home, for I hadn't seen them for about thirty to forty years.

'Do you know a John and Helen Crawford?' I asked in the local shop.

'O yes, I know them. Their house is down that way, I think, but he may be in the art gallery.'

That would not be unreasonable, I thought, seeing he is an artist. I didn't find the house described to me and tried the art gallery, but they were not there. I enquired again about the house, found it the next time and rang the bell. There was no answer and no sign of life round the back, so reluctantly I wheeled the bike back to the road. I would let them know I had called when the next Christmas card was sent. Perhaps John was away playing his bagpipes or sailing on the Clyde.

Moving on I saw Duncryne hill which, I am led to believe, Tom Weir, the well known climber, naturalist, photographer and writer, climbs or climbed everyday. Having read some of his articles and books, I was hoping to run into him, but not with the bike, of course.

Somewhere to the west nearby is the farm where a husband and wife, who disappeared from Aberfoyle in the Trossachs, were found shot and buried. They were said to be involved in drugs. Soon I arrived in Drymen, a one time collecting point for Rob Roy's black cattle, and later where anti-aircraft guns were set up during World War II. Rudolph Hess, Hitler's deputy, was taken to the hospital there during his brief time in Scotland, before being transferred via Euston station to the Tower in London. Billy Connolly, the comedian, also once lived in Drymen but he has never been put into the Tower, as far as I know. I cycled next across country to Killearn via Gartness. It was easy cycling and the traffic was light.

Somewhere near the river Endrick there formerly stood Gartness Castle, where John Napier (1550-1617) once lived. He grew up to be a scientist, theologian, and inventor of weapons of war and of, it is said, the first pump to keep mines clear of water. His great hobby, which he pursued along with his other interests and running an estate, was mathematics. Napier is credited with inventing logarithms (or at least his was the first system published, for a German was also working on a logarithm system) and the decimal point. On the other hand I read once that the Mayans in South America used decimal points long before then. Once Napier is reported to have asked the local miller to stop his mill wheel, for the noise was irritating him as he worked out his logarithms. That reminds me incidentally of a past Pope, who ordered the birds in his garden to be killed to give him peace and quiet when he was thinking. Napier also invented what is believed to be the world's first mechanical computing device, a series of numbered rods called 'Napier's Bones'.

'Excuse me, but do you know where Gartness Castle is?' I asked a country lad.

'Oh, it's long gone. They used the castle stones to build some of the houses.'

So that's how one becomes a builder. It didn't take long to reach Killearn, a small village, where I tried to extract some cash from the machine in the wall. I didn't do it right so I must have tapped in the wrong numbers. I wasn't in the mood to try again, for it was raining quite heavily and awkward, though not impossible, working with the cycling cape flapping about. I was, however, able to draw out money inside the warm bank, after making the excuse that I had had a problem outside.

'Can you tell me where the George Buchanan monument is?' I asked a man in the bank.

'Just outside the bank here,' he said, looking rather amused that I had missed such a large structure.

This monument was another of my 'must see' attractions. The 100 foot monument was in behind a locked gate but there was an information board. Buchanan (1506-82) was a scholar, poet, philosopher, linguist and historian, who had studied at the universities of St. Andrews and Paris. He held various appointments in France and Portugal, before becoming the tutor in classics to Mary Queen of Scots, and then tutor to her son, who became James VI of Scotland and I of England. The obelisk was raised in 1788 and is a copy of one built in 1690 to William the Third. It was Buchanan, who made out the first Scottish case for constitutional monarchy.

I had just left the monument, when I met up with my Buchanan 'guide' in the street. He grinned as he saw me.

'Well,' he said, 'did you find your monument?'

'I could hardly miss it, could I? Actually I hadn't looked for it when I asked you. Do you happen to know where he was born?'

'Over at the farm of Moss, less than a mile and a half south of Killearn. If you have a map I'll show you.'

I undid a pannier hood, took out my map enclosed in a map case, an invaluable item when it rains, and handed it to him.

'There it is,' he said, 'just over Blane Water. You can please yourself, but the original house has gone. It's maybe not worth your time going there.'

He asked a few questions about my trip and talked about Buchanan being a Latin scholar. My 'guide' and I then discovered that we were both among the dwindling number of people who had studied Latin. In my case I had seven years of the language and learned that 'amat' was not something on which you wiped your feet.

Being unable to visit Buchanan's house where he was born, I decided to do something else memorable. I went into the village coffee shop, where I took off my waterproofs and ordered coffee and cake. Two ladies were on duty and soon we got chatting about my trip. When the time came for me to leave, they had a surprise for me.

'Take this scone and pancake with you,' they said and handed me a small wrapped package. I noted their names - Jacqueline Morton and Pat Sutherland.

I thanked them and donned the waterproofs again, although the rain had subsided a bit by the time I came out to the bike. I led my 'friend' along to the old toll house, and began recording details about the tolls from a board on the wall of the building. As I did so a man stopped in his car, wound down the window, and had a short conversation with me about my journey.

Bearing in mind the time, I realised that I wouldn't make it to Crianlarich that day. It remained for me to decide what else I would try to see in or near Killearn. I wouldn't have minded seeing Killearn Hospital, built during World War II to house the expected wounded from Glasgow. Then there was Glen Goyne and its connection with Lord Tedder. Just over two miles south of Killearn down the A875 and on to the A81 was, marked on the map, the distillery of Glen Goyne. Its old name was Glenguin, a title which Lord Tedder, Marshall of the RAF assumed when he became a peer. Tedder, who was born in 1890 in one of the houses overlooking the distillery, worked with Auchinleck and Alexander in N. Africa during World War II, and became Eisenhower's Deputy Supreme Commander in Europe from 1943-45. His daughter was for a while a resident of Alastrean House, recently threatened with closure but now saved, at Tarland in Aberdeenshire. Later she moved to England.

Of course, there and back meant another five miles plus the time tracking down the house. I had to draw a line somewhere, however reluctantly, and decided to move on northwards. I just wished later that I had remembered that one of my classmates from The Gordon Schools, Huntly, a fine vet by the name of Eric Brander, lived in Killearn. Alas he died some time after my trip.

On leaving Killearn, I followed the A875 and went only a short distance into the open countryside, before looking back to the south-east. Away in the distance lay the Campsie Fells, where during World War II decoy fires were to be lit (I'm not sure if they were actually lit) to draw German bombers away from Clydebank and Glasgow. A secondary road then took me across to the A81, which I followed northwards until I took another secondary road to Gartmore. I wondered if there was any connection between the village and the financial organisation of the same name.

On arrival, I locked the bike outside the village shop where my attention was drawn to a notice, which said that the shop had featured on T.V. and was a community shop. Inside I bought some juice and a Mars bar. I was hungry enough to eat food from any planet, in fact.

'How exactly does the shop work as a community shop?' I asked the lady after referring to the notice.

'We all own the shop and we decide on the purchases and policy.'

'Right, that's a good idea. Am I on the right road for the Don Roberto Memorial?' I asked.

'Yes, go right on until you come to a stone arch over the road and it's beside that on the left.'

This wasn't the first memorial to the man. There had been one erected in 1937 in Castlehill Park, Ardoch, Dumbarton, but it was moved from there to Gartmore in 1981 because of vandalism. Don Roberto had been laird of Ardoch as well as laird of Gartmore.

I soon arrived at the arch and confirmed I was in the right place by asking a motorist, who was bringing his car slowly through the arch. I was hungry and started on the scone and pancake from the coffee shop, before disposing of the Mars bar and the juice. A boy came out of a nearby house and greeted me, but he was too late if he wanted a bite, for everything was consumed and in any case I don't bite people. Before entering the wood to find the memorial, I read a N.T.S. interpretative board by the roadside and then 'binned' my bike or, more accurately, locked it against a bin.

A short walk through the roadside wood brought me to the memorial, designed by Glasgow architect Alexander Wright, and it incorporates stones from Argentina and a portrait by Alexander Proudfoot. Robert Bontine Cunningham Graham (1852-1936) was the last family head of Gartmore House, which was taken over by the army during World War II. He was very fond of horses and in his young days lived in Argentina, where he was known as Don Roberto. At one time he represented Lanark in Parliament, was connected with Keir Hardie from Cumnock near Sanquhar, with the establishment of the Labour Party, and with the foundation of the Scottish National Party. He became the First President of the Scottish Labour Party in 1888, and the First President of the Scottish National Party in 1928. He was also the author of several books.

In the quietness of the wood, I stood before the memorial, which had been unveiled by Argentina's ambassador to Britain, a man called Señor

Ortiz Rozas. Don Roberto's love for his horses was clearly shown in the words on the stone: 'To Fama – to Pampa – my black Argentine whom I rode for 20 years without a fall. May the earth lie on him as lightly as he once trod upon its face. Vale...or until so long. Don Roberto.' Buried there, I believe, is a hoof of his horse Pampa, presumably so named from the South American word 'pampa', which the 16th century Spanish invaders used for the great, almost treeless South American grassland plain. Pampa was a mustang, which Cunningham Graham had saved from pulling a Glasgow tram. Real horse power!

After leaving the memorial, I cycled on until I reached the A81 once more and this led to Aberfoyle, which by then was past its busy time. I wanted to see first the manse, kirk and kirkyard of Kirkton of Aberfoyle to the south of Aberfoyle. Robert Kirk (1614?-92) served as minister of that church from 1685-92. In 1684 Kirk produced the first complete translation of the metrical psalms into Gaelic, but he was a bit of a crank in that he wrote another book 'The Secret Commonwealth of Elves, Fauns and Fairies'. No wonder he was described as the 'Fairy Minister'.

Round the side of the old kirk (church) I found his grave, but there's a story that he was spirited away to the fairy world while walking on nearby Doune Hill, which is visible from the cemetery. A tree on top of the hill is called the Minister's Pine. As other people came into the churchyard, I hoped they wouldn't take me for a fairy.

By the church door I found two mortsafes, which were used to protect bodies from grave robbers in the early 1800s. From the churchyard I cycled into Aberfoyle, along the main street and on to the Lake of Menteith erroneously described, I believe, as the only lake in Scotland. Apparently there are several named lakes, but they are not marked on the 1:50,000 O.S. maps as far as I know. I wanted to see the island of Inchmahome on the lake where, in the 16th century, the royal court was in residence for about six months. That was also where Mary Queen of Scots was taken as a five year old child for safety from the English, after they defeated the Scots at Pinkie, and from there she went to Dumbarton Castle.

Don Roberto and his wife are buried in the ruined 13th century priory on the island and, I have been told, some hairs from a favourite horse were dropped on his coffin. In 1878 he married Gabrielle de la Balmondiere, described both as a penniless orphan and of noble Chilean birth, but now known to be Caroline Horsfall, the runaway actress daughter of a Yorkshire surgeon. Gabrielle was also a traveller, writer and campaigner for women's rights. She died in 1906 and Don Roberto died in Buenos Aires in 1936.

As I stood looking across to the island and using the camera, a car drew up and I was joined by a middle aged man. It was amazing, but he didn't look as if he had been born hundreds of years ago.

'Hello,' he said. 'Are you interested in fishing?'

'No, I'm just looking at Inchmahome.'

'I've newly arrived,' he added. 'I love fishing. Some say the lake is the best piece of water for rainbow trout in Scotland. This is where they hold the Scottish Inter-Club Championship.'

'There must be more than rainbow trout here surely,' I said.

'O yes, there's brown trout.'

'Are there still big fish in the water?'

'I heard they took out a brownie weighing over five and a half pounds and a rainbow of 12 pounds. They stock the lake with fish weighing about one and a half pounds and these are allowed to grow. It's quite common to take out three pound fish. Oh, and you're only allowed fly fishing and from a boat.'

I swallowed all this hook and line, if not the sinker, and realised how ignorant I was. I had always believed that a brownie was a little girl in a brown uniform waiting to go into the guides. After the man departed, I cycled back into Aberfoyle where I booked into a hotel in the main street. It was raining and I didn't fancy travelling through to Callander, for it was already 8.00 p.m. and it would be late before I reached the town. Besides, if I continued, there would be no time to visit anything on the way.

I was told to leave the bike round the side and take it into the hotel front hall last thing at night. As I wheeled the bike round to the appointed spot, I noticed two drunks mouthing off just along from the hotel, but they had not seen me or the bike. I put a lock round both wheels and as usual removed my computer, lights and pump. The panniers were already inside upstairs.

Back in the hotel I had a tomato juice and peanuts in the bar, and imagined myself sitting above Jules Verne's fictional coal mine beneath Aberfoyle. I then went upstairs to bed, ready for a sound sleep and hopefully far enough away from Doune Hill to avoid being bothered by fairies. Still, it might have been advisable to have had a small rowan tree in the bedroom for protection. On the other hand, if a Rowantree was meant, what good would a fruit gum have been if I were in danger?

11 June   Aberfoyle – Crianlarich   O.S. 57, 5I, 50

After breakfast in a room overlooking the main street, I left the hotel and paid a visit to the Scottish Wool Centre after phoning through to Crianlarich hostel to book a bed for that night. Inside the Centre a theatre presents 'The Story of Scottish Wool', a 2000 year history of sheep in Scotland. Beside the theatre is a craft display area in which spinners and weavers invite visitors to try their hand at making wool into yarn in the traditional way. Outside a notice said that youngsters could feed lambs and goats. Surely the animals could get something better to eat. I must phone the R.S.P.C.A. .

Sheep, I learned, were domesticated at least 10,000 years ago and in

86

Britain sheep were kept as far back as 2500 years ago. Before the Romans came to Britain, British sheep were smaller with short, dark fleeces and tails. Four horns were common and some even had as many as ten. The sheep the Romans brought to Britain were larger with heavier fleeces and longer tails, and had only two horns or were hornless. Today there's plenty 'roamin' sheep in the hills. I write this sheepishly.

There too I learned about the different breeds of sheep. For example, the Soay (an old Norse word for sheep island) is the most primitive of our sheep. The Boreray is the rarest breed of sheep on display at the Centre, and is usually found on the isle of Boreray in the St. Kilda group of islands. The Scottish blackface is the most numerous breed in Britain and has been developed from Roman breeds, although its black face indicates its pre-Roman origin. This is the main hill breed in Scotland and its wool is used for making carpets and, in Italy, for stuffing luxury mattresses. The merino was unknown in Europe until the Moors invaded Spain in A.D. 711. It has at least five times as many wool fibres as all the other breeds. Wool from the Shetland sheep is so fine that a large christening shawl can pass easily through a wedding ring. In 1792 Sir John Sinclair (mentioned in the Ellisland Farm exhibition) took 500 sheep from the Cheviot hills to Caithness and, by bringing in Lincoln, Ryeland and Merino sheep, produced the North County Cheviot.

A skilled sheep shearer can remove a sheep's fleece in two minutes and do up to 200 a day. Now when I was a young boy, I used to get my hair cut by a barber who was reportedly an ex-sheep farmer, but he couldn't have been a skilled shearer, for he needed ten minutes for my tonsorial operation.

By the time I left the Wool Centre, it was a nice day and I looked forward to cycling along the A821 from Aberfoyle. The road climbed up through the Queen Elizabeth Forest, which is about the size of Glasgow, and I soon reached what was marked on my old map as the David Marshall Lodge. David Marshall had been the chairman of the Carnegie Trust and it had been Carnegie money that had paid for the building. A name change has since occurred and it is now known as the Queen Elizabeth Forest Park Visitor Centre. There I found information and maps of waymarked walks and cycle trails, and looked at the exhibition and forest craft shop.

I was reminded that birch is the first tree to move into unwooded areas and colonise poor soils. It gives shelter to oak and ash which eventually crowd out their protector. I learned that if you see a wind twisted tree growing higher up a hill than any other species, the chances are it is a rowan. It is often found at the entrance of a sheiling, because particularly in the past people believed that it could protect people, sheep and cattle within from evil. Even now some Scottish foresters are not keen or will refuse to cut down a rowan. The Scots pine was described as a hardy tree to be found also throughout most of Europe and in Siberia. There are also spruces and larches in the forest.

I read too about caterpillars, which eat oak leaves to such an extent that they can defoliate an entire woodland, and leave the trees by the end of May as bare as in mid winter. At the height of an infestation the caterpillars are audible as well as visible, for you can hear a faint munching as millions of them chew through the leaves. However, the oak tree is not defenceless. It can produce more leaves later, by which time there are fewer caterpillars around and, as the leaves grow, they contain more and more tannin, a chemical unpalatable to caterpillars.

Then there is the kindle fungus, a parasite which lives on birch trees. It acquired its name, because its dry, fleshy parts could be mixed with saltpetre and used to help light fires. It could also be ground to powder and used as snuff.

Anyone observing peregrines was asked to record the sighting in a book supplied. Apparently in the 1950s and 1960s their numbers were reduced by poisoning from organochlorine pesticides, which accumulated in their bodies and resulted in egg shell thinning and subsequent breeding failure. After restrictions on the use of these pesticides were imposed, the numbers of the peregrines rose.

By this time my head was becoming poisoned by an overdose of facts, so I called a halt and went for coffee.

After leaving the Centre I cycled through the Duke's Pass, named after the Duke of Montrose, who built this toll road from Aberfoyle, the road being rebuilt in the 1930s. Soon I was in the Trossachs, the area strictly between Loch Achray and Loch Katrine, although the term now popularly covers a wider area. The Dane, Hans Christian Andersen, went there once.

According to one source the word 'Trossachs' means 'bristly', presumably because of the rugged nature of the land, and 'Katrine', it has been claimed, comes from the Gaelic 'cateran' meaning a 'Highland robber'. However, there are other possible derivations.

In the 18th century many trees were planted by the Duke of Montrose for commercial reasons, and it was the Duke who maintained the ancient coppice of oak near the Queen Elizabeth Forest Park Visitor Centre. Oak bark was used in the dyeing trade, timber for shipbuilding, and wood was burned for charcoal needed in the area's once flourishing iron industry.

Loch Katrine is about ten miles long, about a mile wide, and about 495 feet deep, of which 17 feet was a later addition after the loch was raised three times. On the north side of the loch, there is public motor vehicle access to the head of the loch at Glengyle where Rob Roy was born. In Glengyle House today lives or lived John Barrington, shepherd and author of 'Red Sky At Night', an interesting book.

Today Glasgow gets its water supply from the loch. In spite of objections from salmon fishermen and local enterprises depending on an uninterrupted supply of water, work began on the scheme which put the city ahead of the rest of Britain. In less than four years Loch Katrine was dammed, a 26 mile long acqueduct was built to the reservoir at Milngavie in Glasgow, and 46 miles of distribution pipes leading through the city were constructed. The acqueduct was tunnelled through the solid rock of the Trossachs and taken across 26 iron and masonry structures, the work being carried out by 2000 or so Scottish and Irish labourers.

In 1859 Queen Victoria sailed on the 'Rob Roy' on Loch Katrine and, afterwards at a ceremony, opened the sluice gates to let the loch's pure water, its 'living gold' reach Glasgow. The water was so soft that it was said that Glasgow's consumption of soap halved. As I stood looking out on the loch, there were cars parked and people waiting at the pier, presumably to board the 'S.S. Sir Walter Scott', named after the great Scottish writer. I fell into conversation with a man who asked me if I had come far.

'I'm from Aberdeen and I'm on my way from Land's End to John O' Groats. I've just come from Aberfoyle today.'

'Well, I live in England now. I used to live in Glasgow. I'm back up here on holiday and thought I would come and see the loch again. It might be my last time.'

There was no need for him to be so pessimistic, for I had no intention of cycling anywhere near him.

'It sure is a beautiful part of the world,' I said.

'You know about the "Sir Walter"?'

'Not much,' I replied.

'Well, as far as I know it's the only surviving screw steamer in regular passenger service in Scotland. It was built by William Denny and Brothers at Dumbarton and was launched in October 1899.'

'Oh, I've just been to Dumbarton. How did they get it to Loch Katrine if it was built there?' I asked. I was puzzled because the loch is landlocked.

'I believe it was taken in pieces by barge up Loch Lomond and then by horse and cart overland from Inversnaid to Stronachlachar. The boat burns special clean briquettes, you know. No oil is allowed for fuel because the loch supplies the water for Glasgow, which is only about 35 miles away.'

That said he caught the eye of his wife (an agile chap) and moved off.

If you are a cyclist, you can take your bike on the boat from the pier up to Stronachlachar, then cycle back on the road which passes Rob Roy's birthplace. I thoroughly enjoyed the run, when my wife and I did it on a different occasion.

Queen Victoria was charmed by the loch and the Trossachs, as were many famous people in the past. Sir Walter Scott, the writer, who stayed at Kirkton manse several times between 1790 and 1809, wrote poems and novels which showed his interest in the landscape and folklore of the area. He wrote about Loch Katrine in his poem 'The Lady of the Lake' and the lady referred to was a certain Ellen Douglas, who is remembered in the name 'Ellen's Isle' out in the loch. In the poem it was the heroine's prayer which inspired Schubert to write his 'Ave Maria'. William and Dorothy Wordsworth thought the Trossachs were wonderful, and Coleridge, a fellow poet and friend of Wordsworth, walked in the Trossachs to try and break his opium habit, which was to enslave him for about 33 years until his death.

I had seen and heard enough and pedalled away from the loch. A quiet and easy run took me past Loch Achray to Brig O' Turk, where I went into a café to enquire about an iron eating tree I had heard about. It certainly wasn't seated inside and iron was not on the menu.

'Excuse me, but do you know where I'll find the iron eating tree?'

'It's farther up the road,' I was told by the lady in charge. She was referring to the side road on which the café was situated.

Cycling on, I came upon an old lady working in the front garden of her cottage and I engaged her in conversation.

'My uncle,' she said, 'lived in the house where I a MacGregor now live. He was the blacksmith in the smithy next door. He threw out bits of iron among the trees and they became part of the tree.'

'Where exactly is it then?'

'Just down there,' she said pointing clearly in the direction.

'Do you know anything about Kate Ferguson, said to be in her time the fattest lady in Britain at 25 stone? Queen Victoria visited the woman at her inn at Brig O' Turk.'

'I know who you mean,' she said. 'One of my relatives knew her but I don't know more than that.'

After thanking the lady, I cycled back to see the tree and sure enough pieces of iron were incorporated into the trunk. I protected the bike and, glad that I was carrying no iron pills, returned to the café where I ordered coffee and a biscuit. As I sat there another man came in and he started talking to myself and to the café lady.

'I used to come here when I was a boy,' he said. 'Paraffin lamps were used to light the place long before your time.' He looked at the lady as he said that.

'If you like I'll show you the old Brig O' Turk,' he added, this time directing these words to me. 'I used to fish there. I once saw an otter there and a salmon with a bit out of its neck.'

When we had finished our coffee, he led the way in his car and I followed by bike back along the road I had come to the café. He turned off the main road and soon we were at the old bridge. Standing there I told him what I used to work at, my name and where I came from and he did likewise.

'I'm from Drongan,' he said. 'The name's Ian Anderson. My father used to be the Inveramsay station master. It's amazing that you're a Philip for my wife is a Philip as well. I used to be in the business of putting bums on seats on airlines, but I gave up work because of a heart attack.'

My mind boggled at his anatomically selective occupation. Was this his attempt at synecdoche (the part for the whole – e.g. 'all hands on deck')? He was a nice chap, however, and I made no comment, for it wasn't as if he was boasting or, as we say in north-east Scotland, 'bumming' about his work.

'Believe it or not,' I said, 'but I used to live in Insch which, of course, is just along the railway line from Inveramsay.'

We finally parted company after a party of handicapped people and their leaders came by. As I cycled back towards the café, I remembered that the Glen Finglas reservoir lay to the north and beyond it Glen Finglas. Somewhere I read that the glen had the distinction of having Europe's largest sheep owner. Luckily sufficient oxygen was reaching my brain to realise that this meant only that he had more sheep than any other owner. The glen was also the setting for Scott's first ballad.

The Woodland Trust is hoping to create there one of the biggest broadleafed forests in Scotland. Golden Charter, the U.K.'s biggest funeral planning organisation, has promoted tree planting there and a batch of trees has been named in the firm's honour. Perhaps my 'wooden suit' will come from there some time in the future.

In 1999 David Murray, ex-teacher and naturalist, passed through Glen Finglas after setting off from Lizard Point in Cornwall with a few pack animals en route for Dunnet Head. Part of his remit was to give talks to school children about the environment.

In 1853 John Ruskin, the writer, painter and thinker, and his wife Effie (real name, Euphemia) took a cottage in the glen and John Millais, his artist friend lodged in an inn in Brig O' Turk village. Effie and Millais fell in love in the glen and later married after her divorce from Ruskin.

Until recently Scotland, Albania and Iraq were the only countries in the world without National Parks. However, the Scottish Parliament passed the National Parks (Scotland) Bill in July, 2000 and the Woodland Trust's estate in Glen Finglas is included in the Loch Lomond and Trossachs National Park. Some people are happy about the Park, but others are concerned about the increase in tourism and possible interference with their property rights, particularly near Loch Lomond and the tourist parts of the Trossachs.

As I cycled away from Brig O' Turk, I met up with a retired couple on a battered tandem. They were making for Loch Katrine.

'Come far?' I was asked.

'Not today,' I replied. 'Just from Aberfoyle. I started originally from Land's End.'

'If you're going into Callander you could leave the A821 and go via the

Sustrans route on the south side of Loch Venachar.'

I knew I had that option, but the traffic was very light on the A road and I was sure that the run along the north shore of the loch would be pleasant in the sun. Eventually I joined the A84 and arrived in Callander, the 'Tannochbrae' of the old T.V. series 'Dr. Finlay's Casebook'. Well, maybe the doctor liked it there but, according to the press, Peter Irvine in his book 'Scotland The Best' described the town as 'crap', which, if it cheers up the people there, is almost an anagram of Capri.

A certain Helen Duncan, who was born in Callander, was the last person to be arrested under the 1735 Witchcraft Act. She was born Victoria Helen McFarlane and developed a reputation as a psychic with quite important clients. Later she married a cabinet maker by the name of Duncan who, with that occupation, should have become a Prime Minister.

During World War II because of utterances witnessed by Royal Navy personnel, she was considered to be a security risk and was arrested, sentenced in the Old Bailey and sent to Holloway Prison in 1944. She was said to have revealed in seances the sinking of H.M.S. Hood and H.M.S. Barham, before the Admiralty announced it.

She had already been fined in an Edinburgh court in the 1930s for obtaining money by pretending to be a medium. Furthermore she was accused of preying on the relations of servicemen, and was earning more than £100 a week when the average weekly wage was £5. Although a big earner I wonder if she was physically of 'medium' size.

Eventually her sentence was reduced to nine months and the Witchcraft Act was repealed in 1951. Winston Churchill, Prime Minister at the time, is said to have instructed the Home Secretary to report to him why he thought it necessary to use the 1735 Act in a modern court of justice.

I decided next to visit the Rob Roy and Trossachs Centre in the town. For nearly 300 years the life of Rob Roy has inspired writers such as Sir Walter Scott and modern film makers. I wanted to enjoy the audio-visual show, but it was not available due to a technical hitch. Nevertheless, I picked up some information on Rob Roy MacGregor, to give him his full name, often regarded as a rogue or as a romantic hero.

The Centre reminded me again of the origin of the word 'blackmail' and of the Black Watch soldiers. Cattle in Rob Roy's time were small, black and shaggy and were known as 'kyloes'. They roamed wild in the hills unless captured and domesticated. The Highlanders considered cattle to be communal property and thieving was not thought of as being too immoral. Some wealthy landowners paid blackmail, the 'black' referring to the colour of the cattle and 'mail' a Scots word for rent, as was mentioned already in connection with the Border reivers in my book 'Vol. 1 Across England'. Furthermore groups of men became organised as 'watches' to protect the cattle. Hence came the name 'Black Watch'.

Before leaving the Centre, I spotted a notice about international legend research and saw that Callander was linked with Alford, a small Aberdeenshire town. I wondered if that had anything to do with the fact that there was a book called 'Exodus To Alford', a book of tales written by Stanley Robertson (1940-) of Aberdeen. He comes from travelling folk, who each summer camped out in the area between the rivers Dee and Don.

As a boy he became steeped in traveller lore through tales and ballad singing, which his aunt, the well known singer Jeannie Robertson, taught him. He left school at 15 with no academic qualifications and became a fish filleter, but today he is a successful author of several books, a master story teller, ballad singer and piper, and has lectured in universities in this country, as well as in the U.S.A., Canada and on the continent of Europe.

From the Centre I cycled next to St. Kessog's cemetery in Callander to look for Kate Ferguson's grave. I locked the bike against a parapet and asked a few people if they knew her lair, but each time I drew a blank except for one man who offered some hope.

'If it's not here, it might be in the old cemetery back at Kilmahog.'

However, I went down into the Callander cemetery, which was at a lower level than the pavement where I had left the bike. It was hard to concentrate on the job in hand, because I kept looking up to where the bike was out of sight, lest somebody made off with my tent or sleeping bag, which could be quickly released from the carriers. The fact that people kept stopping near the bike, in order to look over the parapet, added to my edginess. Nevertheless, I looked at every gravestone, although some were broken and the inscriptions on others were unclear. I had to accept defeat.

Cycling back out of Callander, I stopped to photograph the Dreadnought Hotel, founded by a McNab and which (the original building) James Hogg, the Ettrick shepherd, poet and novelist visited. However, the most significant place on my visit list was the local bakery.

'A macaroni pie, please,' I said to the lady behind the counter. 'I never eat mince ones now.'

'Why's that?'

'I don't fancy eating infected beef and getting a 'science degree'.'

She looked at me uncomprehendingly and her younger colleague came to the rescue.

'Oh, you mean B.S.E.'

'Exactly.'

I left with my treasured macaroni pie (maccherone in Italian), cycled on to Kilmahog and passed the Trossachs Woollen Mill, whose looms were made in Yorkshire in the 1920s. I crossed the road and made for the old Kilmahog graveyard, where I found the grave of a Christian Ferguson. Was this the same person as Kate, I asked myself? I found no stone with Kate Ferguson's name attached to it, but again some of the inscriptions were hard to make out. The internet, consulted later in my local library, says that Kate is in St. Kessog's churchyard. However, internet information can be wrong.

Beaten once more, I cycled on through the Pass of Leny until I came to St. Bride's chapel near the south end of Loch Lubnaig. Inside the graveyard walls are the outlines of a chapel which dates back to Celtic times. Sir Walter Scott made it famous in his 'The Lady of the Lake' published in 1810. In the poem, a man called Angus crosses over the shoulder of Ben Ledi and arrives with a fiery cross just as a wedding is taking place, and the bridegroom has to abandon his weeping bride to go to war.

I read the plaque erected in 1871 to mark the centenary of Scott's birth and the 150th anniversary of his death. As I stood there a car drew up and a man came in about.

'Hello!' he greeted me. 'I've wanted to see this plaque for some time now but I've never been in the area. People at one time queued to see this, you know.'

'And nowadays I suppose most people just whizz past in their cars without realising what it's all about,' I responded.

I left him to browse among the ruins and returned to the bike. Across westwards are Ben Ledi's wooded slopes which provide shelter for deer. I have walked to the top of that mountain, which is classified as a Corbett rather than a Munro. From the top on a clear day can be seen the Paps of Jura, of which I've climbed the highest on a short, sharp expedition, and the Bass Rock. Pennant, the 18th century traveller and writer, tells us that the May Day festival, Beltane, used to be held at Ben Ledi's summit.

The land close by from where I stood was once in the possession of clan McKinlay, the word 'clan' coming from the Gaelic 'a' chlann' meaning 'the children'. Many of the clan emigrated to America in the 19th century and one descendant was President McKinley, later assassinated (shot) in 1901. Six McKinlay generations are buried at St. Bride's.

I had chosen to cycle up the A84 on the east side of Loch Lubnaig in preference to the Sustrans cycle route on the west side. This decision was based on a warning from a cyclist.

'Part of the route is rough. With that fiercesome load you're carrying, you might put your tyres at risk.'

The cycle route, which I have since walked from Strathyre village to Callander, follows the old Callander to Oban railway route which was opened in 1880. The driving force behind the rail route was a man called John Anderson who, I've been told, wrote some 20,000 letters about its construction. I keep wondering if that figure is somewhere a printing error.

It was a good run up through 'bonnie Strathyre', but I was thirsty by the time I reached the village of that name. I stopped for an ice cream, before continuing then branching off westwards to Balquhidder to see what is described as the burial place of Rob Roy, his wife Helen and two of his sons, Robin and Coll. It was this very same Robin who, as mentioned in R.L. Stevenson's 'Kidnapped', had a piping contest with Alan Breck Stewart in a cottage on the Braes of Balquhidder.

When I arrived, some people were already walking around in the churchyard of the ruined 17th century parish kirk. I locked the bike and entered to look at the medieval grave slabs. Although Rob Roy is buried in the churchyard, his actual grave is unknown. One stone with the MacGregor clan arms does presumably cover a buried MacGregor, but there is no clear evidence that Rob Roy's wife and sons are interred in the churchyard. Rob, aged 80, reportedly died in his bed as his piper played.

I rode back to the A84 and pushed on to Lochearnhead with its water sports centre, then down Glen Ogle. At Lix Toll I turned right and sped down the A827 to Killin. Stopping on the bridge over the river Dochart which flows into Loch Tay, I looked right to the burial island of clan MacNab. Kinnell House nearby was the family home of the MacNabs and in the 1820s the house was sold by the clan chief Archibald MacNab, who emigrated to Canada. It is said that, when the United States invaded Canada, a MacNab put a real damper on the move by driving a burning American gunboat over Niagara Falls.

Away back in 1961, I remember seeing near the bridge a notice saying that the largest vine in Europe could be seen at Kinnell House. Years later in the Dreadnought Hotel, I read there about the Blackburgh vine which was planted in 1882. It reached a length of 190 feet and, even after cutting branches at both ends, it yielded at one time 600 bunches of grapes per year.

After moving to the other side of the bridge, I stood admiring the Dochart Falls or rapids which are reportedly more visited than any others. Once over the bridge, I turned left to an old mill which is now Breadalbane Folklore Centre. Unfortunately it was shut, for I had hoped to see the so called seven healing stones said to have been used by St. Fillan, an Irish prince and missionary, who has been credited with starting the first mill in the area. If true, this must surely have added another dimension to his preaching, for he could claim that in his life he had also been through the mill. Some see in the stones shapes resembling parts of the human body.

After checking the map, I cycled into the heart of Killin and turned off right just before Killin hostel in search of Finlarig castle, which I found on a little raised piece of ground among trees. I set about looking for the beheading pit, which I found after going round one side of the castle. There the rich had their heads cut off, although I am sure they had only one each (the French would agree), and the poor were hanged from a nearby tree. As there was no visible evidence of such executions, I took it that it had happened long ago, or else the Killin district cleansing men had been round before me.

I returned to the bike and cycled back into the village, where in an open area I spotted a van selling fish and chips, which I ordered along with a can of juice. Obviously a smart vehicle, but two girls were helping as well.

'Where do you get your fish from?' I asked one of the girl servers.

'I think it comes from Glasgow,' she said.

'No, I think it's from Peterhead,' said the other.

It didn't really matter but I was just curious. At least I knew where the fish was about to go. It went quickly and, after stuffing the greasy papers into the litter bin, I took off again on a bike by no means battered.

Back over the Dochart bridge, I had to climb Gray Street to get out of Killin. A Dewar, perhaps a distant relation of the politician Donald Dewar, once lived there. The Gray Street Dewar was associated with one of the St. Fillan relics. Tradition says that the saint, before his death in 777 A.D., gave five relics to laymen, who were to guard them and use them to heal people or when swearing oaths. The hereditary guards, who were given land and other privileges, were called in Gaelic 'deoradh' (a stranger) and this was anglicised to Dewar. The 14th-15th century silver gilt head, the Quigrich, of St. Fillan's supposed crozier or staff came in time to be held by a Dewar who lived in Gray Street. Whoever had the Quigrich in 1818 took it to Canada, but in 1877 it was obtained by the Society of Antiquaries, and is now in Edinburgh in the new Royal Museum of Scotland. It is a work of art.

I was glad to end my ascent at Lix Toll and thereafter it was fairly easy on the way to Crianlarich. As I passed Luib on my left, I remembered that Wordsworth and his sister Dorothy spent the night there in 1803 and upset the servant, because they didn't order wine. In time I drew level with Ben More, a mountain I climbed many years before and then I reached Loch Dochart, where there is a ruined castle. A man was looking over at it through binoculars while his wife sat in the parked car. I braked and spoke.

'Excuse me, anything interesting?'

'Oh, I'm studying the castle out there. It was built by a man called Black Duncan Campbell of Glenorchy.'

'Do you know anything else about him?'

'Well, he loved books, was into afforestation and horse breeding. He was also a good business man. I looked him up in a library.'

'When did he live?'

'Let's see now... . He died at the age of 83 in 1631 so you can work it out for yourself,' he said grinning. 'His son was a bit of a scholar as well. He was interested in foreign furniture and paintings. In fact he ordered 16 portraits from George Jamieson, the Aberdeen portrait painter.'

'I take it you're English, aren't you?'

'Yes, from Lincoln.'

'How come you're so interested in this castle?'

'I just love Scotland and I love castles.'

'Thanks anyway for the information and I hope you get round many more. I'm from Aberdeen as a matter of fact. I'm heading for the hostel in Crianlarich.'

I continued on my way, glad to have met someone else interested in our heritage. I wondered if he knew that Jamieson was considered to be the father of Scottish painting.

It was rather late when I arrived at the hostel but the warden Paul Ridley was tremendously helpful. There was just time for a quick snack before the kitchen closed. What a treat the new hostel is compared to the old one I once stayed in. It used to reek with the smell of fries, and the large dormitory was often overfilled with rucksacks and 'cheesy' socks hanging up to be aired. The new one is very fresh with small dormitories. A former neighbour of mine, Douglas Leys, remembers prior to World War II seeing German youths sitting in the old hostel with swastikas on their armbands.

I turned in a short while after my snack and soon fell sleep, but during the night I had an attack of cramp, the first on the whole trip. The ball of my left leg knotted hard and I couldn't get out of my sheet sleeping bag. Some of the others in the room pulled off the bag and helped me deal with the cramp. It was extremely painful and I had wakened up the others. However, they were very good about it and at least I had spared them a nightmare about searching for my cut off head.

12 June   Crianlarich – Glen Nevis   O.S. 50, 41

The morning looked promising when I left Crianlarich, and I took with me my memories of climbing all the Munros around the village. Just over a mile to the south-west of the village is Keilator, where James Hogg from the Borders visited a house during his travels. However, I had no intention of travelling backwards, as it were, and so headed up Strath Fillan on the A82. This strath (wide valley) is the scene of James Hogg's ballad 'The Spirit of the Glen'.

About three miles out of Crianlarich, I turned off right along a narrow road to St. Fillan's chapel. St. Fillan crossed from Ireland to west Scotland in 724 A.D., and the story goes that he came to the watershed near Tyndrum, where the water flows west to the Atlantic and east to the North Sea, and established the above mentioned chapel. Today about 200 yards east of Kirkton farmhouse are the remains of a rectangular wall enclosing a monk's garden, and north of the church is an old graveyard.

When I neared the place, I kept a wary eye open for collie dogs which can sometimes be aggressive, but all was quiet. I locked the bike and set out to explore but failed to find the priest's well. From a signboard, I learned that the chapel was made a priory by Robert the Bruce in 1318. Bruce believed that St. Fillan, whose arm bone is said to have glowed in the dark, had helped him in the Battle of Bannockburn in 1314. The Dewar of the Quigrich is reported to have given Bruce a blessing at the chapel.

About a mile upstream is St. Fillan's Pool, in which a person requiring healing was immersed, and then had to go through a ceremony with stones picked up from the river bed. Those are claimed to be the stones now at Killin. Not only has the Quigrich survived but also the Bernane or chapel bell, which was said to have been left lying on a gravestone. The bell was said to have been used at the coronation of James IV and as a cure for diseases right up to 1798, after which it was stolen by a tourist and taken to England, before being brought back to Scotland in 1869. Immersion at the Pool and the tying of the bell to a person's head was the treatment offered at the chapel for the curing of lunacy.

Personally I would have needed the bell treatment had I tried searching for the Pool, given the limited time I had. Who knows but perhaps the National Health Service will yet need to apply for the use of the bell, judging by the lack of resources available.

When I had seen enough, I biked back to the busy A82 and continued to a bridge west of which is Lochan nam Arm (the small loch of the arms), associated with Robert the Bruce, and in which weapons were said to have been dumped. Beside it is Dalrigh, the King's field. The king in question was Robert the Bruce, who was fleeing west after being defeated by the English at Methven just west of Perth. In 1306 Bruce and his men received a mauling at Dalrigh near Tyndrum from a vastly greater force of MacDougall clansmen. Their chief was the uncle of John Comyn, another Scottish crown claimant who, if you remember, was stabbed to death in Dumfries by Bruce and a supporter.

As Bruce fled from Dalrigh it is said that some MacDougall men tore a brooch, the Brooch of Lorne, from his cloak. Later it was stolen by the Campbells, but returned to the MacDougalls in the early years of the 19th century. Ever since then it was kept in a bank vault for safe keeping, but in recent years there was talk of it being put on display to the public. There is, however, some doubt as to whether this is the actual brooch worn by Bruce, for it has been dated to a later period.

I had climbed a bit by the time I drew level with the glen through which the river Cononish flows and the landscape was now barer. Years ago I walked down that glen after walking over four Munros, including Ben Lui on which a hillwalker was recently killed by lightning. The map shows that there were old mines just beyond Cononish farm but, before setting off on my epic cycle journey, I understood that there was ongoing gold exploration. Thinking that that would be interesting for my story, I wrote a letter to the gold mine manager and asked if I could come and see what was going on. Back came this reply from C.J.S. Sangster, the General Manager.

'We are currently in the 'Exploration Phase' – no operations yet. You

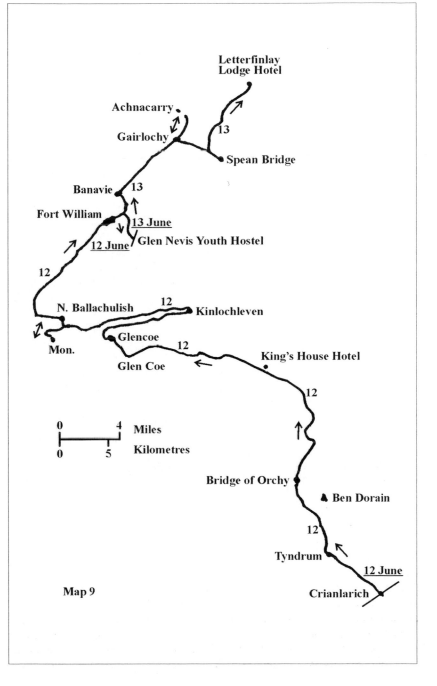

Letterfinlay
Lodge Hotel

Achnacarry

Gairlochy

13

Spean Bridge

Banavie   13

Fort William

13 June

Glen Nevis Youth Hostel

12 June

12

N. Ballachulish   12

Kinlochleven

Glencoe

Mon.   12

Glen Coe

King's House Hotel

12

0   4   Miles

0   5   Kilometres

Bridge of Orchy

▲ Ben Dorain

12

Tyndrum   12 June

Map 9

Crianlarich

are welcome to drop in. From Cononish farm you will see our offices which are just below Eas Anie'.

'Eas' is the Gaelic for 'waterfall' and is marked on the map where the 'old mines' are indicated. There just was no time, however, to go so far up the glen and maybe just as well, for there was probably not much to see and the Canadian based Caledonia Mining Corporation had to abandon its great investment plans, when the price of gold fell. A Mr. Dennis MacLeod, who was at the head of Caledonia Mining at the time of intense interest, left the Corporation and set about trying to raise money for a memorial to those Sutherland people, who were removed from the land during the Clearances.

Instead I stopped for a short break and snack at Tyndrum. In the days of cattle droving in the 18th and 19th centuries, the drovers used to drive their small black cattle through there and stay at the inn. The place has two railway stations and Queen Victoria once visited Tyndrum by rail. I got talking to some ladies about the local mining.

'Do you know anything about the gold mining up at Cononish?'

'No, not really. There's been talk for years of gold under Ben Lui. There used to be lead mines there and down below Tyndrum. Up there, northwards, is Clifton. That used to be a mining village and is named after a Sir Robert Clifton. Lead was discovered there about the middle of the 18th century. Some German miners were employed in the 19th century.'

'Other companies took over after him,' chipped in her companion. 'Lead mining went on for about 100 years up to the middle of the 19th century. It restarted but finally ended about 1925. Long ago they used to take the lead on ponies down to Loch Lomond where they smelted it.'

'I can see that you like history,' I said.

'There's not much else to do in this area especially in the winter, apart from walking, of course. Do you know that William and Dorothy Wordsworth came here once?'

'Not for the lead mining, I hope,' said the other.

'You know, I think some people must feed their dogs badly. I once saw a park sign which read: "Keep all dog on lead." That could poison them.'

They laughed at my word play, and I thanked them for their help before they drove off in their car. Just over three miles beyond Tyndrum, I reached a point where I could look over at Auch and Auch Gleann. Surrounding the glen are the three mountains Beinn Dorain, Beinn a' Chaisteil and Beinn Odhar, all of which I have climbed in the past. From the latter I once sat and watched the train make a U loop round Auch Gleann and over the viaduct. It looked like something from a toy railway set.

At one time there was a royal hunting lodge at Auch and the Campbells of Glenorchy had to supply venison for the royal feasts. Rob Roy, whose wife was a Campbell, once stayed up Auch Gleann when he was under the protection of the Breadalbane Campbells.

Duncan Ban MacIntyre (1724-1812), the Gaelic bard, who fought on the Hanoverian side at the battle of Falkirk in 1746, lived and worked for a time as a forester up Auch Gleann. He was also a gamekeeper in Breadalbane and Rannoch after the 1745 rebellion and was against the Clearances and the great invasion of sheep. Duncan Ban came back to the glen in 1802 and, seated on a boulder, composed his poem and song 'Last Farewell To Beinn Dorain'. He returned to Edinburgh and became an officer of the City Guard. He died there in 1812 and was buried in Greyfriars churchyard. From Dalmally station car park you can walk to Monument Hill to see Duncan Ban's memorial.

As I cranked along to Bridge of Orchy, I looked across to the right and remembered walking that part of the West Highland Way, which uses for the most part the old military road built by Caulfield, who was busy building roads at a time when General Roy was engaged in his military surveying.

My arrival at Bridge of Orchy hotel also brought back memories. My wife and I once had a short holiday in the hotel annexe, and on another occasion I slept in the car (given up 18 years ago) opposite the hotel, after I arrived there about midnight. I had been hillwalking solo in the White Corries area near Kingshouse Hotel and was late in finishing. The White Corries slopes were, by the way, the first in Scotland to be developed for skiing. Another time I camped down by the river beside the bridge and another camper there raved on about how he hated his minister father.

After locking the bike wheels, I had something to eat and drink at the hotel bar and had a brief conversation with a man seated inside.

'Where are you from?' I was asked.

'Aberdeen,' I answered, showing that more than my legs could work.

'Cycling?' Obviously he was observant.

'Yes, Land's End to John O' Groats.'

'Not in one day, I hope.' The chap had his head screwed on, even if the wrong way round. Was he losing the thread?

'No, I'll need at least two.' I was now as smart as he was or perhaps I needed a course with the healing stones.

I had heard that there were seaweed drying sheds at Bridge of Orchy, but the chap I spoke to said that he had not heard of them.

Bridge of Orchy is mentioned in Neil Munro's novels and, in 'John Splendid', the bridge itself is mentioned and a coded message was left on it. Aeneas Macmaster in 'The New Road' spent the night in the inn before crossing Rannoch Moor to Kingshouse.

Over the bridge and about three miles along an unclassified road is Inveroran, which drovers once used as a stance for resting sheep and cattle. William and Dorothy Wordsworth had breakfast in the Inveroran inn in 1803, after coming from Glencoe by way of Loch Tulla's shore. Also

Robert Southey, first mentioned by me in my book 'Vol. 1 Across England' in connection with Bristol and Great Crosthwaite, Cumbria, came to the inn with his friend Thomas Telford.

One of Duncan Ban MacIntyre's poems, 'Mairi Bhan Og' (Fair Young Mary), describes the beauty of the woman there, the innkeeper's daughter who became his wife. Duncan Ban's best poetic writing has been compared to Scott's 'The Lady of the Lake' and to that of Burns. MacIntyre also wrote 'Mairi Bhan' which may refer to the innkeeper's daughter but an Angus MacLeod, who edited MacIntyre's poems, is not so sure, it seems.

I pedalled off again and after a few miles crossed over Water of Tulla at the northern end of Loch Tulla. Away to the east stands Beinn Achaladair, over whose cliffs a man once fell and a psychic pinpointed where his body could be found. Soon I turned left and, after a long haul upwards, I reached a fast food van in a layby. I was fast as well – fast wasting away from hunger and so I bought two bacon rolls and tea.

By the time I was over the A82 bridge between Loch Ba and Lochan na Stainge, Ba Cottage beside the West Highland Way was over on my left. Near it is a memorial cairn to Peter Fleming, brother of Ian Fleming the novelist of James Bond fame. Peter Fleming himself had an interesting life for, among other things, he went looking for the explorer Colonel Fawcett, who became lost in the Amazon jungle, and during World War II Fleming escaped several times from occupied Europe. He died later of a heart attack when on a shooting trip in the Black Mount forest. The two Flemings are of the same family as the Flemings of the Fleming Banking Group, which bought 100,000 acres of land around Glen Etive, 12 miles south of Glencoe village.

Just before Kingshouse Hotel, I drew level with Blackrock Cottage which is used by climbers, and I was able to look up to the White Corries. Higher up is Meall a' Bhuiridh, which I have also climbed, a mountain painted by Horatio McCulloch in 1846. A ski tow was set up in 1950 and in 1960 the chair lift was installed by White Corries Ltd.

I turned off the A82 to include the Kingshouse Hotel in my travels. This hotel began as an inn and was in use at least 200 years ago. In 1803 Dorothy Wordsworth disliked the place, for the standard then was very poor. I had been to see the hotel years previously after climbing some mountains and was impressed by the place, when I entered to enquire about bunk accommodation. Two climbers staying there gave me some information about past inn keepers and visitors.

'The inn keepers here used to smuggle salt. At that time, it was heavily taxed except when it was used to preserve fish for export.'

'And a writer called Southey,' said his companion, 'wrote that one of the inn keepers made enough money from smuggling salt to retire and buy a farm. Have you heard of a climber by the name of Bell?'

'Oh yes,' I replied, 'I've come across the name.'

'Well, in the 1920s when conditions in the inn weren't quite tip-top, Bell complained about the smell of bacon coming up from a hole in the floor. In another room you had to use an umbrella if it rained.'

Little did I foresee at that time that I would one day visit the homes and graves of the Wordsworths and Southey, or that Wainwright would visit the hotel for the launch of his book on Scotland's mountains.

I left the hotel behind and cycled on to Altnafeidh, which is the starting or finishing point of the hill military road, whose zig-zag part is known as the Devil's Staircase. This was built in 1750 possibly by Major Caulfield and several hundred soldiers and is marked on Roy's map. Stopping there I looked over at Buachaille Etive Mor and Buachaille Etive Beag, respectively the Big and Little Shepherd of Etive, and recalled the day I spent in mist walking solo over all their peaks.

Cycling on I went through the Pass of Glencoe to view the famous Aonach Eagach (notched ridge) on my right. This is the narrowest ridge on the mainland and one which has claimed a few lives even in summer. I set out along it once and retreated, because the thick mist made it more risky, particularly when travelling on it for the first time and by myself. However, let me echo the words of the American General MacArthur (of Scottish descent) who, when he left the Philippines during World War II, said: 'I shall return.'

I stopped to speak to a hillwalker making for Glencoe village.

'That's Achtriochtan down there on the left,' he said. 'That's the home (no more) of Hamish McInnes, the international climber and author. He's the former leader of the Glencoe Mountain Rescue team and he has designed mountain equipment. He was awarded a doctorate in science because of his technical achievements. His mountain expertise has been used in several films, including 'The Eiger Sanction' in which Clint Eastwood starred, and he also runs his own film production company.'

The glen has featured in many documentaries and films, including Hitchcock's 'Thirty-Nine Steps', 'Rob Roy' and 'The Highlander' series starring Christopher Lambert. It also comes into R.L. Stevenson's book 'Kidnapped'. Although the glen is attractive to film makers, Charles Dickens wrote in 1841 that it was terrible and awful.

Just over a mile farther on, a secondary road going off to the right leads to the Clachaig Inn, a stopping place in 1839 for coaches travelling between Fort William and Glasgow. Farther along still on that road is Glencoe Hostel. However, I continued on the A82 and was soon in a position to see the Signal Rock, said to be the place where the signal was given for the infamous Massacre of Glencoe.

I've lost count of the number of times and accounts I've read about this massacre, but recently in the Glencoe hostel I listened to a bearded (of course) hillwalker describing the reasons for the slaughter.

'Behind it all was bad feeling between Highlanders and Lowlanders, among the clans themselves and between Jacobites and Hanoverians. MacIain, chief of the clan MacDonald, was loyal to the exiled James VII and he failed to swear an oath of allegiance to William III by the deadline of 31 December, 1691. More important chiefs had also not met the deadline, but the Secretary of State for Scotland decided to punish the MacDonalds as an example, in spite of their oath of allegiance being accepted a week after the deadline. On 1 February, 1692, 120 soldiers led by Captain Robert Campbell of Glenlyon were billetted on the MacDonalds of Glencoe. The latter suspected nothing, partly because Robert Campbell was related by marriage to MacIain, and partly because such a cowardly action was considered contrary to Highland hospitality.'

'So how many were killed?' I asked.

'About 40,' he continued. 'Those not slaughtered died of starvation or exposure in the blizzard raging outside. At 5.00 in the morning, Campbell ordered that everyone under 70 years old was to be put to the sword. MacIain was shot in the back, his wife stripped and her rings ripped off her fingers by the teeth of the soldiers. She escaped only to die outside in the snow. Some people believe that some of the MacDonalds were warned by some soldiers and were able to escape.'

The story teller was a mine of information and, when I asked him how he remembered so much, he said that he had told the story so many times. I thought of the words of the well known Corries' song 'O cruel is the snow... '.

For centuries the Campbells have been regarded as villains and stories have circulated of the local hostelries not welcoming Campbells. To clear their name somewhat, the Campbells have pointed out that the worst atrocities were committed by Lowland soldiers, that the MacDonalds were a thieving lot who had bankrupted the leader of the Campbells and that, not being guests but soldiers billeted on the MacDonalds as a punishment to the latter for not paying their taxes, they could not have broken the Highland code of hospitality.

When I reached the National Trust property in the glen I locked the bike and went in. I knew by then that my membership receipt was missing, but I didn't want to pay again.

'I am a member,' I insisted, 'but I must have left it at the last property I was in.' In fact I found it later when I arrived home.

'You've an honest face,' said the lady in charge. 'You can go in.'

The siting of the old National Trust property was criticised for being an intrusion in the glen, but I was glad of its presence both for the food available and for the knowledge gained there. A row developed later over plans to demolish the visitor centre and replace it with something bigger nearer to Glencoe village. Originally the idea was to create some community facilities, but the National Trust wanted more of a retail development, and the Glencoe shopkeepers and caterers felt threatened. Today the old property is gone and the new one is beside the camp site on the A82.

Before leaving the visitor centre, I had a snack then cycled on until I reached Glencoe village. I wouldn't say that I was glad to be off the main road but, on the stretch from the Signal Rock to the village, I encountered the worst driving I had experienced since leaving Land's End. Some of the drivers seemed to be eager for a new kind of massacre.

I cycled to the far end of the village and sought out the memorial to MacIain of Glencoe. There I read the writing which said: 'This cross is reverently erected in memory of MacIain Chief of the MacDonalds of Glencoe, Who fell with his people in the Massacre of Glencoe 13 Feb 1692, by his direct descendant Ellen Burns MacDonald, August 1883. Their memory liveth for evermore.'

A Commons enquiry into the massacre said that it was wrong to ignore MacIain's oath, although late, and Parliament voted that the execution of the people in Glencoe was murder. The King was asked to send home from Flanders the men in charge but, although William of Orange signed the document, nobody was prosecuted.

Later as I stood at the Bridge of Coe, I recalled how years ago I had cycled up and down the secondary road which leads to and from the hostel. I later learned that along by the river there is an avenue of surviving beech trees, planted to commemorate the soldiers who fought in the 18th century with Wolfe in Canada. I also found out that six poplar trees, brought back from the Continent by men who fought with Wellington in the Napoleonic Wars, were planted in memory of the soldiers who were there. Regretably the last poplar died more than twenty years ago at Invercoe.

When I returned to the heart of Glencoe village, I paid a visit to the Glencoe and North Lorn Folk Museum which was opened in 1967. The original museum was at the other side of the road before it moved to the present building. A Mrs. MacDonald Clarke, who was directly descended from MacIain, opened the new museum.

'The Crown Prince of Japan visited the museum in July 1984,' said a cyclist I spoke to outside. 'That was the very year the museum was deliberately set on fire. Maybe that was a protest by some former prisoner of war against the atrocities committed by the Japs.'

'Could be. British prisoners were badly compensated by the Japanese government, but our own government of the time must bear some responsibility, As far as I know, former British prisoners of the Japanese were each initially given £76 compensation in 1952, but I believe more money has since been given.'

'Anyway,' said the cyclist before he departed, 'with these bikes of ours we're not prisoners.' Very true, I thought.

The museum has an example of hard tartan whose texture is hard and the material is very tough. Queen Victoria is said to have noticed that her soldiers' legs were cut by the hard tartan and she ordered a softer weave to be used. In an age when table legs were modestly covered, what was she doing looking at the soldiers' legs? Also in the museum is a chair which belonged to Bonnie Prince Charlie. There are costumes, embroidery, guns, toys, farm implements, a dairy, a laundry and a blacksmith. I saw also a rush light holder and a clamp to hold the rush in the middle, so that the candle could be burned at both ends, hence the expression 'burning the candle at both ends'. The rushes were coated in fat. I also learned that the tailor's goose got its name from the fact that the iron was heavy and did a better job, and so the tailor could afford to have a goose at Christmas.

After leaving the museum, I cycled out of Glencoe village and then braked at the bridge over the river Coe, where a man was looking out over Loch Leven. It wasn't that he had super eyes, for it wasn't Perthshire's Loch Leven, where Mary Queen of Scots was once held prisoner in a castle on an island. Instead it was the loch which connects Ballachulish and Kinlochleven.

'Excuse me, is there something happening out there?' I asked.

'No, I'm just looking out to the islands. The big one out there is Eilean Munde. Have you been to the Ballachulish slate quarry by any chance?'

'Yes, some years ago.'

'Well,' he continued, 'did you learn about the young slate worker killed there. According to legend, a dove flew down and placed an ivy leaf on his forehead. He's buried on that island and the dove, the leaf and the dead man are shown on the gravestone. I'd love to get out there.'

'Are you on holiday then?' I asked.

'I'm in a caravan here for a few days. A fascinating area this.'

As I just said, I had already been to the slate quarry at Ballachulish and the exhibition centre which explains its history. I decided to leave it out of my journey for that reason and the fact that time was limited. Suffice to say that the slate was originally mud on a sea bed 550 million years ago and the quarry first opened in 1693. In the 19th century the quarrymen wore white 'moleskin' trousers, which were not actually made of moleskin but cotton. It seems an odd colour to choose for such a dirty job, but the women folk took a pride in sending out their men so attired. The slates, of course, were used for roofing and farmhouse floors, but the development of Marley tiles led to the decline of the industry.

Leaving the island spotter, I sped along the A82 north of the Pap of Glencoe and along the south side of Loch Leven. This used to be known, and still is to some extent, as the 'German' road, for that road between

Ballachulish and Kinlochleven was built by 1200 World War I German prisoners who arrived at Ballachulish. It was quite exciting cycling downhill on the final stretch into Kinlochleven, and I remembered that the first time I ever saw the village was about 8 p.m., when walking one year high in the Mamore hills.

At one time drovers used to pass through the town, for the drove road passed by Fort William, then came through Kinlochleven before going on to the Devil's Staircase, then Inveroran and Bridge of Orchy. Pennant, a well known traveller, said that he had a breakfast of minced stag in Kinlochleven. I hope that didn't decrease his ability to have hindsight. My chief interest there, however, was neither cattle nor stags but aluminium, for it was the production of this which increased the size of the village.

First I went to 'The Aluminium Story' Visitor Centre where I met Margaret Donaghy, manager of the centre. I took particular note of her name, because she gave me so much interesting information, in fact more than I could use.

'Aluminium is a great metal, for it can be used to make everything from toothpaste tubes to the space shuttle. It's got great properties. Compared to other metals it's very light. A piece of aluminium is three times lighter than a piece of steel the same size. It doesn't twist and alloys of aluminium can be stiff or supple, it's easily cut and shaped and can be worked using different metal working techniques. For example, it can be rolled into foil so thin that 200 sheets would be needed to make up a thickness of 1 millimetre and it is a good conductor of electricity. An aluminium cable can carry twice as much current as a copper one of the same weight. It's also very attractive in its own right without any extra finish.'

I learned that nearly 230 centimetres or 80 inches of rain fall on Kinlochleven, and it was the potential of the area to produce cheap and plentiful electricity that attracted the British Aluminium Company to the place. In the 1890s the Company bought the Blackwater Valley, 1000 feet above Kinlochleven, and in 1904 work was started on the largest hydro scheme in Europe. An 8 mile long reservoir was created to supply the water power to drive the turbines, and the electricity produced allowed aluminium to be produced in the Kinlochleven smelter. In less than 8 years the dam, the hydro scheme power house, the factory and village were built.

It is said that 3000 navvies were used, including Islanders, Irishmen and local labour taken from the Ballachulish quarries. The men were organised in teams of 40 each under a ganger, who usually spoke Gaelic as well as English. The shifts of work were interrupted by quarrels, gambling and drinking. Some men were so desperate for a drink that they walked over the hills to the Kingshouse Hotel, or swam under the pier and bored holes in the base of alcohol filled barrels placed there. They lived in tents or huts with rats and seagulls, scrounged for waste food amongst the rubbish and suffered the cold of winter and the midges in summer. One Irish navvy called Patrick MacGill wrote a book about it called 'Children Of The Dead End', published in 1914 when he was 24. Near the dam today is a graveyard where lie those killed accidentally or otherwise.

Loch Leven was dredged and bauxite (named after Les Baux in France) was brought in by water from Ghana in West Africa. From it the aluminium metal was extracted in liquid form. A small amount of aluminium was produced on Hogmanay 1907, some of it being made into lucky horseshoes, but full scale production did not begin until March 1909.

A pipeline carrying water from Loch Eilde to the dam was later built by World War I German prisoners, who almost doubled Kinlochleven's population. For some years the Company provided electricity free to the villagers, and Kinlochleven, which was nearly renamed Aluminiumville, was one of the earliest villages in Britain to have electric street lighting. In 1937 the factory closed because of drought, for the dam water dropped by 72 feet.

During World War II, German planes flew over Kinlochleven and photographs were taken for a possible bombing mission later. Today some hillwalkers sometimes bomb down from the Mamores to the nearest pub.

Ian MacGregor of the Coal Board, a man often in the news at the time of the miners' strike during Margaret Thatcher's time in power, was born in the place. Neil Gunn, the writer, lived there for a time and Edward VII stayed at Mamore Lodge on the slopes above Kinlochleven. Hopefully he didn't think the place was called 'Mammoth' Lodge. Apparently Edward once shot an elephant, stood on it and cut its tail whereupon, to his surprise, it took off still alive. Lest you are confused, this did not occur in Scotland.

'What's that building over there?' I asked.

'Oh that's going to be developed into a bunkhouse for hillwalkers and cyclists who pass through.'

The bunkhouse is now up and running and of great benefit to those engaged in outdoor activties.

Learning about aluminium and the dam was interesting, but I didn't mind leaving the village itself for it is not, in my opinion, an attractive place. I next cycled along the wooded north side, until I reached North Ballachulish from which I crossed over the bridge to the south side. As I did so, I remembered crossing the water by ferry in 1961 before the bridge was built. Crossing by ferry or bridge saves about a 2 mile journey round the loch.

I was on the hunt again but this time for the memorial cairn erected to commemorate the murder of Colin Campbell of Glenure, the 'Red Fox', in 1752. This became known as the Appin Murder and is mentioned in R.L. Stevenson's novel 'Kidnapped'. Campbell, it is said, was the King's factor of some confiscated Stuart estates and, on the day of the murder, he along with others crossed by the Ballachulish ferry of the day to the south side of Ballachulish. About a mile west of the present bridge, the party entered the Lettermore wood and shortly afterwards Campbell was fatally shot in the back with two musket balls.

It was a question of finding the right entrance and track in the wood. My first search took me past the correct opening but I succeeded on my second attempt, after a man clearly described to me how to find the cairn. When I arrived at the right place, some people were coming down the track and I waited until they were gone, before I left the bike and luggage. There was no escaping the risk of theft. I hurried up through the wood and where the track swung left I found the cairn.

The murderer or accessory to the murder was said to have been a James Stewart who had fostered Allan Breck Stewart, an army deserter and waster, and very different from the person described by the writer Stevenson and portrayed by Michael Caine, the English film actor. James Stewart was hanged after an unfair trial, for it is now known that the prosecution knew he was innocent. Witnesses lied or were not called for and evidence was falsified. In reality Stewart was put to death for his Jacobite activities, but to try him openly for this would have made him appear as a martyr. It was easier to condemn him for a terrible crime. Some people believe that Robert Oig MacGregor, the younger son of Rob Roy or that Alan Breck was the killer.

I was relieved to find everything intact when I returned to the bike, and I then set off back to the Ballachulish bridge to look for a plaque and memorial to James Stewart. Outside the hotel built near the old ferry inn I asked for some direction.

'Excuse me,' I asked a man, 'but do you know where the plaque and memorial to James Stewart are?'

'Yes, go up the steps there at the end of the bridge and you'll find them both,' he answered.

I found them. The hanging took place on 8 November, 1752 quite near to where the memorial stands today. Soldiers were posted to guard the body and when the body began to disintegrate it was bound with wire. By 1756 only the bones were left on the gibbet.

By the time I descended to the road I encountered my informant again.

'I can tell you more if you want,' he said.

'That would be fine,' I said. 'The more the better.'

'There were three Ballachulish brothers by the name of Livingstone and they decided to take down the bones and give them a decent burial on Eilean Munde. One brother enticed away the sentry for a drink in the inn. The other two took down the gibbet and bones, which they took with them as they rowed away from the shore. The gibbet was then thrown into the water but the bones were buried on another island, because the tide made it impossible for them to reach Eilean Munde. The bones are said to have been removed later and carried to the old churchyard at Keil in Duror. Frightened of being suspected, the two brothers who removed the bones fled west and finally arrived in Ulva, an island close to Mull. They became crofters there, but the son of one of the men moved to Glasgow and then to Blantyre. This son married an Agnes Hunter and their son David, born in 1813, became the famous African missionary and explorer.'

'That's really interesting. Thanks very much. Do you live in these parts?'

'I was born and brought up near here.'

I bade him goodbye, took off again and cycled over the Ballachulish bridge. It was now non-stop to the Glen Nevis Youth hostel, which I had last visited with my girl friend, now my wife. We were making a scooter tour of Scotland in 1961 and I was the pillion passenger. Ladies first, as they say.

When I finally cycled up the green, wooded glen, it was quite busy with vehicles and walkers, for Ben Nevis and other great mountain ranges in the area attract many tourists, as do the Nevis Gorge and the Steall Falls. I booked in, made up my bed and went out on the bike again to cycle up the glen to where the film 'Braveheart', concerning William Wallace, was partially filmed. There was no time, however, to cycle up to the gorge, beyond which a dam might have been built years ago, had there not been a public outcry against altering such a scenic place.

Back in the hostel, which was quite full, I settled down to a snack before going off to bed. It had been a busy day since leaving Crianlarich but a rewarding one. All the gold of Cononish could not buy what I had seen and experienced that day.

13 June   Glen Nevis– Inverness   O.S. 41, 34, 26

When I came down for breakfast next morning, I was surprised to find that some of the breakfast tables were covered with rucksacks and some of the hostellers were seated on the tables. I'm perhaps old fashioned, and I make no apology, but I was brought up to believe that bums and particularly rucksacks, which might have sheep dirt sticking to them, should not be on dining tables. (Note that the previous relative clause is meant to apply only to the rucksacks.) Nevertheless, the continental breakfast was as tasty as any served in a hostel, and having plates greatly dispelled most of my anxiety.

When I came out of the hostel to get the bike, I stood looking up at Ben Nevis and recalled the day I climbed it and two other Munros on the same day after a midday start. At the summit of the Ben, I saw a woman in a bathing costume and she had no rucksack with any spare clothing. She was lucky to get away with that, for the top is often shrouded in mist and the mountain has to be treated with respect, considering that the weather can change so rapidly. Speaking of weather, there was once a weather observatory at the top and a man by the name of Wragge used to climb the mountain daily to take readings, until it closed in 1904. In 1911 a model T Ford car was driven to the 4406 foot summit, the highest in Britain. There was once also a hotel at the summit. The Ben is the ruin of a earlier great volcano, and I remember the time when there was an April hoax story about the mountain releasing steam due to more recent geothermal forces at work.

At the back of the hostel I took the bike out of the shed and loaded it, then cycled down the sunny glen and into Fort William. Coming down Belford road, I spotted and visited on my right at Craig's cemetery the re-erected stone archway or gateway, which is part of the old fort of Fort William. The original fort was built by General Monk in 1635 and General MacKay established its replacement in 1690. The fort was named after William of Orange and the town itself was originally called Maryburgh after William's wife Mary, who was the daughter of King James VII of Scotland and James II of England. Next I went looking for the old fort walls, which I knew overlooked Loch Linnhe at its eastern end.

I found them without much effort and then made for the quieter pedestrianised High Street, where I used the Post Office and bought some spools for the camera. Some people at the time were concerned about the number of so called tourist tartan shops in the street and the risk of losing other traders.

One place I was determined to revisit was the West Highland Folk Museum, which I had been in many years before. I locked the bike outside and waited until opening time. The museum, founded in 1922, has items from the islands in the west to Loch Broom in the north, the Crinan Canal in the south and Badenoch in the east.

As I stood outside the locked door, I started speaking to a man who was also waiting to go in.

'This building is one of the oldest in Fort William,' he said after preliminary queries about my journey. 'It was built when the town was part of the Duke of Gordon's estate. It was a British Linen Bank before it became a museum. The reason I know that is because an uncle of mine used to work in it.'

We then moved to the subject of bikes, before he decided he wasn't going to wait any longer.

'I'll come back later,' he said. 'I hope all goes well with you on your trip.'

I was banking on that, so to speak, as I waited until the doors finally opened. I could leave my luggage inside, I was told, but photography was out. I didn't collapse with surprise.

Inside I learned that Fort William claims that in 1896 it was the first town in Britain to have electric street lighting generated only by water power. Incidentally Mount Stuart, a stately home in the island of Bute, is said to be the first house in Scotland to be lit by electricity, although that is disputed. Inside I saw a dress which once was worn by Queen Victoria's daughter, Princess Louise, and a sporran and dirk given by the same queen to John Brown, her personal assistant, friend and, some say, lover. His grave, which I have twice visited, is in the cemetery next to Balmoral Castle.

I noticed also a hand tinted engraving of the Battle of Culloden where Bonnie Prince Charlie was defeated in 1746. Very interesting too is the Secret Portrait of Prince Charles Edward Stuart, to give the Bonnie Prince his fuller title. This was painted by some unknown 18th century artist. On a tray-like panel is what resembles a blur of paint, but when this is reflected in a polished cylinder placed vertically on the panel, a picture of the Prince appears. It was used when drinking a toast to the Prince, at a time when it was risky and could lead to jail or a whipping.

There were also bagpipes from Culloden field, a silk waistcoat and tartan trews said to belong to Charlie. I saw too the type of gun used to kill Colin Campbell in the wood near Ballachulish.

Tucked away in the museum, and unknown to me at the time, was a bronze ruler spotted in 2001 by a Dr. Martin of St. Andrew's University. This object originated from a Spanish Armada wreck found in Tobermory Bay, off Mull and was used to measure the bore of cannons. By comparing that ruler with a wooden one found in the waters off Donegal and by studying records, he concluded that the Armada had had a mismatch of cannons and cannonballs, and this could have been the reason for its defeat.

I realised that the Ben Nevis Visitor Centre was open by the time I finished in the museum, and I sped back a short distance up Glen Nevis to the building. There, apart from the geology, history and wildlife (the latter not including the tourists) of the Glen), I learned that through the Nevis range there is a 15 mile long 15 foot diameter tunnel, built to bring water from Loch Treig to Fort William's aluminium smelter, and to the pulp and paper mill built at Annat Point at Corpach. The mill was the largest of its kind in Europe when built but it was set to close in September, 2005.

Back in Fort William, I came along by the pier from which boats leave on cruises, sailing past fish farms and on towards Seal Island, the home to common and grey seals. Today on the bed of Loch Linnhe some World War II tanks and armoured cars, deliberately placed there, provide a habitat for about 40 species of marine life.

It was time, however, to leave the town, a starting point for steam train trips to Mallaig and a starting point for those going south on the 95 mile West Highland Way walk to Glasgow. My route out of Fort William by the

A82 took me up near the distillery (the first legal one in the district) started in 1825 by Long John MacDonald, so named because he was well over 6 feet tall. He was the great grandson of MacDonald of Keppoch, the chief who was killed at Culloden near Inverness. I once went to a tartan centre at Aviemore and was told that I belonged to a sept attached to those MacDonalds.

As I cycled left to cross the bridge over the river Lochy, I was aware that Inverlochy Castle was roughly just over a mile away. It was there that Mel Gibson, who acted as William Wallace in the film 'Braveheart', stayed while filming was necessary in Glen Nevis.

Pedalling along the A830 I arrived next at the Caledonian Canal at Banavie. James Watt of Greenock had made a survey in 1773 with a canal in mind. Such a waterway was to provide a link between the North Sea and the Atlantic Ocean. However, it was Telford (who else?) who designed the 60 mile long canal, 22 miles of which had to be cut. The canal uses three lochs, namely, Loch Lochy, Loch Oich and Loch Ness which lie in a glaciated valley. Begun in 1803 and opened in 1822, the canal has 10 swing bridges and 28 locks, 8 of which form the so called Neptune's Staircase at Banavie. As I stood marvelling at the locks I was joined by another cyclist.

'Fantastic, isn't it ?' he said. 'There's so many interesting things to see. I've just been to the geology place in Corpach before coming here.'

'I've been there,' I said but, before I could say that it was some time ago, he continued.

'There were diamonds there,' he said, 'that took half a million years to form ten miles underground. Amazing! And there was something about Europe's largest uncut emerald weighing 26 lbs.'

It was obvious he was fired up but I understood where he was coming from and it wasn't just Corpach. I was excited too when I learned about the 6 foot 700lb amethyst, which took a quarter million years to grow. In the grounds of the museum there are or were four 20 cubic feet tipping tubs, used at one time to mine barytes at Eaglesham near East Kilbride. Perhaps Hess who landed near there was a secret mineral collector. The other cyclist was heading into Fort William and he wasn't even a footballer.

It was a pleasant run along the B8004 towards Gairlochy. Away to my right I could see Aonach Mor, the mountain with the gondolas (why bother with Venice?), which carry passengers about half way up to 2000 feet or so. At the top of the lift there are walks, a restaurant and the highest post box in Scotland. Aonach Mor is a Mecca for skiers some of whom irreligiously land on their knees in any direction. I could have gone by the canal path, for I found it in good condition when I cycled it on another occasion. This is all part of the Great Glen Cycle Route. At Gairlochy a boat was passing through a lock and some people had parked their cars to watch.

'Fishing boats from Aberdeen also come through the canal at

Gairlochy,' said a man I spoke to. 'Coming from inland and nowhere near boats, I love watching them.'

Leaving Gairlochy I cycled through woods along the B8005 with the intention of going through the Mile Dorcha or Dark Mile near the east end of Loch Arkaig. Bonnie Prince Charlie once passed through the Mile Dorcha which is closed in, and I once camped in a grassy field near the Eas Chia-aig waterfalls. When I was about to leave the next morning with my bike, Cameron of Lochiel, the clan chief and a real gentleman, approached along the road with his black labrador.

'Good morning,' I said. 'I hope you don't mind that I camped in your field there. I've removed other people's litter including thick plastic bags and put them in the bin by the bridge beside the falls.'

'Not at all,' he replied. 'Were you in the Commandos?'

'I'm afraid not. I was too young to serve in the war.'

That was a reasonable question considering my rolled up woolly balaclava and weather beaten face, plus the fact that I had told him I had been hillwalking and had been to the ruined house in the hills to the north, where the Commandos practised night attacks and the disposal of sentries.

'I'd like to visit your Clan Cameron Museum as well but I can't spare the time just now. I'll come back some day to see it.'

It was my plan this time to visit the museum on the way back from the Dark Mile, but I saw a notice saying that the museum wouldn't be open until the afternoon. I couldn't wait again and also abandoned the visit to the Dark Mile. Had I continued to there, I could have branched off and followed the Great Glen Cycle Route through the forest on the west side of Loch Lochy, but I had been told that it was rough in places. It wasn't the place for a breakdown and the bike wouldn't have been happy either. I was short of time and if I had become irritable, I might have disturbed any wildlife such as a passing puma, whatever that means.

I did manage to see the museum after the trip. Inside are Jacobite artefacts, clan and regimental history, Commando mementoes and a bridesmaid's dress worn at the wedding of Charles and Diana. If my memory serves me right, the dress was worn by the granddaughter of the above mentioned Cameron of Lochiel. Sadly that grand old man passed away recently.

An earlier Cameron of Lochiel supported Charlie, when the latter raised his standard at Glenfinnan in 1745 in his attempt to regain the crown for the Stuarts. After Culloden Charlie returned with Lochiel to Achnacarry. Beside the museum are trees with trunks swollen near the base. The popular story is that Cumberland's Hanoverian forces, whose job it was to crush the Jacobites, had lit fires at the bases of the trees and hung their kettles from the branches to boil water, and so badly damaged the trees. Apparently it's not a view held by arboriculturists.

Returning to Gairlochy, I passed again Loch Lochy, where World War II Commandos practised assaults and beach landings. South of Gairlochy is Kilmonivaig which is said to be the largest parish in the UK. From Gairlochy, I cycled along the B8004 to Spean Bridge but first made a stop at the Commando Memorial, which is near where the B8004 road meets the A82. Erected in 1952 the Memorial, designed by a sculptor by the name of Scott Sutherland, shows three Commandos looking over to Ben Nevis, where they practised some of their cliff climbing.

Recently in November, 2002, the Memorial was visited by an 83 year old Norwegian, one of three survivors who attacked the Vemork industrial plant near Rjukan, Norway, in 1943. He and other Norwegians, who escaped from Norway, trained in Scotland and were sent back to their country to destroy the heavy water being produced by the Germans for developing an atomic bomb. That water slowed released neutrons which split further atoms more easily. (See 'Vol.1 Across England', page 66.) The successful attack was featured in 'The Heroes of Telemark', a film in which accuracy was subject to Hollywood's needs.

Less than one mile roughly south-west of the Memorial and at the river is High Bridge, where the first shots of the 1745 rebellion were fired. The last time I was there was in 1961, so I gave the place a miss and sped down the slope to Spean Bridge to revisit the Commando Museum, which is incorporated into the Spean Bridge Hotel. Inside the museum I was able to see photographs, maps, uniforms, weapons, medals and stories all relating to the Commandos and their exploits. Would be World War II Commandos had to get off the train at Spean Bridge and do a quick march to Achnacarry about six or so miles away. Achnacarry Castle, the seat of the Chief of Clan Cameron, became the headquarters and officers' mess.

Inside the museum are photos of the Commandos doing their training, which was tough and specialised and included the use of live ammunition, unarmed combat, rock climbing, assault landings and forced marches. The tough regime resulted in several deaths. I also learned in the museum that the Commandos are also remembered by the memorial of a Commando soldier in the cloisters of Westminster Abbey.

The Commando training at Achnacarry and in the Fort William area was only part of the World War II training, which took place in that Highland area. About 35 miles west of Fort William at Arisaig, agents were trained for dropping into continental Europe. Two Czech agents went from Arisaig to assassinate the notorious Nazi Heydrich, the governor of the Czech part of Czechoslovakia. On the outskirts of Prague, Heydrich was injured in an attack and died a week later in hospital. The agents were caught and executed and, as a further reprisal, two villages were destroyed and about 5000 people were killed.

On leaving the museum I raided a small supermarket store close by and

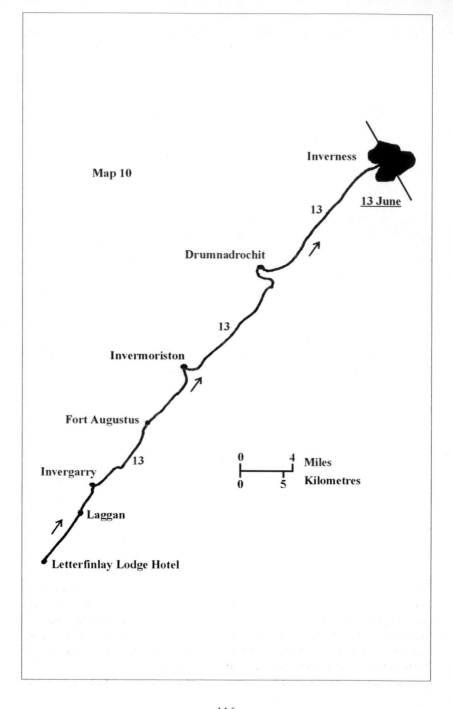

Map 10

Inverness

13 June

13

Drumnadrochit

13

Invermoriston

Fort Augustus

13

Invergarry

Laggan

Letterfinlay Lodge Hotel

| 0 | | 4 | Miles |
| 0 | | 5 | Kilometres |

bought some milk and sandwiches. Outside I sat in the sun eating and drinking, and watched the bus party tourists walking about or visiting the tourist shop or tea room.

'Have you come far?' I was asked by a backpacker.

'From Land's End.'

'You must be fit,' he laughed.

'Not really. I've taken more than a day. I'm getting that way.'

'Are you going to the Hoares' hotel?' he asked laughing again.

'The what?' I replied puzzled and taken aback. If only I had taken my prayer beads.

'I'm only joking,' he said, laughing even more. 'That's the name of the people who run one of the hotels up the road there.'

He spelt out the surname and all became clear. I realised that I had been fooled by a homophone and said so.

'What do you mean by a "homophone"?' he queried with a look of anxiety encroaching on his face. Perhaps he thought I was insulting him.

'A word sounding the same as another but spelt differently.'

'Oh, I see. Well, all the best,' he added, a little of the wind out of his sails.

I observed that some of the bus passengers could have done with some physical challenge, but it was obvious that all they would be doing would be to haul themselves aboard and waddle to their seats. However, if they weren't going to exert themselves unduly, I had to. After all did I not look like a Commando, even a half dead one?

I set off again and urged the bike up the slope leading from Spean Bridge. Soon I was past the Commando Memorial and heading out the A82 on the east side of Loch Lochy. This was a straightforward route which I had cycled up before, when I pedalled north to Invergarry and then west to Knoydart. For a large part of the way there is a roughly two foot wide strip between the white line and the grass verge, and I claimed that space for myself. It is, however, a busy road, but for a great stretch there is a clear view of Loch Lochy.

At its northern end are the Laggan locks and, just beyond that, Loch Lochy hostel in which I last slept in 1961. There my girl friend and I met from the U.S.A., Fred Neumann who was cycling around Scotland. We had to shelter in the bicycle shed from the rain until the hostel opened. The hostel was pretty full and I was put into the annexe. During the night, in order to get to the toilet, I had to step over the bodies of Germans sleeping on mattresses on the floor, something that would not be allowed now with more stringent fire regulations. I corresponded for a while with Fred, but the last time I heard from him was about 40 years ago, when he was an assistant or associate professor at Harvard University.

Just past the hostel I braked to a halt at the Laggan swing bridge, which was closed to road traffic to allow a boat to pass through from Loch Oich into the short section of the canal, which links with Loch Lochy. When I was able to continue, I arrived at the Tobar nan Ceann or Well of the Heads monument less than a mile farther on. From the shop opposite I bought a Mars bar, which I ate before reading the well inscription written in Gaelic, French, Latin and English. Seven brothers were slaughtered for killing the chief of Keppoch and his brother. The story is that the family bard, who arranged the seven murders, washed the heads in the well, which is still there under the road, and presented them to the Chief of Glengarry. Was that an example of poetic licence or justice? That is said to have happened in 1663 but the inscription dates the event not far into the 16th century. The monument was erected in 1812 by Colonel MacDonnell of Glengarry, who was a friend of Sir Walter Scott. The latter is said to have based the character of 'Fergus MacIvor' in 'Waverley' on MacDonnell.

I cycled on, soon leaving behind the boats near the monument, and entered Invergarry, where I had a light snack before continuing to Fort Augustus. This place was formerly known by its Gaelic name 'Cill Chuimin' or Cummein's Church, St. Cummein being the seventh Abbot of Iona, and thought to be the author of the first book ever written in Scotland. Between 1729 and 1742, General Wade built a fort to replace an earlier barracks, and he named it Fort Augustus after the King's third son, William Augustus, later known as the Duke of Cumberland or Butcher Cumberland, because of the atrocities he permitted at the Battle of Culloden in 1746. The first fort was destroyed but was replaced. In 1867 the government sold Fort Augustus to Lord Lovat whose son handed it over to the Benedictines. Much of the Hanoverian fort is included in the Fort Augustus Abbey, which was opened in 1878 and later enlarged several times. From 1878 the monks ran a boarding school until 1993 when it closed, but now they run a heritage and conference centre.

Once the bike was locked, I spoke to two ladies who were on duty at the abbey entrance.

'I'm sorry,' said one of the ladies, 'but we're closed now.'

'Can you give me any information about the abbey?' I asked.

'Oh yes, we can do that.'

One of them proceeded to give me some facts about the place and then the conversation turned to the trip.

'You've cycled from Land's End? That's marvellous. Do you hear that?' she said, turning to the other lady.

I was outnumbered and didn't argue with her. They were so enthusiastic for me or more precisely wished me all the best on the remainder of my journey. I wanted to ask more questions but they had to shut.

'There's just time for you to see into the church, though.'

I went over and entered. It was interesting but I was dissatisfied. Where outside was the Battery Rock where the Jacobites placed their cannons and fired on the fort's powder magazine? That took place in 1745 when the fort surrendered to an Irish regiment fighting for Prince Charlie. Where were the Camp Fields (later the playing fields of the abbey Roman Catholic school for boys), where Cumberland's men had to sleep after the Jacobites had destroyed so much of the fort? This Hanoverian defeat led to the officer in charge being court-martialled and thrown out of the army. Lastly, where was the green lawn, which replaced the original fort's barrack square? What makes fields 'camp' anyway? I should have quizzed the ladies more.

From the Abbey's own harbour you can take off with the 'Catriona', a former Cornish crabber now used for pleasure trips on the loch. Time, I was aware, was short and I was still only half way between Fort William and Inverness. I thought perhaps I would have to stop at Loch Ness hostel at Alltsigh about ten miles farther on. However, before leaving Fort Augustus, I went into a café for two bacon rolls and tea. That would keep me going during the evening. When I emerged from the café, the air was cooler and it looked as if the weather might change.

As I cycled on, I was passed by a young couple, a male and female, then I overtook them. So this continued until it was my turn to catch up with them outside Loch Ness hostel. Another couple had been turned away from the hostel and the two cyclists, with whom I had been playing a sort of leap frog with bikes, were wondering what to do.

'We're hoping that some folk who have booked won't turn up. We'll maybe get in yet or maybe we'll have to look for a B&B,' they said.

'I'm going on to Inverness,' I added. 'If I don't get into the hostel there, I can camp or there's plenty B&Bs in the city.'

I said goodbye knowing that I had a long haul ahead of me. About 12 miles on from Fort Augustus, I was at a point of the road opposite Foyers on the east shore of Loch Ness, which has about three times as much water as Loch Lomond. In fact, Loch Ness is the biggest body of fresh water in west Europe. The loch has a depth of about 754 feet, a length of 23 miles and is 1.5 miles at its widest. Southey the poet visited the falls at Foyers with Telford, and Pennant gave a good description of the falls, which had then a 200 feet drop. However, in 1894-5 the falls were interfered with, when the water power was used to produce hydro-electricity (the first time in Scotland) for industry, in this case for the production of aluminium. The villages of Foyers and Glenlia were established, but the factory closed in 1967.

Less than two miles farther on from Foyers is Boleskine House, which was once the home of the satanist Aleister Crowley who, some believe, called up evil forces which still haunt the house. Long after Crowley had left, a workman there claimed that he felt fear, when he saw a dark shadow and was aware of a presence near him. I could have taken that B road from Fort Augustus, but the roads department might not have been too pleased, when I passed Boleskine House.

More than two miles from Drumnadrochit I stopped at the memorial to John Cobb, who died on Loch Ness on 29 September in 1952, while attempting to break the world water speed record. His boat disintegrated after hitting waves at 240 m.p.h. Very soon after that I drew level with Urquhart Castle, beside which there is now a new visitor centre. There had been a vitrified fort there long ago, followed by a motte and double bailey and then the 13th and 14th stone defences. From the time of Edward I until the Jacobite rebellion of 1689 the castle was involved in conflict. After that date the castle was blown up, which perhaps shows that rubber technology and wind power must have been more advanced than deemed then possible.

Considering all the encouragement I received throughout my journey, I was a bit miffed that the Loch Ness monster, whose favourite hideyhole is in Urquhart Bay beside the castle, didn't turn up to greet me. Perhaps it took the hump. Some people have suggested that the creature in question is a plesiosaurus, one of a family of such creatures, but it has even been proposed that it is an evil spirit conjured up by Crowley. That for sure is a monstrous idea. One American invested 80,000 dollars in a project to find the 'monster' and sold his house to put another 120,000 dollars into completing a 40 foot submarine. In recent years Hollywood produced a fictional film 'Loch Ness', starring Ted Danson in his search for 'Nessie'.

Some years ago I had a nasty experience which eventually brought me some pleasure. I was cycling south just past the castle when my back carrier broke. The weight of the two back panniers bore down on the rear mudguard, which then pressed against the tyre and prevented the wheel turning properly. I tried tying the carrier with cord but that didn't work. Luckily I came to a small petrol station where the man put my bike into a trailer, which he then towed with his car to the Bught Park, Inverness. The driver was £15 richer and I was £15 poorer, but was I glad to set up my tent. Next morning I wheeled the bike into town to get a new carrier and walked straight towards a T.V. camera, which was filming the headquarters of a firm that was paying off employees. The result was that I appeared on the B.B.C. news at 6.00 p.m. and 9.00 p.m. I didn't get the new carrier I wanted, but was very glad to have with me my 70 litre rucksack into which I put my belongings from the rear panniers. Back in Aberdeen later I bought two better quality Blackburn carriers and these have served me well.

Away on my left, as I approached Drumnadrochit I could see Balmacaan woods, the first acquired in Scotland by the Woodland Trust. When I entered the village that evening, I was glad it wasn't as busy as it is during the day, when tourists flock to the shops and the two Loch Ness monster exhibitions, one of which is the official one. One of the past visitors to the official exhibition was a young marine biologist, who today is the present Emperor Akihito of Japan. Others have included the film actor James Mason, the T.V. actor Tom Baker, who acted in 'Dr. Who', and Ian Botham the England cricketer. I got talking to an old gentleman who asked why I was doing the trip and he offered me some interesting information.

'You should go to the Divach Falls. They're worth seeing. They're just south of here and up above the falls is Dhivach Lodge. That's where Millais the artist used to go on holiday, and Barrie, who wrote 'Peter Pan', and Captain Scott of the Antarctic used to spend time there too.'

'Thanks very much but I don't have the time. I've got to move on and reach Inverness tonight.'

In any case I had been there before with my wife, when some years earlier we had stayed at Cannich Youth Hostel on a cycling holiday exploring the surrounding countryside. Barrie came to Dhivach Lodge in 1907 with his wife and a family they befriended, and so a summer holiday was spent there with the five young Llewelyn-Davies boys, who were later cast as the 'Lost Boys' in 'Peter Pan'.

I exited from Drumnadrochit by way of the A82, which I had been following for the most part from Fort William, but I had intended originally going up the A833 and on through the parish of Kiltarlity, where families had to live on berries and herbs for two famine years at the beginning of the 18th century and were thus forced to beg. From Kiltarlity I was going to cycle west to Eskadale House and Eileanaigas House, which is on an island in the river Beauly. On that island there lived in a lodge two brothers, who claimed to be the sons of Bonnie Prince Charlie and they ended up in a tomb at Eskadale House. From there I meant to cycle to Beauly (the name said to be derived from 'beau lieu', the French for 'beautiful place', or from Gaelic), then to Muir of Ord where the brother of Alistair MacLean the novelist once lived, and then a few miles north-west of Muir of Ord to South Arcan farm where Helen Keller, the famous blind and deaf woman, came to live for a while with her servant, the Dingwall provost's (mayor in England) daughter. Back in Muir of Ord, I was going to cycle on mainly by a secondary road along the north shore of the Beauly Firth to Inverness, where Alistair MacLean himself received some schooling at Inverness Royal Academy.

All that had to be omitted and could only have been done by overnighting in Drumnadrochit, but I was concerned that I wouldn't be able to return on the 18th to Aberdeen, in readiness for the already mentioned holiday my wife and I had booked in Chester and Wales. I made the right decision as it turned out.

Consequently I cycled along on the A82 and came in past Tomnahuraich cemetery, which has been described as the most beautiful in the world. At Tomnahuraich there once lived a fiddler known to the Gaels as the second

Scott Skinner, the famous Strathspey king who was born in Banchory.

After much pedalling I reached Inverness and made my way to the new purpose built S.Y.H.A. hostel, which is more on the outskirts of the city in contrast to the old one along from the castle. The receptionist had a foreign accent, in fact she sounded French, but her English was fluent. I took the bike to the shed, where I found the bikes suspended by the front wheel, but I thought this would put a strain on the wheel and left the bike standing in the normal way at the end of the shed. Back in the hostel I was impressed by the security card system for gaining entry beyond reception, and I was pleased to see a drinks machine offering tea, coffee or hot chocolate, and there was also a biscuit and sweets machine. I made good use of the facilities until it was time to go to bed and I was ready for it.

What would tomorrow bring, I wondered? Perhaps it would start with a monster breakfast. Yes, that would be really appropriate. I made my way to the dormitory and, as I settled down (a natural activity when one is supplied with a duvet), I hoped that I wouldn't dream of 'Nessie' crossing my road, for the creature has been reported out of the water.

14 June   Inverness – Culloden – Clava Cairns – Inverness   O.S. 26, 27

Sunday was a black day in some respects, not that the weather was bad, but I discovered that my bicycle computer was no longer working. It had been going perfectly at bedtime, but perhaps I had stood on it at some time in the morning, or the batteries were done. From Inverness onwards, I would have to calculate my road distance from a road map only, but at least for the most part, the mileage between places was shown clearly, and I had kept a written record of the total computer mileage covered since leaving Land's End. My camera too was causing problems for it wouldn't rewind. I couldn't imagine going on without being able to take pictures. Lastly my back tyre was a bit soft and I would have to get it seen to, if I wanted a hassle free conclusion to the last stages of the journey.

I went for my continental breakfast (no longer served in the hostel today) and found a contrast to the situation in Glen Nevis hostel. Some of the Inverness hostellers, who wanted to dump their rucksacks on the tables, were left in no doubt by the kitchen staff that this was forbidden. I started a conversation with two chaps sitting at a table and I learned that they were cyclists, who had gone from Land's End to John O' Groats.

'How long were you on the road?' I asked.

'Four days. We did it in four. We just bombed along hardly stopping. How long have you taken?'

'I'm in my sixth week, but I've done over 2000 miles already. I've been doing a winding route, tracking down and investigating interesting things.'

There was no arguing about that. Had I not tracked down fish and chip shops in Exeter and Glasgow?

It was obvious that I would probably have to stay another night, and so booked again and left my luggage in the dormitory. I got out the bike after breakfast and went in search of a bike shop. First I tried the one I had gone to some years earlier, when the back carrier broke south of Drumnadrochit.

'It's no longer here,' I was told. 'Try the shop along that other street.'

I did so and found a chap waiting impatiently outside, for the shop was still shut.

'I wish he'd hurry up, for I've been waiting quite a while,' he moaned.

At last a man appeared and opened up the shop with an apology and he used a key as well. The man who had been waiting outside handed in a wheel and collected one. As for me nothing could be done. He hadn't the right size of tube and he didn't have a cycle computer, but he directed me to 'Bikes Inverness' in Grant Street, a fair distance away. When I arrived there it was shut, but I made an enquiry at a nearby general store.

'Is the cycle shop over there open on a Sunday?'

'Can't say, but it might open in the afternoon if he doesn't open in the morning. He used to open in the morning for the Sunday cyclists.'

Meanwhile I increased the profits of the shop by buying some crisps and a can of juice. At least I wouldn't die of starvation while I waited, and wait I did until 2.00 p.m., hoping that a miracle would occur and I'd get my bike and camera seen to. I was out of luck and would have to try again next day.

As already stated, one of the aims of the trip was to see interesting things. I had already been to the battlefields of Sedgemoor and Solway Moss, so I resolved to cycle to Drummossie Moor, usually known today as Culloden Moor, five miles out of Inverness. If the bike failed I could always walk back.

Twice before I had been to Culloden Moor when it had a good covering of conifers. Once was on the pillion seat of my future wife's scooter during a 1000 miles tour of Scotland, and the second time was on a school trip. Since then many trees have been removed to try and restore the moor to the state it was in at the time of the battle.

There on the moor the last great battle on British soil took place in 1746 between the forces of the Duke of Cumberland, (son of George II, King of Great Britain) and Charles Edward Stuart, a Jacobite and grandson of James VII of Scotland and James II of England. (For those who find the double title too cumbersome, I am quite willing to use James VII only instead of the usual James II, but I do not think that that would go down too well in England. In Scotland we have to endure the constant use of English titles and post 1603 references to the English throne and monarchy.)

To understand the meaning of 'Jacobite' and why the battle took place, let us go back to 1688. In that year the King James referred to above was forced into exile after he tried to make Britain a Roman Catholic country.

Leaving aside who and why certain people succeeded James, let it suffice to say that thereafter Parliament enacted in 1689 and in 1701 that all British monarchs had to be Protestant. Those who supported the exiled king were called Jacobites because the Latin for James is 'Jacobus'. Later the name was given to supporters of his descendants.

His son James Edward Stuart, known to his opponents as the Old Pretender, meaning 'the Old Claimant' (to the throne), had lived in France, then Italy, but came to Scotland in support of a Jacobite rebellion in 1715 to put himself on the throne. The attempt failed and later in 1745 Charles Edward Stuart, known as the Young Pretender to those against him, landed in Scotland in 1745 to claim the British crown for his father James Edward Stuart.

George II, King of Britain and of Hanoverian origin, was determined that his son the Duke of Cumberland would thwart Charles's plans. After a series of victories, the end came for Charles's army in the spring of 1746 at Culloden Moor. Cumberland's army, among other things, was much larger and better equipped, whereas the army of Bonnie Prince Charlie consisted of men who were hungry and tired after a long march. When Charlie's army was staring defeat in the face, he and his horse were led away. The battle lasted for about an hour.

For five months the Prince was on the run from the mainland to the islands and back with a reward of £30,000 on his head. He hid in caves and tramped the glens and mountains, some of which I have also walked and climbed, and endured the anxieties of dodging soldiers, the rain, the midges and lice. He eventually escaped to France and died, a fat old drunk in Rome, 42 years after Culloden.

Many atrocities were committed on the battlefield and afterwards there were hangings, beheadings and transportations. The Highlanders were harried in their homes, forbidden to wear the kilt, plaid and tartan and had to disarm while the chiefs lost their powers. This led to the break up of the clan system.

If the government forces were hard on the Highlanders, the bike at least was soft with me – not surprisingly considering the state of my tyre. I set off past the old S.Y.H.A. building on the road to Culloden, using the map and street plan. It was practically all on the B9006, but at least the day was warm and sunny and the road not too busy.

Before reaching the National Trust Visitor Centre, which I could see in the distance, I noticed on the moor to the right that there were flagpoles with flags flying to show where the various clans or government forces had been positioned. I was suddenly aware that the hardest thing that a pedestrian needed to do to enter 'illegally' was to jump a ditch. However, I kept on the right side of the law, for just then I imagined I heard my bike singing that old Frankie Lane number: 'Do not forsake me, o my darling.'

Soon I reached the Centre and there I paid the senior citizen entry fee and had a look around outside at the gravestones marking the burial places of the various clans.

'It must have been a bit of a massacre,' said a man who joined me as I studied the gravestones.

'No doubting that,' I replied. 'The wounded were bayonetted, shot, burned and mutilated. Word spread among the government forces that the Jacobites intended giving no quarter. False information, of course, but it explains partly why Cumberland's men were so ruthless.'

I remained there until it was time to see the audio-visual presentation. During the show the commentator said something which caused me to shake my head and mutter: 'Inaccurate.' Probably something about Scottish history was being ignored again and the English aspect mentioned.

After the show, I went back out on the moor and I found myself disagreeing again. You realise, of course, that if cameras, bikes and their computers were unbreakable I'd have such a sweet nature. I heard a little boy speaking to his English father.

'Who were fighting here, Dad?'

'The English against the Scots.'

Now even if some of the English put sugar on their porridge instead of salt like true Scots, I didn't want this man to give his countrymen all the blame for beating the Scots. Or maybe I didn't want him to give his countrymen alone the credit for the Jacobite defeat.

'Excuse me,' I said diffidently, lest I received a beating on the moor, 'that's not quite right about the English against the Scots.'

'Really?' he replied amicably. 'And what's wrong with that?'

'Well, it was a case of government forces, which included English and Scots, against rebel soldiers who were mainly Scots but were also supported by an Englishman, a Frenchman and French speaking Irishmen. It was a fight between Hanoverians, who were in power and on the throne and Stuarts, who were not in power and who claimed the throne.

'Sounds a bit complicated to me,' he replied. 'I'll just stick to the English versus the Scots idea.'

Maybe my version wasn't completely accurate, but it was better than the simple Scots versus English story.

As I walked away, I heard his child asking what the man had been saying and the father saying: 'Nothing.'

Since my last visit it has been discovered that calculations as to the site of the battlefield based on historical accounts are somewhat off the mark. Scientific methods, including radar and metal detectors, have shown that the area of the battlefield is bigger than previously thought, and that a decisive Jacobite charge took place in another field about 80 metres further south.

The Centre was now closing and I set off along a secondary road to the

Clava Cairns about a mile away. These burial cairns surrounded by stone circles date back to before 2000 B.C. . I later heard a story about a Belgian tourist who removed a stone weighing about 2lbs from the cairns. Was he or did he deserve to be stoned? He subsequently posted it back to Inverness tourist office, because he thought his family had become cursed since the theft. I looked around a while then made my way back the way I had come.

I felt peckish after the trip and, after putting my bike into the shed, the food and drink machines in the hostel once again did my bidding, before I went out on foot to check my route out of Inverness. I discovered how to get to Kessock bridge without using a very busy route, and that done it was back to the hostel and hot chocolate. I was going to have to watch my diet or else I myself would become a 'chocolate', an expression, which in Aberdeen at least, is a bit derogatory and suggests one is several neurons short of a brain.

I read a little, including some tourist literature, then began conversing with some hostellers from mainland Europe. I landed up explaining to them that Britain and England were not the same and that Scotland and England were separate countries. I continued by saying that Britain consisted of Scotland, England and Wales, the U.K. was formed by these three countries again plus Northern Ireland, and the British Isles consisted of all that plus southern Ireland or Eire. I also pointed out that Scotland had three languages, namely, English, Scots and Gaelic and illustrated this by translating an English sentence into Scots and Gaelic. They were so impressed that they headed off to the dormitory for bed.

Perhaps it *was* time for bed, I consoled myself, and followed after them shortly afterwards.

15 June   Inverness – Cromarty   O.S. 26, 27

I was in the capital of the Highlands and the weather was indeed capital that morning, as I left the hostel after a good continental breakfast. The first job was to phone my father and wish him a happy birthday. I then returned to'Bikes Inverness' in Grant Street, where I tried a new cycle computer battery, but still the computer didn't work. I left the bike and luggage and found later a photographic shop called 'Click', where my stuck spool was taken out safely from the camera and a new one inserted. I also bought two disposable cameras in case my camera failed completely, for they would provide at least prints of the last stages of my journey.

From there I went to photograph the Town House built in 1878-82. There the first Cabinet meeting held outside London took place. That was in 1921 when Lloyd George (1863-1945), the Prime Minister, who was on holiday in Scotland, had to deal with a letter from Eamon de Valera. I know nothing about the contents of the letter, but 1921 was the year in which the Irish Free State was established. De Valera was the leader of the largest Irish party, Sinn Fein, and he was opposed to the settlement. The Irish problem was pressing and to speed up a reply, Lloyd George called a meeting in the Council Chamber at 11.00 a.m. on 7 September. Among those present were J. Austen Chamberlain, Stanley Baldwin and Winston Churchill. A framed document with the signatures of the Cabinet Ministers who attended is in the Council Chamber.

Next I took a look at the Clach-na-Cudainn or 'Stone of Tubs', where women rested their tubs on the way up from the river Ness. Obviously they had large ice cream tubs in Inverness, if it wasn't their washing that these women carried. Next stop beside the tourist office was the museum where I saw a female puma, which was caught near Aviemore and is now stuffed in a glass case. Even Inverness has its share of 'fat cats'.

Farther uphill from the museum beside the castle, I had a date with Flora MacDonald who met me in statue form. The sculptor's intention was to show her, as if she were outside her house at Kingsburgh in Skye, and watching for Bonnie Prince Charlie's enemies when he was in hiding there. That was when Charlie was on the run as already described. Flora, when questioned later by the king about her part in helping the Prince, said she would have done the same for him or anyone in trouble. It has been suggested, however, that Flora was really a government agent and that she was allowed to get the Prince, a politically embarrassing figure, out of the country. She was pardoned and went with her husband to live for a time in North America. During the American revolution her husband and son were taken prisoner and Flora returned to Scotland in 1779. She was not to see her husband again until 1783, and when she died in 1790 she was buried at Kilmuir in North Skye. She was wrapped in a sheet used by the Prince and over her grave is a Celtic cross. Although I don't get paid for advertising, remember Flora next time you are spreading margarine on your toast.

Seated on a bench in the castle grounds, I ate some sandwiches and enjoyed the view. An old lady sat down beside me to have her picnic and we talked.

'I've just come from Canada,' she told me. 'I'm revisiting the places of my youth before returning. I know because of my age that I won't be back again.'

I felt her sadness as she said goodbye and left me alone on the bench. However, with my sandwiches in their new home it was time to fetch the bike and get on the road.

What a pity I didn't have more time to investigate or track down more in this interesting city. There were so many unanswered questions. For example, where was the house in Bridge Street where Mary Queen of Scots stayed, where was the house of Archie MacDougall, the last survivor of the seven men of Knoydart, who had rebelled against their treatment by their landlord and seized some land? Those seven are not to be confused with the seven men of Moidart, who were counted among the Prince's most loyal followers, and among whom was a Colonel Francis Strickland from Westmorland. Where in Inverness did Lord Irvine once live, a man of humble origins but later a member of Tony Blair's government and famous for his expensive taste in wallpaper? And then there was McIntosh who went to Canada and planted apple seeds to give us the famous McIntosh Reds. I would have liked too to have seen the world's largest kilt making workshop. Perhaps I'll do that some day on another visit to Inverness. The word 'tartan', by the way, is believed to come from the old French 'tertaine', a wool fabric, or perhaps from the old Spanish 'tiritana', a fine fabric. The oldest known dates back to before 250 A.D. .

I said goodbye to Flora as well, left the castle grounds and soon reached the bike shop after a brisk walk.

'That'll keep you going to John O' Groats. You can depend on it,' said the bike mechanic when I called for the bike. He was right for I had no more problems.

After a bacon roll and a pint of milk, I set off along the cyclist's route out of Inverness to the north. I followed the river, went past a boat about to take tourists to see the dolphins off the Black Isle, which isn't an isle, and then past Cromwell's Clock Tower, the remains of a fort built by Cromwell's army between 1652 and 1657. It was a pentagonal fort (the Pentagon of Inverness?) built to hold 1000 men and 600 horses (0.66 horses per man). Very useful. Imagine the conversation which might have ensued.

'Trouble's brewing in the town, sir. Shall I prepare your two-thirds horse, sir, or do I give it a rest and order a whole one?'

'Er, get a whole one. It's fractionally better.'

The fort was demolished in 1661 and the stones ended up in the town's buildings.

Soon I was on the cycleway over the Kessock Bridge, which spans the narrows between the Beauly Firth and the Moray Firth, the latter the deepest of all the Scottish firths, and the most northerly major wintering area for wildfowl in Europe. Once over the bridge I turned left and down into the village of North Kessock where Neil Gunn, a Scottish novelist, lived for a time. I called in by Joe Lindsay, maker of Highland targes.

'In Jacobite times,' he explained, 'this was the Highlander's chief defence in battle. It was about 19 inches in diameter with the front covered in tough hide and the back in deerskin. The front was decorated with brass studs and plates, which occasionally had cut-outs backed with red cloth, traditionally a piece of a redcoat's uniform. The leather was usually tooled in Celtic patterns and some targes had a little spike set in a centre boss.'

I had heard that in 1745 a William Lindsay in Perth made targes for Charlie's army. It was amazing to think that there was another Lindsay who

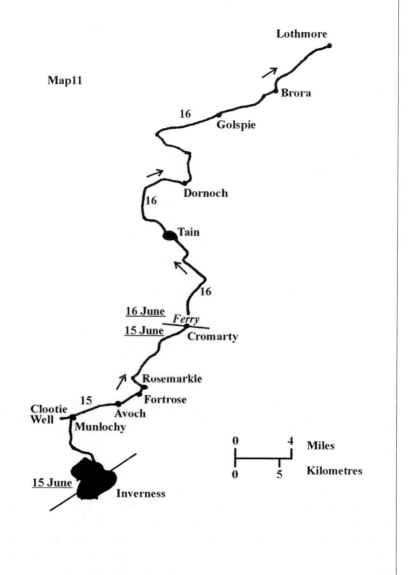

Map11

Lothmore

Brora

16
Golspie

Dornoch

16

Tain

16

16 June
Ferry
15 June
Cromarty

Rosemarkle

15
Fortrose

Clootie
Well
Avoch
Munlochy

15 June
Inverness

0   4   Miles
0   5   Kilometres

was making similar targes only eight miles from Culloden.

'I got into this by accident,' he told me. 'My kids were doing a project in school and I made some models including small model targes. It was then I decided to go in for this in a big way. Here look around. I've a phone call to make.'

I thought he was very trusting and said so, for he had many small things lying around, but he insisted. I learned that the shields are based on shields in private collections, on those in the National Museum of Antiquities or in other museums. Small targes were priced then at £30 (now £35), a fighting targe at £90 (now £100), a clan Ranald one at £170 (now £195) and a Keppoch one at £205 (now £215). Obviously a lot of work goes into them. I think he said that the present Prince Charles had bought one.

The Perth targe is based on an unfinished original in Perth Museum and is possibly one of the last made by William Lindsay. The Cameron targe is based on an original, reputedly carried by Cameron of Lochiel at Culloden, and the MacKay one on an original in the Hunterian Museum, Glasgow.

It was very interesting and I thanked him for his time. Still on the cycleway I continued along the north side of the Beauly Firth, went through an underpass and came out on the other side of the A9 and headed towards Munlochy on the B9161. I was aware that to the east is Mains of Drynie, the 'Mains' coming from the Latin 'mensa' for 'table', for in the days of serfdom the table lands were the lands, which provided the lord with the food for his table. More distant to the west and north-east of Muir of Ord is Drynie Park. All I knew, before setting out on my journey at that time, was that some place called Drynie was Europe's largest exporter of Christmas trees. I had written to Mains of Drynie before leaving home and requested a visit, if that was the right place, but I received no reply. Perhaps I slipped up and forgot to enclose my usual stamped addressed envelope.

On the way to Munlochy I passed the Black Isle Country Park, which had pot bellied pigs, probably through making pigs of themselves. Perhaps some exercise in the form of bacon rolls would have improved their fitness. Also rare sheep and cattle, red grouse, capercailzie, pheasants, ducks, geese and walking street crossings known as zebras were to be seen. Plenty food there, I thought, but I made do with another Mars bar. Some time after the trip, the Park was put up for sale at an asking price of over £300,000.

Once I climbed the little brae in quiet Munlochy, I reached the A832 and turned left. I hadn't far to go to see the famous Clooty Well. 'Cloot' is, of course, a Scots word for 'cloth' and there beside the well the trees are festooned with all sorts of clothing, even handbags, which people have hung on the branches to bring them good luck and keep off harm. I didn't need a handbag for I had four panniers. A couple drew up in a car and got out.

'You could start a shop here,' said the man, grinning.

'It's an amazing collection for sure.'

'You fancy some underwear?' he asked his companion and she blushed noticeably.

Another car drew up and the driver reversed when he realised that he was blocking my view of the well and cloots I was trying to photograph.

From the well it was an easy cycle to Avoch (pronounced as in 'loch', not 'lock', without the 'l'). On the south side of the village is Ormond Hill, where Andrew de Moray (often overshadowed by William Wallace) raised the Scottish Standard in 1297, as he rallied his supporters in the fight for Scotland's freedom from English domination.

Once in the village I stopped for some chocolate at a corner store, before going up a brae at the opposite side of the road. On reaching the top, I turned right into a churchyard and, after a short distance in, again to the right and this brought me to the burial place of Alexander Mackenzie (1755?-1820), who travelled down the Mackenzie river to the Arctic Ocean in 1789, and later crossed the Rocky Mountains to the Pacific. Mackenzie, after whom the great Mackenzie river in Canada is named, came from the Isle of Lewis. He lies behind a walled and iron railed area adorned with several flags, including the Saltire of Scotland, the Union Jack, the flag of Canada, that of the Northwest Territories and, as far as I remember, that of any other part of Canada he crossed.

An easy freewheel downhill took me back to the main road and the Avoch Heritage Centre, which is on the other side of the road but opposite the store. Inside the Centre there was much information about Mackenzie and other matters.

'Did you know,' said a man I spoke to in the Centre, 'that a William Roy or Ray came from here and was a deserter from the 'Bounty' captained by Bligh. In fact it's said that about a quarter of the 'Bounty's' crew came from Scotland, including two from Aberdeen.'

'No, that's news to me.'

Later on B.B.C. T.V., a documentary was shown about 'H.M.S. Jervis Bay' in action during World War II. It told the story of how the ship, although outgunned, in order to protect its Atlantic convoy, attacked the 'Admiral Scheer', a German battleship. The British ship went down but 35 convoy ships made it to Britain. In 1999 the only one left of the survivors was an Avoch man through whom the story was told.

The main road wasn't too busy as I continued on to the royal burgh of Fortrose. First I looked around the 13th century cathedral, which was formerly the ecclesiastical centre of Ross, then cycled down to Chanonry Point, which has been described as the main observation point in Britain for seeing the dolphins which regularly pass by.

Down on the shore I photographed the cairn commemorating Coinneach Odhar, the Brahan Seer. The latter was said to have second sight, which enabled him to make prophecies about the future. In 1699 the Rev. Robert

Kirk of Aberfoyle wrote that people who had second sight were considered to have received this power from their dead ancestors, who lived in knolls beside churchyards. It was believed to be a gift from the fairies. It seems many of the prophecies have come true and some are still not fulfilled. The Seer predicted the depopulation of the Highlands, the coming of rich landlords, the Caledonian canal and the railway going through Muir of Ord among many other events. He warned that 5 bridges across the river Ness would bring disaster and, the day after the 5th bridge was opened in 1939, Hitler invaded Poland.

Why was the Seer put to death? According to the story he quarrelled with Isabella, wife of the Earl of Seaforth, when he told her that her husband was having an affair at the court of Charles II. She was somewhat upset and ordered his death but, before he was burned in a spiked barrel of tar at Chanonry Point, he cursed her and predicted very accurately how all her family would meet their fate. A pity he didn't see his own fate coming.

But how true is all this about the so called Brahan Seer? According to an Alex Mackenzie, who collected prophecies and tales, a Kenneth Mackenzie, better known as Coinneach Odhar, who was born in Baile-na-Cille in Uig on the Isle of Lewis, came eventually to labour on the Brahan estate owned by the Seaforth Mackenzies between 1660 and 1675. However, in the Gaelic tradition there is no word of a person called the Brahan Seer, only mention of a Coinneach Odhar who is sometimes described as a seer. He is also mentioned in a history of the MacLeods as being born in Ness in Lewis in the 16th century. Documentary evidence tells us that he was accused of witchcraft in 1577/78 but, although some witches were burned after being tried at the Chanonry, we don't know if he was ever caught let alone tried. However, the 16th century Coinneach Odhar couldn't have made his prophecy about the Seaforth family for two reasons. Firstly there was no Earldom until 1623 and there was no Countess of Seaforth in the 16th century.

It seems that because Kenneth Odhar was well known, prophecies which didn't come from him were linked with him nevertheless. Some of the prophecies he has been associated with come from Norse folklore or have been made also by Thomas the Rhymer, the Isla Seer, and Michael Scott, a scholar who, as part of his amazing career, wrote a book about magic spells. The evidence suggests that some other person, unless there was some unknown second Coinneach Odhar, predicted the downfall of the Seaforth family, and that this person was confused with the seer Coinneach Odhar, who lived about a century earlier. This prophecy was very detailed and was known before the events prophesied took place. Lockhart in his 'Life of Scott' says that Sir Humphrey Davy and Sir Walter Scott believed it was a genuine prophecy. It is a complicated story, but the Seer is to be commemorated in a Gaelic opera to be presented, when Inverness bids to become European Capital of Culture in 2008.

As I walked away from the Brahan Seer cairn, I was joined by a man with a Glasgow accent.

'I'm hoping to see dolphins today. The last time I was here they were really leaping out of the water. It's best of course when the tide's changing. Do you know that a dolphin can eat about ten salmon in a day?'

'The last time I saw them,' I responded, 'was when I was camping at Rosemarkie and walked farther along the coast. You get schools of between 2 and 30 and you also get porpoises and common seals.'

'Are you touring?' he asked.

'You could say that.'

'Have you been to Fort George across the water?'

'Yes, I once biked there, when my wife and I had a bargain break holiday at Nairn,' I replied.

'Oh that's where Charlie Chaplin used to holiday sometimes.'

I could see that like me he was a collector of information about places. The 18th century fort was built in the reign of George II after the defeat of Charlie at Culloden, and its bastioned defences and original garrison are still there. It stands on a spit of land at Ardersier, and it is claimed to be the mightiest artillery fortification in Britain and perhaps in Europe. The magazine was built to hold 2,500 barrels of gunpowder and these barrels had copper hoops, which were less liable to cause sparks than iron ones. The door of the magazine was also covered with a sheet of copper. Almost a mile around and enclosing an area of 42 acres, its parade ground is large enough to hold Edinburgh Castle. It took 21 years to build and cost £1 billion at today's prices, and it never saw a shot fired in anger.

Readers who have seen the film 'The Bridge On The River Kwai' will remember the tune 'Colonel Bogey' which was whistled. Fort George is said to be where the tune first originated. An ex-policeman, Michael Spence from Aberdeen informed me that it is a piping tune. Like the church in Slaidburn, England, the chapel in the fort has a three decker pulpit. I was very impressed with my visit to the fort.

When I was finished with Chanonry Point, I cycled back to the main road and into the shopping area of Fortrose. Supplied with something to eat and drink, I retreated to the Cathedral grounds for a quick snack. Afterwards I pedalled on to Rosemarkie, which at one time was more important ecclesiastically than Fortrose. The road was pretty quiet which made pleasant cycling. At the Rosemarkie Camping and Caravan Club site where my wife and I once camped, we met a geologist who had been collecting samples of sand wherever he went on holiday. His name wasn't 'Sandy', believe it or not, but he told me of his fossil finds.

'If, instead of going out the A832 to Cromarty, you take a secondary road just over a mile out of Rosemarkie, you'll eventually come to a track on the right before Eathie Mains. Follow that down to Eathie Fishing Station and, if you search along the coast, you'll find trilobites in the blackish slate looking rocks. These creatures died out about 65 to 100 million years ago.'

My wife and I followed his advice and, after leaving our bikes in the wood, went down the winding path to the shore, where we found fossils within ten minutes, and that included some tourists older than ourselves, of course, as well as trilobites. However, there wasn't time on this occasion. The rain came on and I disappeared into Rosemarkie's Groam House museum (opened in 1980) to look at Pictish stones. If I remember correctly, the word 'groam' originates from the Latin for a bog or marshy place. The Romans called the locals 'Picti' or 'Painted ones', because they painted their bodies blue, but we don't know what the Picts called themselves. The 18th century building was occupied once by a man, who came from Groam just over two miles east of Beauly. In its time the house has been a drapery, a grocery, a tea shop and a private house. Now it was 'selling' Pictish stones, but there were no brown paper bags in which to take them away. Two videos were available for viewing, two on the Brahan Seer and one on the Picts in Ross-shire.

'Would you like to see the videos?' I was asked.

'No, I'm sorry. I can't stay too long. I didn't get out of Inverness until the afternoon and I've a long way to go. I'll just have a quick look round at the information, for I didn't see round the museum the last time I was up here.'

Fifteen hundred years ago the Picts were spread out from the centre of Scotland to the Northern Isles. They were farmers, who became Christians in the 6th century A.D., and they built stone monuments, engaged in metalwork and produced weapons and jewellery. About 840 A.D. they united with the Scots and after that they 'disappeared', except for their carved stones scattered across eastern Scotland and traces of their language in place names. Pictish cross slabs are among the first 8th century sculptures in western Europe. The latest stone in the museum was discovered in 1995 in a Rosemarkie garden rockery.

As I left I thanked the lady in charge. Now for Cromarty. I knew that I could cycle there via the attractive road to the fossils but the road was rather steep initially, so I chose instead the A832. In any case, had I gone fossil hunting, it would have been too easy to steal stuff from the bike, as there was no place to hide my luggage easily in that remote spot.

Nearing Cromarty I looked over the Cromarty Firth to Invergordon, a port for cruise liners, and once the home of possibly the largest distillery unit in Europe. From 1863, the Cromarty Firth was often used by the British fleet, and it became a naval base after Winston Churchill visited

Cromarty. At one time it was a larger naval base than Scapa Flow.

'During World War II,' said a cyclist I met, 'the entrance to the Firth was protected by anti-submarine nets and there were gun emplacements on the headlands. They're said to have inspired Alistair MacLean to write "The Guns of Navarone".'

I wondered if they were ever used on the 'Glorious Twelfth' of August and later, for the Firth is internationally important as far as birds are concerned. Thousands of duck, geese and waders winter here or pass through. Mudflats and the abundance of food attract many species to the reserves, which are managed by the R.S.P.B. or Scottish Natural Heritage. Killer whales, the type made famous in the film 'Free Willy', come into the Firth.

Once in Cromarty, I cycled down the High Street, where a young man in a hurry nearly became acquainted with my bike, and then I turned into Church Street where I stopped at the 1772 Cromarty Courthouse. This is the town museum, and inside is a recreated trial from the 1770s with moving figures. There too are prison cells and information on Cromarty itself. I could have had a Walkman and tape but just read the wall displayed information instead. Outside and farther down the street I came to Miller House but went to Hugh Miller's Cottage, now a museum in the care of the N.T.S.

Hugh Miller (1802-50) began life as a stonemason, but he was also a geologist, writer, journalist, folklorist, accountant, church reformer, lecturer and editor, a man who made his mark in life. Back at Eathie, Miller used to explore the fossil beds and his pioneering work in geology was recognised throughout the world. One of Miller's geology books even found its way to a log cabin deep within the heart of America. Miller also became the leading lay member of the Free Church of Scotland after the Disruption. As an important Victorian literary figure, he was recognised by men such as Darwin, Carlyle, Dickens and Ruskin. He was also known to that great Scottish environmentalist John Muir, who in 1879 named one of the North American glaciers in Glacier Bay after Miller.

In 1856 Miller committed suicide by shooting himself in his chest. He had been very worried about the safety of himself and his family and kept weapons in his house. The gun dropped into his bath water and lay there rusting several hours before it was discovered. A professor friend, another Miller, was one of four doctors who carried out a post mortem, and evidence of brain disease was found. The gun was then taken to the gunsmith from whom Miller had purchased it, because the professor wanted to know how many bullets had been fired. Bad handling of the gun led to Thomas Leslie getting a bullet through his right eye and he was killed immediately. Four thousand people formed a funeral procession, which went from Miller's Portobello home to Grange cemetery in Edinburgh.

Thomas Leslie was buried shortly before him. Carlyle said that Miller's death was 'the world's great loss'.

So well thought of was Miller in Cromarty that, apart from his cottage which is in the care of the N.T.S., there is a tall column with the figure of Miller atop just south of the cottage. This is the Hugh Miller Monument set up in 1859.

Outside the cottage I got talking to a man and his dog or rather to a man with his dog, for the latter was uninterested in the conversation as far as I could tell. Perhaps I should have held a dog-eared book in my hand.

'If you're interested in writers,' he said, 'go farther along the street and you'll come to a church, which has a memorial to Sir Thomas Urquhart of Cromarty. He was the first to translate the work of the French writer Rabelais into English.'

He departed with his dog and wished me all the best on my journey, but not before directing me to the roofless Gaelic chapel beyond the Hugh Miller Monument. I went along to see the Monument and the chapel built in 1784 for Gaelic speakers from neighbouring parishes, so that they could worship in their own tongue before going to the East Church. I learned that the memorial to Urquhart was placed there by the Saltire Society, and that Sir Thomas's translation was one of the best translations made of any work.

Cromarty is the Highland's best preserved 18th century town, and 200 years ago it was a busy commercial centre and port. It was George Ross of Cromarty who really created the town. He built one of Scotland's first factories and employed several hundred people to spin and weave hemp from St. Petersburg in Russia. For centuries Cromarty exported salt, cod, herring and salmon to the Baltic and the Mediterranean. It was Ross again who built the Court House, a brewery, the harbour and the Gaelic Chapel. I cycled to the Old Brewery, now a study centre, then pedalled back to Marine Terrace to see the old factory, now mostly converted to houses.

From there it was a short run to the lighthouse, which is now Aberdeen University's base for sea mammal research. Boat trips are run from the harbour by Dolphin Ecosse. Tapes are available in French, German and Italian and hydrophones are available for listening. It is claimed that dolphins are seen on nine out of ten trips and whales, seals and porpoises are also spotted. Although dolphins have been sighted in various places on Scotland's west and east coasts and off Cornwall, the Moray Firth and Cardigan Bay in Wales provide clear evidence of a substantial residential dolphin population. Those in the Moray Firth are being threatened with extinction, for some are already showing signs of skin disease, which could well be caused by pollution.

It was time to continue on my journey to Tain and that meant I had to use the ferry across to Nigg. I cycled to the terminal and studied the notice board, which gave the time of the last crossing as 6.00 p.m.. What I wasn't sure about was whether this last crossing was from Nigg to Cromarty or vice versa. As I stood at the notice board, which is about 100 yards from the actual boarding point, a man, whom I took to be a ferry boat crewman from his dress, came walking from the town end towards me. At the same time a ferry boat was approaching the Cromarty terminal.

'Excuse me, is that the last crossing?' I asked, referring to the boat coming in at just before 6.00 p.m. .

'Yes, that's it,' he replied disinterestedly and without stopping.

'That's a pity,' I said, 'for I was hoping to get across tonight for I have far to go.'

He went down to the boat and I assumed that he was going to check that it was moored properly, before finishing for the night. I stood watching him board the boat and wished that I could get across, and I noticed that he was looking across at me but he didn't shout over. If he was finished he had no reason to. To my surprise the boat took off and started another crossing. I could not believe it. Why hadn't he shouted to ask if I was coming aboard? I was really upset and stood there a while before heading back to the harbour area. If I wanted to go north that evening, I would have to go back about 18 miles to a bridge to get to the other side of the Cromarty Firth, and then cycle the same distance forward to draw level with Cromarty. I found this idea hard to stomach, because it was raining and after 6.00 p.m., and it would have been a waste of time and energy. The only sensible course was to stay overnight in Cromarty.

I was so mad that I waited to see the crewman, when I realised the boat was on its way back. Once he docked he walked towards me with another man and I spoke angrily.

'I thought you said that was the last crossing when the boat was coming in. You went and did another crossing.'

'That was the last crossing,' he replied dourly.

'You knew I wanted to cross. Why didn't you give me a shout?'

'I thought you didn't want to come on.'

'I didn't come on, because you said that was the last crossing as the boat was coming in. I'm going to take this farther.'

'Are you on something?' he asked angrily and marched off.

I had to find accommodation for the night. Back in Church Street I had noticed a hotel 'The Cromarty Arms' opposite the Courthouse. I booked a room for the night and, unlike the Manx cat which has no tail, I had a tale which I readily unrolled. Several people were puzzled as to why I should have been left and some people, thinking they knew who it was, said that that person was a nasty bit of work. I was glad to be in, however, to enjoy a delicious bar supper and this time it wasn't a Mars bar.

The fact is I was lucky to miss that ferry for, had I gone on, I might have missed seeing some of the things, such as the Tain Heritage Centre, which were only available during the day. Without much prophecy, I knew that I would sleep well and so hung up my cloots and deposited my near fossil frame into the bed.

16 June   Cromarty – Wick   O.S. 27, 21, 17, 12

After a good breakfast I went to catch the 9.00 a.m. ferry and, before going down the sloping concrete ramp, I read something of the ferry's history on a notice board. Back in the time of Macbeth and Robert the Bruce, the early settlement at Cromarty was already into ferry crossings. James IV used the ferry on his 18 visits to worship at the shrine of St. Duthac at Tain and his last visit was in 1513, just before he was killed at Flodden. It was the Scottish Crown that established a frontier post at Cromarty, a colony of southerners, as a move to subdue the Highland clans, and it became a Royal Burgh with trading rights. In the 19th century Cromarty became a major port for ships carrying emigrants to Canada.

At breakfast I had had time to reflect, and I came to the conclusion that the previous evening's incident was perhaps due to a misunderstanding. Mind you, I still thought the crewman could have asked whether I was going to board the ship before he crossed again. After all, had I not expressed disappointment and said that I wanted to cross that night. Perhaps he hadn't been paying attention. Once on board the boat, I went up to the cabin and made it up with the crewman, who may have been the owner himself. It seems he had had a good breakfast as well, for he was pleasant and the bike and I were not forced to walk the plank.

The crossing to Nigg was quick and I soon got on the way past the fabrication yard and oil terminal, but stopped briefly to question a security man at a kiosk at the entrance to a yard. He saw me taking a photograph and I felt I had to give some explanation, especially when I wasn't wearing a placard with the words 'Industrial Spy'.

'Is it true your firm may be taking over the running of the ferry in the future?'

'Yes,' he replied.

So ended my brief interrogation. About a mile from the ferry there was the oil terminal on my left, and on my right, about a half mile from the road as the crow flies, there was Pitcalzean House, at the time a posh guest house, but formerly the Nigg home of the writer Eric Linklater (1899-1974). Although born in Wales, Linklater's forebears on his father's side were Orcadian, and he spent a good part of his childhood and later life in Orkney. Particularly after 1930 he broadcast and wrote novels, popular histories and books for children.

Soon I was away from the industrial area and was cycling across flat country on the B9175, when I passed Arabella. There was no greeting, smile or wave, but then I was perhaps expecting too much from a place name.

It wasn't long before I left the B road for the A9 at Calrossie Woods to head for Tain, which claims to be the oldest royal burgh in Scotland, for its charter goes back to 1066. Just over 4 miles to the south-west of the woods is Balnagown Castle, connected with the Brahan Seer and owned by Mohammed al-Fayed, the proprietor of Harrods store in London and father of Dodi, who was killed along with Princess Diana in a controversial Paris car crash. I had no intention of going to the castle, however.

Before going to Tain, I had meant to cut across country to Inver which is just over 5 miles east of Tain. Inver and the area were evacuated in 1943, and the people were told that the area was to be used for military training. What they didn't know was that the area around the village had been chosen from the air, as the nearest thing to the Normandy beaches. Unfortunately because of secrecy, the locals were not consulted about the tides which moved the sand and water channels. Barges were sent from Invergordon but, when a barge opened, a tank disappeared into a channel and the idea of practising tank landings there had to be abandoned. The tanks were then brought by land and the area was used for shooting practice. However, there was no time to visit the area and I continued on the road for Tain.

Upon arriving there, I went into the heritage centre for the 'Tain Through Time' experience. There was much to learn from the photos, artefacts and examples of local crafts such as Tain silverware. The Clan Ross Centre is also there plus information about the origins of Tain. A mural and video explain why James IV came regularly to Tain on pilgrimages from 1492 to 1513. A sound and light show tells of St. Duthac or Duthus, Malcolm Canmore and Robert the Bruce. A bone of St. Duthac was said to have curative powers and his shirt was supposed to protect its wearer, North American Indian or not. Mind you, it didn't stop Hugh, Earl of Ross, from being killed at Halidon Hill in 1333. Perhaps he was wearing it round the wrong way or was a mere mortal, who was too far away to get the Duthac bone treatment.

Next to the museum is the St. Duthus Collegiate Church, whose restoration was approved by the Pope of the time in 1492. His Papal Bull, conferring status on the Church, is in the museum. Cardinals beware!

When I came out, I started speaking to an elderly couple and the lady was amazed by my driving skill.

'How on earth do you manage to balance your bike with all that load?'

I felt like telling her that I was more unbalanced than she realised, but I simply said that it was just a matter of practice.

After leaving Tain, I gripped my handlebars tightly as I passed some buildings. The map showed the words 'distillery' and 'morangie' and, although teetotal, I called upon St. Duthac to save me from temptation. As I started on the Dornoch Firth bridge, my eye caught sight of a plaque with a legend. I can't remember the details now but I noticed the word 'Bavaria'. Just over the bridge to the left the map showed Lake Louise. Wow! Had I suddenly moved into Canada? Was I going in the wrong direction after sniffing some heady air?

About a mile farther on and about a mile to the west is Skibo Castle. This was where Andrew Carnegie (1835-1919), the Dunfermline born multi-millionaire, lived for a time. Carnegie had gone to America where he made his fortune, some say rather ruthlessly, from investment in the railways and from the steel industry in Pittsburg. Married to a woman aged 40, Carnegie became a father in his early 60s, and bought Skibo and Lake Louise in 1898 to make sure that his daughter Margaret had 'a little Scottish home'. He wanted to stay there for five or six months a year. The castle was rebuilt and enlarged, the first telephone exchange in Britain was installed, and a piper was engaged to march up to the castle and play the pipes at 8.00 a.m. . On July 4th the Union Jack and the American flag were flown. For ten years in the summer there, he entertained people such as King Edward VII, Paderewski, the concert pianist who became Prime Minister of Poland, Rudyard Kipling and Booker Washington, ex-slave and later college head. He left in 1914 and vowed never to return until World War I ended. It was at Skibo that he planned to give away £70 million of his vast fortune, for he once said: 'To die rich is to die disgraced.'

Peter De Savary, a multi-millionaire, turned Skibo into an exclusive country club and planned to spend £22 million developing the estate and castle. He was, however, concerned about the proposed new land reform legislation, whereby the right to roam would compromise the privacy and security of his high profile guests. The new company's Carnegie Club tries hard to maintain the privacy of its guests.

It was rumoured once that the American actor Michael Douglas and the Welsh actress Catherine Zeta Jones were to be married at Skibo Castle in a £50,000 ceremony, but that idea fell through. Mick Jagger, Jack Nicholson, Robert Carlyle, Sir Sean Connery, Bob Geldof, George Bush Sen., Bill Clinton, Bill Gates, Robbie Williams and Ted Danson are among the guests who have stayed there, and the pop star Madonna and Guy Ritchie, her film director partner, were married there.

Beyond the castle, I swung right and cycled towards Dornoch where my first visit was to Dornoch Cathedral, built by Gilbert de Moravia (founder of the Murray clan) at his own expense, after he was appointed Bishop of Caithness in 1222. Two people were on duty inside.

'Good morning. Is the Rev. James Simpson still here?' I enquired.

'No, he retired some years ago and is down south now.'

I was disappointed, for although I was only an acquaintance he always addressed me by my first name. The last time I saw him was when we played table tennis as opponents in a competition organised at a St. Andrews University based, week long Christian Education conference, where he acted as chaplain. I shall always remember him as a good preacher both in church and on ' Reflections' on T.V. He was also a writer of several books on Church and family humour, for he believed in the power of laughter to preserve our sanity in times of stress and adversity, and to relieve irritation and tension. How right he is and yet humour is regarded with suspicion or contempt by some people. I read once that Eric Linklater, that great Scottish writer, was not regarded by some as an important or serious author, because he brought humour into his work. Personally I think people without humour are sadly lacking, not that anyone ought to like all kinds of humour. Above all I shall remember James Simpson as a friendly, down-to-earth man, and I was very pleased when he took his turn as the Moderator of the Church of Scotland.

Dornoch Cathedral began as a Roman Catholic church, then became Episcopalian and then Presbyterian. Although the Cathedral has been the parish church for 300 years, the name 'cathedral', which means 'seat of a bishop', is kept as a reminder of its history.

Inside I admired the stained glass windows commemorating how Andrew Carnegie gave away a great part of his wealth. One window reflects Carnegie's love of music and is represented by a figure holding an organ. He was one of the founders of the Pittsburg Philharmonic Orchestra, the Carnegie Concert Hall in New York and he also gave over 7000 pipe organs. The centre window shows Carnegie's interest in fostering peace on which he spent millions, and to that end he paid for the construction of the Hague's Peace Palace, which my wife and I later went to see after I completed my cycle journey. It was my first time abroad. The third window shows a lady holding a book, which reminds us of the 3000 libraries Carnegie gifted throughout the world. The church organ was reconditioned in 1908 thanks to Carnegie's generosity, and completely rebuilt in 1979 thanks to the generosity of his daughter Margaret.

Little did I realise, when I left the Cathedral to pick up my bike, that the building was later to be the venue for the christening of the singer Madonna's child.

I must have had 'Tourist' written over my face, for a man I engaged in conversation outside asked me if I had seen the windows and the piscina.

'The Carnegie windows, yes, but what's this piscina?' I said.

After seven years of Latin and some study of Italian, I knew that 'piscina' could mean 'fish pond' or 'swimming bath' but I was puzzled, as I had neither seen nor expected to see either.

'It's a stone basin and there's one in a niche in the south wall. It was used when this was a Roman Catholic church. If, after Mass, there was any wine left, it had to be washed away into holy ground. The priest poured the wine into the basin and it passed through a central hole and down through a pipe into the cemetery. The basin used to be at the priest's waist level but, as you'll see if you go in again, it's at a lower level now. That's because the floor was raised in the 19th century to make room for vaults for the Sutherland family.'

'O thanks,' I said, 'I'll go and see that.'

'I have to go now but, if you've time, I'll show you the ell measure in the cemetery. That's where they used to measure plaids long ago.'

'I saw an ell measure in Dumfries on the Tolbooth wall,' I said.

'Well, this one's sort of horizontal.'

He led me to it and then said that he had to dash. I photographed the stone then went across to the Castle Hotel opposite the Cathedral. That was where a new bishop's palace was erected, for before then the Bishop of Dornoch stayed in the castles of Skibo or Scrabster.

I then enquired locally about the Witch's Stone, which is said to mark the spot where Janet Horne, the last witch in Scotland, was burnt in 1722. She was accused of turning her daughter into a pony shod by the devil, but that was perhaps her way of saying that her daughter was a nag. Once informed I set off and found it in a garden to the south side of Dornoch. I was near the golf course by then, and remembered that the Rev. James Simpson was a keen golfer on this, the third oldest golf course in Scotland after St. Andrews and Leith. It was because of its golf course and castle that Dornoch became known as the 'St. Andrews of the North'.

Had I visited the Dornoch Craft Centre, I could have spent time in the jail which is housed in the building. I had heard that you could try the birching table there but decided that I would be 'whipped' enough by the end of the day. My father as a lad remembered being horrified at seeing the birch marks on a young man's back. That was the latter's punishment for stealing a butterie (a bread roll made of a high-fat, croissant-like dough).

Having seen enough, I left Dornoch by a secondary road running parallel to the coast. On the outskirts of Dornoch, I first stopped at a small shop where I mastered a heated chicken pie and a can of juice. It was just then that I realised I had forgotten to go and see the piscina after looking at the ell. Too bad, I thought, but there was to be no backtracking. I had probably looked at it anyway without being aware of its significance. When I thought of the wine going into the cemetery soil, the expression 'dead drunk' took on a new meaning. Moving on, I was soon cycling along the peaceful south side of Loch Fleet and it didn't take long to get back to the A9. I crossed the Mound, a causeway built in 1812 by the Duke of Sutherland over the western end of Loch Fleet, and pressed on to Golspie, a quiet Highland village and seaside resort.

The first time I ever visited Golspie, I was amazed by the number of jelly fish on the shore. I had never seen anything like it before. At that time it was also the farthest north I had been. This time, however, I was more aware of Golspie's nearness, when into view came Ben Bhraggie with its summit statue dedicated to the 1st Duke of Sutherland who died in 1836. This statue has been the centre of controversy, for it was on the Duke's estates that people were cleared, sometimes extremely harshly, to make way for sheep. The Duke's statue stands with its back to the glens that were cleared and looks towards the sea, which was offered as an alternative livelihood.

A man called Patrick Sellar (1780-1851) was against the statue being erected, because he said it would spoil the beauty of the area. A landowner set on improvement evicted Sellar's father, who had been a stonemason, but by his endeavours the latter became a successful lawyer in Elgin. Obviously this was an argument for clearing from the glens people often thought of as barbaric, uncivilised and slothful. They would be forced to improve themselves.

Sellar also qualified as a lawyer, became the factor for the 1st Duke of Sutherland and was given the task of clearing people off the Duke's land in the name of improvement. It was argued that the land was better suited to sheep and that those evicted would be better off employed in fishing at the coast, or in the coal mine at Brora, or even emigrating to the New World. In the pursuit of evictions, Sellar was accused of acting viciously in Strathnaver (he has been compared to the Nazi Heydrich, although I think that is over the top) and was even taken to court because of the burning of cottages, the destruction of barns and kilns and the deaths of people hastened by being rendered homeless. Sellar was acquitted by a jury but it has to be said that more than half of the members were landowners.

The Countess of Sutherland persuaded Harriet Beecher Stowe (1811-96), an American woman who wrote against slavery in her novel 'Uncle Tom's Cabin', to write 'Sunny Memories', a sanitised account of what occurred on the Countess's estate. Families were not evicted but took an unmissable opportunity to begin a new life in a New World. To counter this viewpoint, a Highland stonemason called Donald Macleod wrote 'Gloomy Memories'.

There are arguments for and against the Clearances, but probably most people would disagree with the violence and ruthlessness in its execution. However, those evicted were not themselves all paragons of virtue. Some of those who went to the New World were quite ruthless, when removing people from land they wanted. Furthermore some of those, who were cleared off or their descendants, became fishermen or tradesmen in the likes of Wick and were by 1900 better off than some labourers in south England.

Golspie is a favourite place for fishing and has its own golf course. Golf has been played in Golspie since 1892, but the present course was remodelled in 1924. For beginners there is at the sea front a small course known as 'Gleneagles'. Somebody obviously had a sense of humour.

The Orcadian Stone Company Limited there is a family business open to the public, and visitors may watch stone cutting and polishing. I gripped my wallet tightly and merely looked in at the window. Up Dunrobin Glen at the north end of the village, the stream sometimes uncovers semi-precious stones such as smoky quartz and amethyst. Geodes of the latter are on display in the workshop.

The village was at the time of my visit the only one in the Highlands with a kart circuit up to championship standard, and the new extension allowed karts to reach speeds of over 100 miles an hour. There is also a 25 metre swimming pool, fitness suite and sauna available. The village has or had at one time the only water powered flour mill in the Highlands.

While in Golspie I asked two people what they thought of the statue on the hill.

'I'd have it pulled down,' said the first I spoke to.

'I agree,' said the other, 'but I wouldn't say that everything the Sutherlands did was bad. The 3rd Duke built a gas works, one Countess founded the residential Sutherland Technical School and the 4th Duke and Andrew Carnegie paid for it.'

'Maybe so,' came back his companion, pointing in the direction of the statue 'but my forebears were cleared off the land by him.'

My mind went into overdrive and I wondered what had subsequently happened to his four bears. However, I gave nothing away facially or verbally, which is perhaps just as well after hearing that a man in Golspie was sacked for using bad language. Perhaps I could have landed in trouble for playing with words. Later I asked the opinion of a third person who showed a deep feeling for the history of the area by providing a well considered, balanced answer.

'I couldn't give a ..... '

From Golspie I cycled on to Dunrobin Castle. Open to the public during the summer months, this ancestral home of the Earls of Sutherland is the most northerly and largest of Scotland's great houses. The Castle has 189 rooms and is one of Britain's oldest continuously inhabited houses, dating in part from the early 1300s. Dunrobin was captured by Bonnie Prince Charlie's men and has the vague claimed distinction of being the last castle captured in war. During World War I, it was used as a naval hospital before becoming a boys' boarding school. The Victorian museum contains a collection of Pictish stones, local history, geology and wild life specimens. Outside there are formal gardens modelled on those at Versailles Palace in France and designed by Barry, the architect of the Houses of Parliament.

Opposite the castle driveway and back at the road, I viewed the statue of George Granville, 3rd Duke and 12th Earl of Sutherland. Beside the statue is the Castle's own railway station which was built by him in 1870. It has the distinction of being the only one on the railway network, privately owned by the same family since it was built. There is an exhibition in the waiting room. In the York National Railway Museum, which my wife and I once visited, there are models of the Duke of Sutherland and Edward VII looking at plans of the railway.

For many years the 'Dunrobin', a steam engine, pulled a single carriage from Inverness to Dunrobin. The likes of Edward VII, Kaiser Wilhelm, George V, George VI and King Alphonso of Spain used to sit and travel on the leather covered seat above the coal box. Wilhelm used to travel elsewhere and, before World War I, would spend part of his summer up the Sogne fiord in the village of Balestrand in Norway. There in the Kwiknes Hotel, although I was not staying there, I once sat in the chair he used to occupy, before he returned to Germany upon hearing of the assassination of the Archduke Ferdinand at Sarajevo in 1914.

The train's final journey took place in 1938, and the engine was bought by a businessman from Canada and transported to Vancouver Island. Later it was purchased by the British Columbian government, and the last time I heard of it it was in the Fat Steel Museum.

Cycling on I came next to a broch on the seaward side of the road. I parked the bike and went to take a look at that circular defensive tower from the Iron Age. A young couple came over and we spoke briefly.

The next halt was in Brora, and the only thing I knew about the place was that coal mining had taken place there. As a matter of fact coal has been mined there since 1529 and, at the beginning of the 17th century, James VI of Scotland and I of England was already aware of the worth of Brora's coal. Extraction of the coal took place from a strip of level ground above the beach. Later a John Williams took over the mines in 1746 but the coal gave him a problem because, when it was piled up and exposed to moisture and air, it caught fire by spontaneous combustion. It has been claimed that until recently Brora had the oldest working coal mine in the world.

'Excuse me,' I said to two men working in a yard, 'but there's absolutely no coal mining here now, is there?'

'No, it stopped a long time ago. In the 1970s, I think,' said the taller of the two.

'And is it true about the coal catching fire by itself?' I asked.

'Well, there was something about a ship carrying coal from Brora to Portsoy,' he added. 'I heard that the ship sprang a leak and the coal got wet and started to burn.'

'Who told you that?' queried his workmate.

'Don't remember exactly.'

'Is this place famous for anything else?' I asked

'Well, maybe not famous but they had woollen mills.'

'And there was salt for the Moray Firth fish.'

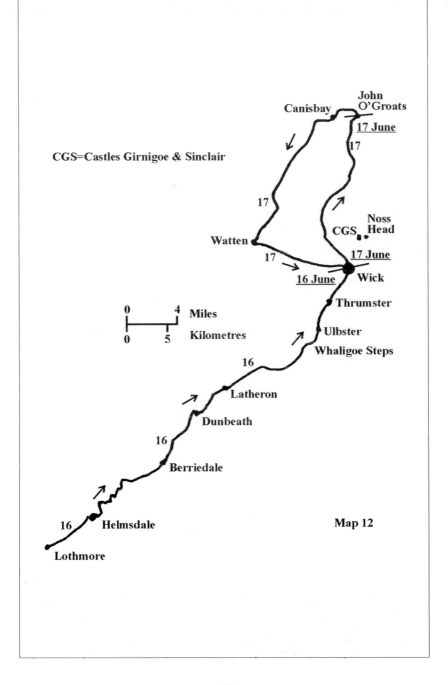

CGS=Castles Girnigoe & Sinclair

John O'Groats

Canisbay

<u>17 June</u>

17

17

17

Noss Head

CGS

Watten

17

<u>17 June</u>

<u>16 June</u>

Wick

Thrumster

0   4 Miles

0   5 Kilometres

Ulbster

Whaligoe Steps

16

Latheron

Dunbeath

16

Berriedale

16 Helmsdale

Map 12

Lothmore

'Maybe the Clynelish distillery is famous for its single malt Scotch whisky.'

'You should know!' said the younger of the two. With that remark they both laughed.

I thanked them both and left. I was surprised that they didn't mention that the local sandstone was used in the extension to Dunrobin Castle, in the statue of the 1st Duke of Sutherland on Ben Bhraggie and in London Bridge.

After I finished the trip, Brora was in the news, when a group of vigilantes called the 'Disciples of the Fiery Cross' were said to have threatened a troublesome teenager with death. They were reported to have guns and explosives and were determined to stop city violence spreading into rural areas. It was reported that a cross was set ablaze outside the teenager's house and a brick was hurled through his window. Let's get serious. Does the end justify the means? That incident reminded me that the Klu Klux Klan in America has also burned crosses, and a Scotsman has the dubious distinction of being the founder of that movement.

It was time to leave Brora, for I had still a long way to go to Wick. Just before Lothbeg, I parked the bike at a monument to my left near the road. The inscription said that the monument was set up 'to mark the place near which (according to Scrope's "Art Of Deerstalking") the last wolf in Sutherland was killed by the hunter, Polson, in or about the year 1700'. Thank goodness we are not menaced by wolves roaming around this country, although someone has already reported seeing one in the wilds. It's all very well for those who are not farmers or hillwalkers or who mouth off from urban Scotland and England, as I have read, to advocate the return of wolves to the Highlands and Islands. We're told how safe it would be and that wolves are much maligned animals. Well, the 'experts' can keep them as far as I am concerned. Red Riding Hood wasn't impressed either.

Right next to the monument was a small portacabin type toilet. I entered and exited, and wondered if an escaping smell had been the cause of death of the last wolf but, when my head cleared, I remembered the true reason.

When I reached Helmsdale, I wished I could have stopped in the hostel for the night, but I had to keep going. Helmsdale has one of the best harbours on the east coast of the Highlands and boats have long engaged in fishing. Schooners used to ply between there and Leith and Newcastle, exchanging fish, mainly herring, for timber and slate. I was too late to see 'Time Span', a new visitor attraction with a heritage centre, a herb garden beside a Telford bridge, an art gallery, restaurant and shop.

Helmsdale was the setting for the first part of Gunn's famous novel 'The Silver Darlings'. From there Catrine in the novel set off walking to the village of Dunster, the fictional name Gunn used for Dunbeath.

I had cycled over the river Helmsdale just before arriving beside

Helmsdale youth hostel, and I realised that following that river back inland on foot would bring one to Strath Kildonan, famous for its gold rush there in the second half of the 19th century.

In 1868, a Mr. Gilchrist, who hailed originally from Strath Kildonan, returned home after working for almost twenty years in Australia's goldfields. After being granted permission by the Duke of Sutherland, he explored above the Helmsdale bridge. This was no haphazard search for, about 50 years before, a gold nugget was found in the river Helmsdale. He was lucky and found gold but the best was in the Suisgill tributary. The Duke granted licences for prospecting at £1 a month per claim, and by Easter 1869 almost 500 prospectors were working for gold. Some lived in wooden houses at Baille an Òr (town of gold), near the meeting place of the river Helmsdale and the Kildonan burn. Others camped in tents at Càrn nam Buth (cairn of the shop), also near where the waters met. Back in Helmsdale's shops and pubs, the prospectors received food and drink for gold. A good amount of gold went to P.G. Wilson in Helmsdale and he turned it into jewellery.

The Duke also offered £10 to anyone who found the source of the gold. The Director of the Geological Survey, Sir Roderick Murchison, about whom in 'Vol. 1 Across England' you may have read in connection with the Ludlow rocks, became interested and came to believe that the gold was of local origin.

The prospecting led to complaints about deer being frightened off to other estates, about salmon being affected, and shepherds complained about their ewes being disturbed. Accordingly in 1870, the Duke of Sutherland ordered all the prospecting to stop.

That evening, however, the richest find for me would be Wick, but that was still miles ahead. Farther on I passed the signposted path to Badbea, now a ruined village, where the houses were so close to the cliffs that the children were tethered lest they fell over the edge. Miles on again, I received an almighty shock when I came to Berriedale that evening. I phoned home to say that I was going to Wick and then I tackled the scenic, but long and steep Berriedale Brae. There was no way that I could cycle up it with the load I had, probably even without a load. It was a case of pushing the bike all the way and it took ages. This is the way Gunn's Catrine in 'The Silver Darlings' walked, at a time when there was no road but merely a dirt track along the cliff top.

Once beyond the Brae I passed the Kingspark Llama Farm, but it was too late to visit it. Had I been able to stop overnight at Helmsdale hostel, I could have gone there the next day. The last time I had seen real llamas was beside St. Mary's Loch in the Borders. As I cycled on towards Dunbeath, I consoled myself with the thought that llamas probably don't like being interviewed anyway. On reaching Dunbeath, I paused to eat a

Mars bar and asked a passing man if he knew anything about the llamas.

'The llamas? They breed them back at the farm,' he said. 'They use them for carrying people's belongings. They go walking with them. They get a picnic lunch and a guide to point out interesting things and at the end they visit the farm and the shop. They've also got parrots, chipmunks, pheasants and raccoons.'

'Do you know where Neil Gunn was born?' I enquired, forgetting about llamas.

'No, but when you cross Dunbeath Water by the bridge, the house he lived in is somewhere in the row of houses on the north side of the valley. Also down at the harbour near the river mouth there's a statue or sculpture commemorating his work.'

I started down the road to the harbour but it seemed a long steep descent, and I reckoned it would take some time to get there and return to the main road. Reluctantly I abandoned the idea and left that piece of the Neil Gunn story for another day.

Gunn was born in Dunbeath in 1891, one of a family of nine brothers and sisters. His father was the skipper of a local fishing boat and the first 13 years of his life were spent in Dunbeath. When he was 13, Gunn moved to Galloway and in time he entered the civil service. After a while in London and Edinburgh, he returned to the Highlands and became an excise officer at the Glen Mhor distillery in 1921. Eleven of his 20 novels were produced at Braefarm, a former farmhouse in the hills above Dingwall.

After leaving Dunbeath behind I cycled to Latheron, where there is the Clan Gunn Heritage Centre and Museum established in 1985 in the 18th century parish church. The Centre here has a clan shop and is the base of the Clan Gunn Society, of which there are others throughout the world. The clan claims descent from Norse jarls. In the Centre can be seen some of the evidence for claiming that the discoverer (at least European) of America was not Columbus but a Scot. There you can learn about the 600 year old portrait of a Scottish knight, known as the Wesford knight, marked on stone on a quiet roadside in Massachusetts. America was still considered undiscovered then and 94 more years passed before Columbus came to America. Unfortunately for me the Latheron centre was closed and I marked it down for a visit at some future date.

I pushed on and came to a roadsign for Lybster, a small fishing village where the Gunns lived for nearly a year in 1922. This was where his work took him and he was shocked by the poverty caused by the fishing port's decline. This experience appeared in his first novel 'The Grey Coast'.

Just before Ulbster I passed the entry to Whaligoe at the coast. The village is famous for its 365 steps (approx. 365 days in a year) leading down to the small harbour, where fishing was more important in the past, but I had no time to see the steps where women used to carry up the landed fish.

After that I pedalled through Ulbster, a small community noted for its Ulbster stone now in the museum in Thurso. It is a Pictish stone from about the 7th or 8th century AD, is made from sandstone and has more symbols carved on it than any other known stone of its kind.

About a mile beyond Ulbster, I was within a mile as the crow flies of Mains of Ulbster, where there is a mausoleum to Sir John Sinclair (1754-1835), who was born in Thurso Castle. He became an M.P., initiated the First Statistical Account of Scotland, was an agricultural improver, a town and village planner and became the first President of the Board of Trade.

I cycled next into Thrumster, where it has been claimed the first automatic telephone exchange was installed. I stopped at a shop for something to eat and drink.

'I hope I can get some accommodation in Wick at this late hour,' I said to the lady behind the counter. 'It'll be a while before I get there.'

'You're right. I'll tell you what. I'll phone somebody I know in Wick and see if she has a vacancy.'

She phoned and told me that, if I could get there by a certain time, I'd get accommodation. I thanked her for her help.

'Here's the card of the person in Wick,' she said before I left.

By the time I was approaching Wick, I was very cold in my shorts and my hands were frozen. I stopped and for the first time in the whole journey from Land's End I put on my gloves. It was really dark now and I had on my lights. Strange, I thought, not many cyclists going about. In the darkness it was at least encouraging to see the lights of Wick in the distance. At last I entered the town and wondered where I would spend the night. I didn't really fancy cycling through the streets in case I met some undesirable characters, who might mug me and steal some or all of my valuable equipment. Nor did I fancy having to put up the tent in the dark, should I once find the camp site marked on the map, as being to the west of Wick. It might even be closed or not exist any more. I even thought of standing in a telephone booth, if I could find one in the quiet part of Wick I had entered, but that could have invited trouble as well.

It was past the time set by the shop lady's friend for accommodation and I hadn't spotted the place anyway. Just then I saw a B&B sign in the garden of another establishment and noticed a light on in the front room and hall. I approached the door and heard a lady speaking on the phone and, when I rang the bell, she eventually appeared at the door.

'Good evening,' I said. 'I'm sorry to be calling at such a late hour (it was then midnight), but do you have a bed for the night?'

'Yes,' she replied, 'but you're lucky I'm still up. I was just about to go to bed.' She didn't express disbelief that I was really the 'knight'.

I had to leave my 'steed' tethered outside and hidden behind a hedge, and then she showed me upstairs to my room where I deposited all my luggage. I so much wanted to get warm that I would have slept with a llama that night. Probably the feeling would not have been mutual, but one can never tell. Perhaps my animal magnetism might have created a certain level of tolerance. On the other hand the Royal Society For The Prevention Of Cruelty To Animals might have put a spoke into such a move, even although I had a four-legged bed.

17 June   Wick – John O' Groats   O.S. 12

It was a lovely morning when I headed for the harbour after breakfast. No, I did take a shower before leaving the B&B.   Like Helmsdale, Dunbeath and Lybster, Wick was very much involved in the herring fishing in the 19th century. In fact Wick was once the busiest herring fishing port in Europe, if not the world. In the novel 'The Silver Darlings', set when the herring fishing was at its peak, a character called Finn was obliged to walk from Dunster (Dunbeath) to Wick to get a doctor, and he was shocked by the sight and noise of the harbour after the peacefulness of the moors. Many of the old harbour buildings are still there. The area on the south side of Wick was once known as Pulteneytown and was a fishing village, built under the charge of Thomas Telford (he also designed the original Avoch harbour) and named after Sir William Pulteney, the Fishery Society chairman.

In 1862 there were 1122 boats operating from Wick at its busiest but, with the arrival of the steam engine, many of the steam drifters were too large for the smaller harbours, and Scrabster with its deeper water became more important. Once diesel power came into use, this enabled a change in operations and herring was replaced by white fish such as whiting and cod.

I paid a visit to the Wick Heritage Centre, which is run on a voluntary basis by the Wick Society, and is the largest of its kind in the North of Scotland. While there I spoke to Iain Sutherland, the author of the 'Wick Heritage Centre Guide', and he and his publication helped greatly in my tour of the Centre.

On the ground floor I studied a large photograph on the wall. It showed the scene in 1865 when 1000 boats were based in Wick. At the height of fishing activities in the last century, over 6000 fishermen and fish workers came to the town each summer. The fishermen lived in their boats, but as many as 2000 women were accommodated in dormitories above the yards or in attics. Some women, however, lived in more comfortable rooms. As many as four girls or women would live in such a room, as shown with its typical box bed in the museum. Some of the women walked over 100 miles to Wick and slept outdoors on the way. Wick's population would more than double at busy times.

In another part of the museum is an actual reconstructed kiln used for smoking herring (smokers can become very desperate) which were thought to be too poor in quality to be cured in salt. These were smoked and called kippers. The kiln on display could hold 10,000 herring which were smoked for 24 hours. The largest kiln in Wick could hold 90,000 herring. Herring were exported from Wick to Germany, Russia, Poland, Lithuania and Latvia from about 1820 to about 1953.

The gutting girls could gut and clean herring at the rate of 35 a minute. In the 1860s there were 650 coopers in Wick producing about 125,000 barrels a year, and the girls were paid according to the number of barrels they packed with gutted herring.

Many fish curers went bankrupt when they were paid with German paper money, which lost its value in the years 1922 and 1923. One Wick curer who lost everything papered his house with the notes, and the notes displayed in the museum were what were left over after 'decorating'. Long before Lord Irvine expensively papered his house, it seems then that this Wick man tried to 'cure' his house with a paper of 'note'.

The word 'herring' is an interesting word and is connected with the old German word 'Heer' meaning 'host' or 'army', an appropriate meaning when one remembers that herring travel in shoals.

On the walls of the Centre are examples of the Johnston Collection of photographs, taken by three generations of a local family between 1863 and 1977. Of their 100,000 negatives, 50,000 are owned by the Society. Alexander Johnston (1839-96) worked in the family plumbing business until 1863, when he fulfilled his ambition to set up a photography business with his brother James.

Wandering through the museum and into a parlour generally typical of about 1900, I came across a long case clock made at a time when Alexander Bain was an apprentice. It is claimed in Wick that he invented the electric clock, the fax machine and an early electric typewriter.

In a kitchen typical of the 1920s there was a radio, the second to be bought in Caithness about 1926, and examples of chairs known as Caithness chairs. At the top of the building there is a model of the Whaligoe Steps, which are for real 7 miles south of Wick, and for repairing those the Wick Society won the 'Shell Best Of Britain Award'.

In another room there was the reconstruction of the battlefield of Altimarlach, the last major clan battle fought in Scotland. However, the claim has been made that the last clan battle was at Mulroy near Roy Bridge.

Also in the museum is part of a lighthouse dating from the middle of the 19th century and on loan from the Lighthouse Commission. It was built and designed by Alan Stevenson, uncle of Robert Louis Stevenson, the author, and it came from Noss Head.

'You see that lifeboat made from 'H.M.S. Hampshire' as a memorial to Lord Kitchener,' said an elderly visitor who spoke to me. 'I've seen where he was killed when his ship sank off Marwick, Mainland, Orkney.'

'My wife and I once cycled in Orkney,' I replied. 'We read the words of the Kitchener memorial and also saw from the cliff top where the ship went down. We saw as well a relic from the ship in Stromness Museum and, at the naval museum, (now called the Scapa Flow Visitor Centre), at Lyness on the island of Hoy, we saw the Hampshire's propellor.'

Somewhere in the Wick Heritage Centre I read about a Captain John Hood, a personal friend of William Smith (1854-1914), the founder of the Boys' Brigade. A plaque is set into the wall of Smith's birthplace in Thurso. Hood, I learned, was a B.B. officer for over 60 years.

'This is a display of their old fashioned transfer certificates, badges, chevrons and uniforms they don't have now,' said Iain Sutherland.

In the harbour area I went looking next for the house in which Robert Louis Stevenson lived briefly. I read somewhere that the house was in Shore Road.

'Excuse me,' I asked a man, 'but is Shore Road along here? I'm looking for the house where Robert Louis Stevenson stayed.'

'O that's No. 9 in Harbour Terrace,' I was told.

That reminded me of the situation in Hereford, when I was looking for a house in which Nell Gwynne stayed and found that the street name was changed. Eventually I found the Stevenson house with a plaque erected by the Literary Society of Wick in 1907. Young Robert, a student, came north to Wick in the autumn of 1868 and stayed for six weeks. His father's firm was involved at the time in constructing a breakwater, where Robert spent two tiring days. He donned a diver's suit and helmet and went down with a man called Bob Bain. Stevenson was amazed how buoyant he was under water in spite of all his diving weights. I had already bought at the Heritage Centre Stevenson's account of his dive, an account taken from his 'Random Memories'. The breakwater was damaged in storms and was eventually abandoned by Stevenson's firm.

As I stood outside No. 9, the man who had directed me there caught up with me and passed on some more information.

'You know the story of "Treasure Island"?' he asked.

'Yes, I've read it.'

'And you remember Ben Gunn in the story?'

'Yes,' I replied.

'Well, the story locally is that Stevenson used to listen to tales from an old sailor here by that name.'

A Mr. Sutherland, head of Wick Academy, once travelled to Edinburgh with his son Scott. The latter was hoping to become an artist and attended a class held by Alexander Carrick, who designed the Killin war memorial and the bronze soldiers at Dornoch. As said earlier Scott Sutherland later became noted for his Commando Memorial at Spean Bridge.

In Stafford Street, if my memory serves me well, I noticed a plaque to Bain. It read: 'The inventor of the electric clock and the electric printing telegraph. Alexander Bain was born at Watten, Caithness in 1810. Part of his apprenticeship as a clockmaker was served with John Sellar, watchmaker in this building 1829-1830.' I wondered if the watchmaker was a relation of Patrick Sellar.

Near the railway station I came across a memorial stone with the names of famous people who had visited the town. Among the politicians were three former British Prime Ministers, namely, Gladstone, Rosebery and Lloyd George, two former Chancellors of the Exchequer, a Viscount Peel, who was the Speaker of the House of Commons, Sir Stuart Knill, Lord Mayor of London and the foreign leaders Sir Oliver Mowat, Premier of Canada and General Grant, President of the USA. What had brought them there? Did Wick become wild and need some super governing powers? Did Wick become such a den of iniquity that William Booth, the founder of the Salvation Army, and Randall T. Davidson, Archbishop of Canterbury, had to pay a visit? Was it such a remote place that Sir Ernest H. Shackleton came to explore? And what about John Bright, Joseph Hume, Professor Huxley, Andrew Carnegie, Sir H. Rider Haggard, George Borrow, Hugh Miller, Thomas Carlyle, Robert Louis Stevenson and Sir Roderick Murchison, President of the Royal Society, some of the people already encountered in my story? Were they all secret End to Enders, who stopped at Wick before leaving for John O' Groats?

'That's some list, isn't it,' said a voice behind me. It belonged to a perky sort of chap with a ladder. 'There's one bad mistake, though.'

'What's that,' I asked out of curiosity.

'They didn't leave a space for my name.'

A reasonable enough point perhaps. I could have offered my deepest condolences but decided to humour him before taking off.

'Aye, a serious mistake right enough.'

Back in the heart of Wick, I noticed a plaque in the wall of the Alliance and Leicester Building Society. It was a quote from Neil Gunn's 'A Ton Of Delight' and it read: 'In communal life it is quite simply the recognition of the others, the need to be one with them and to enjoy the work and gains, to contribute what one can to increase the mutual delight.'

Before leaving Wick for John O' Groats, I entered the tourist office and booked a B&B, for I intended coming back to Wick for that night in preparation for catching a train home next day. When I eventually left Wick and cycled towards John O' Groats, I felt excited about nearing my goal but, at the same time, I was anxious in case anything went wrong with the bike and complicated the day. I decided that if the chain broke, I would load the big rucksack and push the bike if necessary. I would worry about getting back to Wick once I arrived at my destination.

Next I decided to take a look in by the Caithness Glass Visitor Centre (now closed in Wick), which was on the A99 out to John O' Groats. I was surprised to learn that the firm had also branches in Oban and at Inveralmond in Perthshire.

I learned that the Inveralmond branch had made a replica of a famous goblet originally made in Venice. This very fine glass goblet was a present from James VI of Scotland, before he became also James I of England, and it was given to Sir Robert Halkett of Pitfirrane, whom he highly esteemed and had recently knighted. The goblet was said to have had the magic property of being able to change colour, when it came in contact with a poison. It is a wonder the king gave up that goblet, considering how superstitious he was and how much he feared the spells of witches and the threat from would be assassins. The sacrifice showed the depth of the king's feelings towards Sir Robert. Strangely enough the replica goblet was again the work of a Venetian glass maker, who came to work for Caithness Glass which was founded in 1966.

Through a glass window I could see the craftsman at work shaping the glass for jewellery, bowls, glasses and paperweights.

After leaving the Centre, I got talking with a couple of cyclists who were, they said, making for Wick.

'Are you going to John O' Groats?' one of them asked. 'I'd like to ask a few questions. I'll maybe do the End to End run some day.'

'Such as?'

'How far is it from Land's End to John O' Groats, and how long does it take?'

'Well, the shortest distance is about 874 miles, and how long it takes depends on how fast and far you cycle each day. Do about 63 miles a day and you'll bike it in about a fortnight, if it's just straight cycling you're doing.'

'Right, and is it better to cycle from south to north or vice-versa?'

'Well, if you go from south to north, you have the south-westerly winds sort of behind you. On the other hand if you're English you're going farther away from home. I liked going north because of the wind factor and psychologically it was good coming back to my own country.'

Conversation over, we said our goodbyes and I set off again. Not far past Caithness Glass I was level with Wick airport. It was from Wick that the first batch of Commandos flew off in gliders on a mission to destroy the Norwegian heavy water plant at Vemork. This water or deuterium oxide was essential to the Germans for developing their A-bomb. The mission failed badly and it was left to a later one to succeed. Just beyond Wick airport is Noss Head, where during World War II an alert radio operator picked up a message, which when decoded told us of the location for the launching of either the V-I or V-2 rockets.

I knew that there were two castles there as well, namely, Castle Girnigoe and Castle Sinclair. Iain Sutherland, the author, tells us in his booklet 'Sinclair & Girnigoe Castles' about many famous Sinclairs of the past. In 1057 one of them took the Saxon princess Margaret to Scotland to marry Malcolm Canmore, King of the Scots. Another Sinclair was one of the escorts carrying King Robert the Bruce's heart to the Holy Land for burial, and he died defending it in Spain in 1330. Then there was the Sinclair, known as Henry the Navigator, who is said to have discovered Greenland and reached America in 1398. In 1446 another Sinclair established Rossyln Chapel and it became the world headquarters of the Freemasons. A Sinclair raised 300 men to fight at Flodden in 1513 and the story goes that only one returned. Until relatively recent times, some people used to refuse to cross the southern border of Caithness on a Friday (the day the 300 left) wearing green, the predominant colour in the Sinclair tartan, because it was deemed to be unlucky to do so. A Sinclair was also involved in the relationship Mary Queen of Scots had with Darnley, David Rizzio and Bothwell.

Castle Sinclair became uninhabited because of a land quarrel between one of the Sinclairs and Campbell of Glenorchy. This Sinclair either sold or promised his land to Campbell of Glenorchy to pay off debts, but there was opposition from another Sinclair and his people, who objected to Glenorchy becoming the Earl of Caithness. A court ruled in favour of Campbell, but the rebel Sinclair would not give way and Campbell marched north and seized the castles. The piping tunes 'The Campbells Are Coming' and 'Breadalbane Gathering' were written on the way.

Approximately 11 miles on I came to the Northlands Viking Centre, where there was an exhibition about chambered cairns, brochs and Picts of pre-Viking Caithness right through to the late Norse period. Norsemen began to arrive in Caithness from the 9th or 10th centuries, some of them interested mainly in plundering on the way south to the monasteries and their treasures. The Norsemen had a greater influence when they settled in Caithness and took up more peaceful occupations. The native Picts seem to have been overwhelmed by them. Many of the place names derive from the Norse language and thus we have names like Scrabster, Lybster, Thurso, Wick and the 'dale' and 'goe' endings as in Ousdale and Whaligoe. Sutherland was the southern limit of their main influence.

There too in the Centre I learned about the great contribution to archaeology made by John Nicolson (1843-1934), the local Victorian artist and historian. Nicolson was born at Stemster near John O' Groats (also a Stemster west of Wick) and attended the old Free Church in Canisbay as a child. He later took a certain pride in being bottom of the class there. He became a farmer but collected many old documents, and became during his lifetime acknowledged as an expert on Caithness ancestry. He started a debating society and, after developing an interest in archaeology, he became involved with the excavations of the brochs at Keiss and Nybster. Nicolson also became a recognised artist both as a painter and as a sculptor. He obtained clay from a hill at Stemster and his first efforts produced pipes for smoking. They were in great demand from the local fishermen and crofters. He sketched and painted most of the local worthies or characters such as the pilots of the Pentland Firth and many of the public men of Caithness. Not only was he interested in the pilots, who worked from Sinclair Bay and took ships through the Firth, but also in the pilots who operated from the small harbours below his house. To help them in at night he built a small lighthouse on the cliff top. When this was lined up with a light in his house window, the pilots knew that they had a safe passage into the harbour.

'The lighthouse and the barometer house can be seen from the Nybster broch car park,' said Elizabeth Munro, the lady in charge of the museum.

She even came outside the museum to point me in the right direction and told me more.

'The community hall was once a Nissen hut but it was improved. Nicolson sculpted two busts, one of a soldier and one of a sailor to represent those who died in World War I. Coins were found in one of the pillars here. Nicolson kept a record of those who came back from the war. There was one man called Alex Begg, an ambulance driver, who came home on leave and he didn't want to go back. He went into hiding in the peat hag but they found him and took him away.'

Nissen, by the way, was a World War I Canadian captain who designed the hut named after him. When Nicolson died, he was buried in Canisbay churchyard where there are some of his sculptures. Scott Sutherland produced a bust of Nicolson but the latter died before it was completed.

'John Nicolson's daughter lives just along the road there,' said Elizabeth Munro. 'She works in the shop at the other side of the road.'

I thanked her and cycled along to the shop, where I bought some chocolate and asked the lady who served me if she was John Nicolson's daughter. She confirmed that she was and I felt privileged to have met a living link with her father.

'Your father was an amazing man for his time,' I said, hoping that she would feel good about hearing her father praised, but I am sure she was well accustomed to it.

I left the shop and cycled non-stop to John O' Groats. I had expected a very easy run there, but I was quite surprised at the climbs on the way to the coast. If I had studied the contours I would have known what to expect. On the final run down from Warth Hill, I was surprised too that day by the force of the wind blowing towards me, and I had to keep a good grip of the handlebars. At least the traffic was reasonable.

At last I entered John O' Groats with a controlled excitement and a sense of anticipation. I even took the bike. I sought out the signpost on the raised piece of ground and a man came out of the little kiosk beside it.

'I'll take your photo if you like,' he offered and I gratefully accepted and gave him my camera.

'Are you heading south?' he asked.

'No, I've just finished.'

Later I wondered if he had meant that he would take my picture with his own camera in order to sell me the photograph. Perhaps he thought I was just about to set off for Land's End, or perhaps he was simply being kind and helpful.

I then went round the various buildings, including the hotel, to make sure that I had been to the correct or official finishing point, for I had heard that people sometimes quibbled about that. In 1995 Peter de Savary, said to be the 17th richest man in Britain, purchased the John O' Groats House Hotel, as well as the Land's End tourist complex in 1996. The Snowdon mountain railway was also his at the time. Reportedly he promised to upgrade the John O' Groats House Hotel and build a visitor centre like the one at Land's End, but he was later criticised for doing almost nothing.

I noticed a museum and had a look inside, then had another look towards Orkney. The sea and sky were blue, as they were when I set off from Land's End.

It was time to 'celebrate', so I parked the bike outside a restaurant and went in for something to eat and drink. The luggage went inside with me.

'Coffee and some sandwiches, please,' I ordered.

While this was being prepared, I had a look at some information on the interior wall. The name John O' Groats, I learned, was derived from Jan de Grote, a ferry man of Dutch origin. Jan de Grote charged 4d a trip and this became known as a groat. In 1498 he was granted land by the Earl of Caithness and legend has it that he built an 8-sided house with an octagonal table, so that each of his eight sons could claim to be seated as the head of the family. The site of the octagonal house is now the mound with the flagpole.

When the mature waitress brought my food, I told her I was going to enjoy it especially, for I had just completed the End to End. Hungry and thirsty, I didn't consider how much Dounreay nuclear contamination I might have in my coffee and sandwiches. There had been concern for some time over radiation leaks from the power station, but I would have at least cycled past Dounreay in my tour had I had the time.

A criminal investigation was ordered in May 1998 by the Wick Procurator Fiscal, for a back up safety system failed to work when there was a power cut, and over 300 staff were evacuated. A series of radiation leaks and dissatisfaction with the recording system led to Dounreay's licence to reprocess nuclear waste being suspended. Decomissioning of the plant could take up to 100 years and many years may pass before existing waste is reprocessed. A radioactive particle could burn a hole in the skin, cause an ulcer and increase the risk of cancer. These have been found on public beaches near Dounreay.

'You've done well,' said the waitress. 'You're no spring chicken. You're looking tired. Eat up now.'

She was very kindly but also observant and knowledgeable, I thought. No doubt it was through working in the catering trade that she knew I wasn't a chicken. On the other hand she maybe thought I was a summer one. I tried not to worry about it, for I could always go to the toilet and check my appearance in the mirror. Maybe there was something wrong with me. She was definitely right about me looking tired even if I didn't feel it. I discovered later that I had lost two stones in weight mainly by not eating proper meals, coupled with the exercise involved. I could have become a weight loss guru, I thought. Bike over 2000 miles, usually have a poor breakfast and for lunch and tea have the occasional sandwich and eat plenty Mars bars or KitKats. She was a decent woman and I smiled and thanked her for the food, making it obvious that I wasn't in a 'fowl' mood.

I was in the course of leaving the restaurant when I suddenly came face to face with my daughter's fiancé, Tony. My mouth nearly fell open.

'How did you find me here?' I asked.

He didn't answer but probably had inquired at the tourist office or phoned my wife. His work at the time also took him to different parts of Scotland.

'I'm going to treat you to dinner,' he said, 'and I've arranged sandwiches at 9.00 p.m. at your B&B.'

He'd even found out where I would be staying for the night back in Wick. Officially my trip was ended, but I explained to him that I wanted to see two more related things on the way back to Wick. He set off ahead by car and was soon out of sight. I took the A836 out of John O' Groats, then branched off to Canisbay to find its 15th century Scandinavian looking church, in which the Queen Mother used to attend services. When I arrived, Tony and I scoured the churchyard for Jan de Grote's grave. Eventually we found his gravestone inside the church itself. Apparently when the church was being repaired, the stone was removed from under the church floor and placed in its present position by John Nicolson, who was later buried in the churchyard.

'I'm going next to Watten to see a monument to Bain the inventor,' I said.

Tony went on again but it took longer to reach him that time, because I had to cover about 16 miles to meet up with him. My route was partly along a small secondary road and partly along the B870 to Watten. The monument, overlooking the main road in the village, was easy to find. The inscription read: 'Erected 1943 by public subscription in honour of the distinguished Caithness man Alexander Bain inventor of the electric clock and the electric printing telegraph. Born at Leanmore parish of Watten 1810. Died at Kirkintilloch 1877.' It is also claimed that Bain introduced for the first time the rubber insulation of electric cables which lasted until plastic was used years later. Watten, like Comrie in Perthshire, was also a place where some hard core Nazis were held in a camp during World War II.

Considering the time that evening and the distance back to Wick, we decided we had better have dinner in Watten. The meal over, Tony said that he would drive to Wick and suggested that I could follow him along the A882, and meet him at a fixed time and place to be guided to the B&B. I had a street plan of Wick but obviously it was quicker following him. When I did reach the town, I had only ten minutes to wait before he appeared and we soon arrived at the B&B, where the host was very friendly and the accommodation excellent. There was just time to get the luggage in and the bike locked up under cover, before sandwiches and tea were brought into the lounge.

As I lay in bed later that night, I turned over some thoughts in my mind. I wondered how many groats I would need to be ferried home in the 12.04 p.m. train next day. Also what better way was there to finish and mark an epic journey than a tasty supper in Wick? A good enough reason for doing the End to End, I thought. No pain, no gain as they say. Yes, what better way to finish, unless Wick Council....was working through the night....to cement on an extra slab of stone at....the top of the memorial....near the station.

It was obvious I was starting to dream. So what? It is important to dream, to have a goal, to be inspired and had I not indeed fulfilled my own dream? Yes, and there was more to come, for the dream was to lead to two books, not one, about the trip. Anyone requiring a set of book ends?